Managing the Dually Diagnosed Patient: Current Issues and Clinical Approaches

Managing the Dually Diagnosed Patient: Current Issues and Clinical Approaches

David F. O'Connell
Editor

The Haworth Press
New York • London

Managing the Dually Diagnosed Patient: Current Issues and Clinical Approaches has also been published as *Journal of Chemical Dependency Treatment*, Volume 3, Number 2 1990.

The Haworth Press, Inc., 10 Alice Street, Binghamton, NY 13904-1580
EUROSPAN/Haworth, 3 Henrietta Street, London WC2E 8LU England

Library of Congress Cataloging-in-Publication Data

Managing the dually diagnosed patient : current issues and clinical approaches / David F. O'Connell, editor.
  p. cm.
  "Has also been published as Journal of chemical dependency treatment, v. 3, no. 2, 1990" – T.p. verso.
  Includes bibliographical references.
  ISBN 0-86656-918-9 (acid-free paper) : – ISBN 0-86656-978-2 (pbk. : acid-free paper)
  1. Narcotic addicts – Mental health. 2. Mentally ill – Substance use. I. O'Connell, David F.
  [DNLM: 1. Mental Disorders – therapy. 2. Substance Abuse – therapy.
W1 J058L v. 3 no. 2 / WM 270 M2664]
RC564.M256 1990
616.86 – dc20
DNLM/DLC
for Library of Congress
                                                          90-4613
                                                            CIP

Managing the Dually Diagnosed Patient: Current Issues and Clinical Approaches

CONTENTS

Schizophrenia and Substance Abuse   **163**
George S. Layne, MD

Substance Abuse and Personality Disorder   **183**
Edgar P. Nace, MD

ABOUT THE EDITOR

David F. O'Connell, PhD, is a licensed psychologist with 13 years of experience treating dually diagnosed patients. Currently he maintains a private practice in Reading, Pennsylvania, and is the consulting psychologist for the Caron Foundation, as well as a consultant to the MICA Project (Mentally Ill Chemical Abuser) of Trenton, New Jersey. He is also an instructor in the addictions program at Alvernia College, Reading, Pennsylvania, and a trainer for the Health and Education Council, Baltimore, Maryland. He was formerly the staff psychologist at New Beginnings at Hidden Brook in Bel Air, Maryland, and at ARC/The Terraces in Ephrata, Pennsylvania.

Dr. O'Connell has published in the *Journal of Alcohol and Drug Education, Journal of College Student Personnel*, and *Alcoholism Treatment Quarterly*. He is presently writing a book directed specifically to addictions counselors on treating dual disorders. He is a member of the American Psychological Association, the Society of Psychologists in Addictive Behavior, and a Fellow and Diplomate of the American Board of Medical Psychotherapists.

Managing the Dually Diagnosed Patient: Current Issues and Clinical Approaches

Foreword

It is often the case that increased public awareness and interest in a problem are an indication that society is beginning to marshal its resources to combat that problem. As a reflection of such a trend for the problems of psychiatrically ill substance abusers, this book is most welcome. As a number of the writers in the book indicate, the consideration of the psychiatrically ill substance abuser in itself represents a major change in direction for both the fields of psychiatry and substance abuse. As recently as five years ago, the interested reader would have had to exert some energy to find a single chapter on the treatment of this population. The writings in this book point to at least a serious beginning in this direction.

This book appears to be directed mainly to personnel, professional and nonprofessional, involved in substance abuse treatment, although some of the papers may be of interest to substance abuse researchers and to mental health workers/students in other fields. The papers encompass a wide range of perspectives, content areas, and differences in level of scholarship. Thus, there has been no effort here to produce a textbook which would systematically address a fixed set of content areas. At this point in the development of the field such an undertaking would probably not be very appropriate or useful. The intent, as Dr. Penick and her colleagues suggest in their paper, is "to stimulate interest in a group of chronically dependent individuals who have not always been well served by the health care system and who certainly deserve better." The papers herein and the many references to related work indicate that this is taking place to a greater degree than heretofore and that this problem is being considered from a number of viewpoints.

As the editor indicates in the preface to this volume, "research into what constitutes effective treatment for *dually diagnosed patients* is just beginning." One objective of the book is to communicate to workers in the field, "the wisdom and experience of those individuals who are struggling to understand and provide the best available care . . . for these patients." The book succeeds in providing much useful information and, to at least one reader, the belief that sound research/evaluation in this area is not far beyond the horizon. The editor, Dr. O'Connell, is to be commended on this effort.

Arthur I. Alterman, PhD
Clinical Professor of Psychiatry
University of Pennsylvania
School of Medicine
Philadelphia, Pennsylvania

Preface

Patients who present for chemical dependency treatment with a
co-existing psychiatric disorder have historically been underserved
in our healthcare system. Fortunately for these individuals, health
professionals and researchers have become increasingly attentive to
and involved in their plight. Programs offering state-of-the-art psychotherapeutic and pharmacotherapeutic care for dually diagnosed
patients have been established in many localities. Clinical research
on the course and outcome of treatment for such patients is gaining
momentum. The present volume is a contribution to this growing
body of knowledge.

In this monograph, treatment professionals from a number of disciplines laboring in diverse settings, such as hospitals, medical
schools, addiction treatment programs, and dual disorder units,
have examined the critical issues in the assessment and treatment of
dually diagnosed patients and offer the reader an up-to-date review
of the latest knowledge in research and rehabilitation. The result is a
panoramic view of theoretical, conceptual, and practical issues involved in caring for dually diagnosed patients. Against the back-
drop of a historical review of the problem of dual diagnosis, the
reader is exposed to valuable information on psychopathology, psy-
chodiagnostic assessment, and issues in professional training and
intercollegial collaboration involved in the treatment of dually diagnosed patients. Considerable emphasis is also given to the understanding and treatment of the major psychiatric disorders commonly
occurring in chemically dependent populations.

Dr. Penick and her colleagues at Kansas University Medical Center provide a thoughtful, indepth overview of what is known about
the concept of dual diagnosis at present. Through an exhaustive
review and informed critical analysis of extant clinical and research
literature, the authors systematically explore the scientific politico-
economic and programmic issues that underpin the wide spread lack

xv

of understanding and under treatment of the dually diagnosed patient. The intricacies in diagnosis and treatment and the complexities inherent in clinical research with this population are thoroughly explored. The authors have condensed and clearly explicated a large body of literature and provide the reader with an excellent summary of the nature and scope of the dual diagnosis problem.

Russell Smith's paper on the psychoanalytic theory of substance abuse provides a highly readable, concise, incisive treatment of the often inscrutable psychoanalytic literature on psychopathology and drug abuse. For the reader unfamiliar with psychodynamic explanations of chemical abuse and associated psychological dysfunction, the paper offers a clear, compact introduction. The reader well acquainted with this literature will find a highly focused integration and synthesis of the diverse writing in this field. For all clinicians striving to understand their patients, this article offers illuminating insights into the pathogenesis and manifestations of characterological dysfunction which researchers have established to occur frequently in chemically dependent patients.

A focus on the practicalities, problems and pitfalls in diagnosis and assessment of dually diagnosed patients is given by Dr. Woolf-Reeve. Utilizing a current symptom approach to assessment, common diagnostic problems facing the addictions counselor are clearly portrayed and guidelines for effective assessment are included. Particular emphasis is given to the assessment of the violent patient. The assessment of medical danger, the behavioral signs of psychiatric disorders, and the symptomatology of cognitive and perceptual disorders are included. Clinical vignettes that compliment and illustrate the information on diagnostic decision-making assist the reader to grasp the complexities of this skill. Clinicians working in all phases of addictions treatment will find this article extremely useful.

Working from a multiple perspective approach, Linda Rubenstein and her colleagues at Western Psychiatric Institute explore the problem of assessment and treatment of dual disorders from the viewpoint of the patient, the family, the care giver, and the treatment system. Useful guidelines for patient education, skill development, relapse management, and treatment compliance are included. A large section is devoted to the unique considerations in the treatment of families with dually diagnosed members; a treatment condition that has received very little attention from researchers in the field.

Dr. Hudson reviews the literature on anxiety disorders and translates this knowledge into sound guidelines for the clinical management of this often misunderstood patient population. Dr. Hudson gives particular consideration to how socioeconomic factors affect the nature, course, and type of treatment for chemically dependent patients with anxiety and panic disorders.

Drs. Weddige and Ostrum at Texas Tech University draw out the salient findings of the growing body of literature on affective disorders and alcoholism and relate them to practical strategies in diagnosis and treatment. The problems inherent in the current classification of depressive disorders as well as the complex interplay of depressive symptoms, manifestations of alcoholism, and the diversity of this patient group are recognized and described.

Dr. Layne addresses the hard realities involved in the treatment of the schizophrenic addict. He offers valuable advice on differential diagnosis and a full account of the signs and symptoms of this most crippling mental disease. Three major programs to manage the substance abusing schizophrenic patient are presented along with the author's own ideas on effective treatment based on his experience at Northwestern Institute.

Personality disorders in substance abusing patients is the topic of Dr. Nace's contribution to this monograph. Dr. Nace documents the occurrence and effects of the major personality disorders on the course of treatment with such patients and argues for the recognition of the phenomenon of the substance induced personality disorder. He clearly delineates how characterological dysfunction can predispose an individual to substance abuse and complicate the course of treatment of the substance abuse disorder. The impact of traditional chemical dependency treatment and twelve-step programs on the personality disordered patient is explained and stands as a testimony to the genius of the founders and developers of twelve-step based treatment for the chemically dependent.

Dr. Klee addresses a rather neglected area of concern: training and education in dual diagnosis. A model for graduate level education developed at Chestnut Hill College is portrayed. Dr. Klee shows how a carefully conceived and structured sequence of courses and experiences can provide the requisite knowledge and skills that are required if addictions clinicians are to be effective in treating dually diagnosed and other special patient populations.

Intercollegial relationships is the subject of the article by Drs. Luyster and Lowe at the Charter Fairmont Institute. The authors demonstrate how the team approach can work effectively in a special dual disorder unit at a psychiatric hospital. A series of case examples are provided to illustrate both the problems and the benefits of a multi-disciplinary approach to the treatment of dually diagnosed patients.

The monograph concludes with an article by Dr. Carroll on the treatment of the psychiatrically disabled patient in the therapeutic community setting. The author documents how the problem of severely deficient self-esteem and multiple life problems profoundly impede progress in the recovery of afflicted patients. Dr. Carroll offers solid programmatic guidelines for therapeutic communities including guidelines for psychiatric referral, admissions decisions, aftercare planning, and patient care monitoring. A special feature is the inclusion of several detailed case summaries that give the reader a real feel for the issues, concerns, and procedures involved in treating the mentally ill chemical abuser in the therapeutic community environment.

Research into what constitutes effective treatment for dually diagnosed patients is just beginning. Until the results of such research efforts are available to clinicians, professionals in the chemical dependency treatment field must rely on the wisdom and experience of those individuals who are struggling to understand and provide the best available care for dually diagnosed patients. This volume was conceived with the hope of providing just such guidance and direction. The impact of it, hopefully, will be greater success in our clinical work with this troubled patient population.

David F. O'Connell, PhD
Bel Air, Maryland
December, 1988

Acknowledgements

I wish to thank Michael Barbieri and the staff at New Beginnings at Hidden Brook for their support. Special thanks to Cathy Frazier, Judy Stefl and Barbara Rankin for their assistance in typing, preparing and organizing this volume.

The Emerging Concept
of Dual Diagnosis:
An Overview and Implications

Elizabeth C. Penick, PhD
Elizabeth J. Nickel, MA
Peggy F. Cantrell, PhD
Barbara J. Powell, PhD
Marsha R. Read, MSW, PhD
M. Mickel Thomas, MD

Brenda entered psychotherapy with the complaint that she was drinking "a little too much" and that this was causing "some problems" in her marriage. The therapist advised Brenda to cut down on her drinking while they worked in therapy to discover the underlying causes of her excessive drinking and her anger toward her husband. After 18 months in therapy which focused on unresolved childhood issues, Brenda died in an automobile accident when driving while drunk.

Upon completing four weeks in an inpatient psychiatric program, Harry was stabilized on lithobid for his manic-depressive disorder diagnosed several years previously but never ad-

Elizabeth C. Penick, Elizabeth J. Nickel, Peggy F. Cantrell, Barbara J. Powell, Marsha R. Read, and M. Mickel Thomas are affiliated with the Department of Psychiatry, Kansas University Medical Center, Kansas City, KS and the Psychiatry and Psychology Services, Kansas City VA Medical Center, Kansas City, MO.

The preparation of this chapter was supported, in part, by funds from the Medical Research Service, Washington, DC, NIAAA #1R21 AA07539-01, and NIAAA #R01 AA07386-01.

equately treated. Shortly after his discharge from the psychiatric center, he mentioned his use of lithobid at an AA meeting that he had been attending in the past year. He was told sharply by some of the "old-timers" that you can't solve a drug problem with another drug. He accepted their advice and discontinued his medication. Two weeks later, during a manic episode when he continued to abstain from alcohol, he took the family business's assets and headed to Las Vegas where he lost everything within 48 hours.

Tom, who is an alcoholic and drug addict, was on probation for possession of marijuana when he dropped a dirty urine, thereby violating his probation. Shortly before his arrest, he had suffered a severe psychotic episode for which he had been hospitalized and started on lithium and a phenothiazine. Tom had difficulty complying with his medication regimen and his psychotic symptoms started to return although the urine analyses were negative. Tom's therapist spoke with the probation board about the Tom's need for long-term residential treatment. The probation board agreed with the therapist that Tom was not a "hardened criminal" who should go to prison, but a person in need of treatment for his chemical dependency and bipolar mood disorder. All available publicly funded long-term treatment programs were contacted throughout the state. The residential chemical dependency programs stated they could not accept him if he needed psychotropic medication. The residential psychiatric programs refused to admit a known alcoholic/drug addict. Tom ended up in prison for six months during which time he attempted to hang himself because the "demon voices" told him that he did not "deserve" to live.

I. THE NEGLECT OF DUAL DIAGNOSIS

Dramatic scenarios such as these are not really uncommon. Individuals suffering from other types of psychiatric disorder in addition to a psychoactive substance abuse problem often become the victims of *schisms* which have existed, and continue to exist, between the mental health field and the chemical dependency field.

The historic lack of integration between these two health-care systems and their often differing philosophies toward diagnosis and treatment, frequently prevent the dually diagnosed individual from obtaining optimal treatment (Wallace, 1986). Fortunately, a greater awareness of this problem has emerged recently. This interest is evident in the large number of articles, books, and professional seminars which have appeared in the last 5 years that deal with dual diagnosis. It is also apparent in the development of new treatment programs which specialize in treating individuals who not only abuse drugs and/or alcohol but also satisfy diagnostic criteria for other psychiatric disorders as well (e.g., Daley, Moss and Campbell, 1987).

Obviously, this clinical phenomenon is not "new." The existence of such individuals has been recognized for some time. A series of articles by Freed in the early 1970s summarized much of what was then known about "dual diagnosis" and the major mental disorders (Freed, 1970, 1973, 1975). Instead, the accelerated interest in dual diagnosis reflects a shift in the perception of mental illness, coupled with a recognition of the past neglect of individuals who suffer from two or more mental disorders which can, but does not always, include substance abuse (Boyd et al., 1984). This neglect of multiple psychiatric disorders has been particularly harmful to those who become dependent upon alcohol and drugs. What contributed to this neglect? How is it that so many people, often desperately in need of help, fall "between the cracks" of our service delivery systems? Why has this issue of dual diagnosis been largely ignored in our training programs, mostly overlooked by clinical researchers, and rarely brought to the attention of those responsible for allocating resources for the public good? There are many reasons, most of which are intrinsically interwoven into historical developments which have shaped our present understanding and treatment of "mental illness." We will attempt to focus on those schisms which have influenced the neglect of "dual diagnosis" in the past.

A major reason for the neglect of dual diagnoses among the chemically dependent was the failure of this country to achieve a strong national consensus about "the nature" of alcohol and drug abuse during the first half of this century. Due to this lack of national will, the facilities and people who served the chemically dependent historically were not the same as those serving the mentally ill (Wallace, 1986). For example, formal recognition of alcoholism as a "treatable disease" by the American Medical Association did not occur until 1956. Prior to this time, and even later, hospitals and physicians were reluctant to treat alcoholics for their alcoholism. Similarly, mental health professionals were reluctant to focus on drinking problems *per se*, tending instead to focus upon underlying factors that presumably "caused" the abusive drinking. Typically, such "underlying causes" reflected the theories and beliefs about mental illness that were popular at the time. Thus, mental health professionals were often taught that: "Alcohol addiction is a symptom rather than a disease . . . There is always an underlying personality disorder as evidenced by maladjustment, neurotic character traits, emotional immaturity, or infantilism" (Knight, 1937, p. 333). Acceptance of this belief all too often communicated a message to the alcohol abusing individual that he or she must first "cut down" or "cut out" the excessive drinking and then get therapy for "the real problem." This approach was rarely successful and many mental health professionals in the early days concluded that alcoholics were "intractable" to treatment because they were "unwilling" to stop drinking. The chemical abuser was then placed in an untenable position. He/she was asked to first "give up" their symptoms in order to get treatment for their symptoms, i.e., stop drinking or using drugs in order to get help for their drinking or drug use. Because of the muddled and contradictory attitude toward excessive drinking and drug use, many doors of the traditional medical and mental health establishments were effectively closed to the chemical abuser during the first half of this century. As a result, the training of medical and mental health professionals about alcohol and drug abuse was de-emphasized, public and private monies were funneled away from services which might have benefited the substance abuser and the subject stimulated little interest throughout the research community. There were bright spots in this otherwise bleak picture, of course, such as the pioneering efforts by Jellinek and his colleagues at Yale (1960) and the formation of the Federal hospital for drug abuse in Lexington, Kentucky.

The failure of the medical and mental health establishments to arrive at a concensual understanding and vigorously work together to address the problems of alcohol and drug abuse in the early part of this century produced an enormous vacuum in the health care delivery system. This vacuum was initially filled by the efforts of the Fellowship of Alcoholics Anonymous (AA) in 1935 and later, with their help, by the development of powerful political constituancies such as the National Council on Alcoholism (NCA) in 1944 which came to represent the "special interests" of the chemically dependent individual.[1] Thus, a schism was born. Largely parallel systems of services were developed for the alcoholic (and later for the drug abuser). These systems formed their own philosophies and attitudes toward "the disease" and its treatment. In the early days, relationships between the chemical dependency and mental health professions were far from harmonious. Wallace (1986) nicely summarized this situation when he notes:

> Treatment of primary alcoholism became a specialty in and of itself in which the drinking as such was assigned first priority and dealt with realistically, directly, firmly and openly. Tough love became the standard rather than permissiveness, flexibility and inadvertant professional enabling . . . the here and now of active alcoholism and its consequences became the focus of clinical activity rather than the there and then of psychosocial development . . . First things first, a slogan borrowed from AA, indicated that we had to deal with alcoholism first if any progress could be expected. Alcoholism counseling became a specialty built around the critically important issues of the patient's recognition of the problem, identification of self as an alcoholic, acceptance of alcoholism, and how to live a comfortable, productive and fulfilling life without alcohol. (p. 164)

Gradually, the schism between the "mainstream" medical and mental health establishments and those "outsiders" serving the substance abuser narrowed. A landmark event occurred in 1970 when the National Institute of Alcohol Abuse and Alcoholism (NIAAA) was formed by the Unites States Congress. This event, the result of much hard work by many people, clearly signaled the beginning of a true rapproachment between the "insiders" and "outsiders" (Lewis, 1988). There are many factors which led to the narrowing of this schism. Certainly, the greater public perception of alcoholism as a "disease" rather than a crime or moral failing was one factor, although the disease concept of alcoholism and drug abuse is not without its ambiguities even today (Siegler and Osmond, 1974; Goodwin, 1981; Fingarette, 1988). Another was the growing recognition that the most focused and dedicated efforts to help the substance abuser were not uniformly effective and that the social, economic, personal and medical consequences of substance abuse appeared to be dramatically increasing (Alcohol and Health, 1972, 1974). Clearly, the "outsiders" who had assumed the greatest burden of the care and treatment for the chemically dependent needed help. About the same time, widespread changes were occurring within the mental health field itself which resulted in a re-examination of alcohol and drug abuse from quite different perspectives. The once pervasive psychodynamic theory of human behavior, which had previously dominated the training of mental health professionals and their approach to treatment, gradually gave way to a more eclectic and pragmatic view of deviant behavior that was fueled by failures of the past and reinforced by the discovery of effective psychotropic medications for several of the major mental disorders. The emphasis in the mental health field began to focus much more on specific disorders and their treatment rather than on largely unprovable theories of behavioral deviance to which "generic psychotherapy" was all too liberally applied. In this respect, the substance abuse field can take a certain amount of pride in their pioneering efforts to move "the professionals" away from their preoccupations with general theories of human behavior to a greater concern about specific overt manifestations of personal suffering and dysfunctional behavior which are labeled "mental disorders." As psychiatry moved closer to the mainstream of medicine, clinical description and diagnosis assumed greater importance. Scientific empiricism became the new standard by which "facts" were judged; intuitive inspirations were no longer acceptable. The community mental health movement, promoted by John Kennedy in the early 1960s and implemented into law by the United States Congress in 1963, influenced the narrowing of the schism by establishing a comprehensive health service delivery system which quickly recognized that substance abuse was a ubiquitous problem that could no longer be ignored. The creation of a Central Office within the Veterans's Administration (VA) hospital system in 1967 and the formal funding of VA alcoholism treatment programs in 1970 also served to narrow the gap between those who served the substance abuser and those who served the medically and mentally ill. Public Law 93-282, signed by Richard Nixon in 1974, among other things prohibited hospitals which received Federal funds from discriminating against the alcoholic. Finally, the NIAAA-stimulated influx of monies for research and treatment created an essential link between the fields of substance abuse and mental health.[2]

Although the gap between substance abuse and mental health has gradually lessened, legacies of the distant past continue today and serve to reinforce the neglect of dual diagnosis. What are these legacies? As Stephanie Brown (1985) and others have noted (e.g., Harrison et al., 1985), people who have traditionally served the substance abuser often differed greatly from those who served the mentally ill. These differences included education and training experiences, as well as attitudes and beliefs about "helping" which sometimes led to disharmony or animosity between the two groups. The bulk of the "treatment" given to those who abuse alcohol and/ or drugs is typically provided by counselors with little formal training. (In fact, one of the traditions of AA states that "Alcoholics Anonymous should remain forever nonprofessional . . .") When formal training is provided, it generally consists of on-the-job seminars, lectures or a brief course dealing exclusively with substance abuse. Thus, the formal educational experiences of substance abuse personnel have tended to be minimal and narrowly focused while their experiences "in the field" have been vast. In contrast, the mental health system usually requires more broadly-based education at the postgraduate level in which many aspects of mental disorder are covered; however, the topic of substance abuse is rarely taught in great depth and supervised, longterm training experiences in caring for the chemically dependent substance abuser is often minimal.

Many of the traditional caregivers in the substance abuse field are, themselves, recovering from chemical dependency; they have "been there." Such individuals feel strongly that their personal experiences with "the problem" uniquely prepare them to serve others who abuse alcohol and/or drugs. Despite the fact that personnel in the medical and mental health fields are usually given "scientific" information about substance abuse and its treatment, they typically have limited preparation in dealing with individuals who abuse drugs and/or alcohol on a day-to-day basis "over the long haul." Unlike personnel in the substance abuse fields who feel comfortable with personal disclosure and will freely offer themselves as a role model to emulate, the mental health specialist is trained to assume a certain degree of "objectivity" and "professional distance" when working with others who seek their help. Generally, service providers in the substance abuse field tend to know and use only one approach to treatment. If they are recovering themselves, the approach taken is usually the one that "worked" for them. When confronted with failure, substance abuse workers typically have no "fall back" position to draw upon, continuing instead to do "more of the same" rather than shift to a different treatment strategy. Mental health specialists, on the other hand, are exposed to a variety of treatment modalities but frequently have little "hands on" sustained experience with individuals who abuse alcohol and/or drugs.

In the mid 1970s, Kalb and Propper (1976) provided a useful comment about the tensions created by the sudden influx of mental health professionals into the field of alcoholism treatment after the creation of NIAAA. They noted that the disharmony between the traditional substance abuse provider and the professionally trained mental health worker was an outgrowth of different orientations toward the work they perform. Kalb and Propper compared two orientations: the *craft* model which they associated with the substance abuse field and the *scientific-professional* model which they associated with the mental health field. Craftsmen obtain their knowledge and skills through a prolonged apprentice-like relationship with a master craftsman. Novices are taught to closely identify with, think and perform like their teachers; little flexibility is usually allowed for questioning or deviating from the doctrine presented to them. Their commitment is to the "truth" as perceived by the master teacher. In contrast, the scientist-professional is encouraged to doubt and think independently. Novices are required to critically analyze and weigh equally various viewpoints. Their commitment is to "truth" as provided by "factual" knowledge, regarding with skepticism any premise not supported by objective empirical data. Dissonance occurs when the scientist/professional questions the craftsman's treatment doctrine because the "facts" may be contrary to commonly held beliefs. Dissonance is created when the craftsman dismisses or ignores the "facts" marshalled by the scientist/professional which are contrary to their belief systems. To the craftsman, doubt is an anathema; to the scientist/professional, it is a way of life. Brown (1985) observes that such "defensive separatism" has served to break down communication and collaboration between mental health professionals and chemical dependence providers.

This schism in the background and training of those who care for the chemically dependent has had particularly unfortunate consequences for the dual diagnosis patient. Mental health professionals sometimes fail to vigorously and actively address substance abuse problems when they occur with other psychiatric or personality disorders. Even worse, mental health professionals often feel so inadequate to "treat" the substance abuse problem themselves, that the individual is turned away from treatment and referred elsewhere until the substance abuse problem is "under control." On the other side of the coin, the chemical dependency treatment provider may fail to recognize signs and symptoms of a potentially treatable disorder, assuming that the observed emotional distress or social dysfunction are simply residual effects of the substance abuse problem. The single-minded attention to the substance abuse disorder, which served the field so well in the beginning, can result in unhelpful comments such as: "zip up your fly, tie your shoes and put a plug in the jug"; judgmental statements like: "you're not working the program (AA) hard enough"; or, unusable explanations such as "you're just having a dry drunk." Critical attitudes toward psychotropic medications, various psychotherapies and other psychosocial treatment strategies often discourage the dual diagnosis patient from considering other forms of help. Clearly, a "cross-fertilization" in the education, training and longterm supervised experiences of substance abuse and mental health personnel is needed to overcome this schism from the past.

Another related schism from the past which has influenced the neglect of dual diagnosis has been the development of physically separate "treatment" facilities and programs for chemical abusing individuals. The failure years ago of the medical and mental health establishment to fully embrace the alcohol and drug dependent person into their system of care resulted in the creation of "dedicated" or single-objective programs to fill the gap. Special interest groups and constituencies successfully lobbied for these "dedicated" treatment programs. Often separate funding sources were carved out and set aside for this purpose and later jealously guarded by those who had worked so hard to secure them in the first place. Private and public funds were used to construct "separate" programs which often existed side-by-side, in the same building, with programs that were created to serve other psychiatric disorders. Initially adhering mostly to the AA tradition, these specialized substance abuse programs developed a strength and ambiance of their own. Admission policies, intake procedures, diagnostic philosophies, treatment formats and staffing patterns in these disorder-focused programs often differed markedly from those developed for other mental disorders. Intense loyalties were formed, even among patients or clients who frequently wished to be associated with one type of program and not with another (e.g., alcoholics who do not wish to be associated with "those crazies" on psychiatric units or psychiatric patients who do not wish to be associated with "those bums" on substance abuse units). In time, these programs became quite adept at selecting patients who "fit" the structures they had erected; they also became quite adept at formally or informally excluding those who did not. The perception gradually arose that "only" a well established substance abuse program was capable of effectively treating those with drug and/or alcohol problems while individuals with other types of problems could "only" be helped by programs specializing in "mental health" treatments. These very entrenched perceptions have persisted despite the fact that there is *no* empirical evidence to support the need for separate facilities or programs for the chemically dependent. Dual diagnosis patients were often the losers of this shared misperception. The phrase: "we're not equipped to handle those kind of people" often signified an unwillingness of psychiatric personnel to treat the substance abuser or the substance abuse unit personnel to care for individuals with other psychiatric disorders. As a result, neither the substance abuse field nor mental health field has acquired extensive experience in caring for the dual diagnosis patient; no substantial body of knowledge or clinical wisdom exists about this important and very distressed group of people who frequently "fall between the cracks" of the health care system.

Another legacy from the past which has sustained the neglect of dual diagnosis patients is less direct and immediately apparent, but influential nevertheless. It involves the manner in which clinical research has been supported and maintained in this country. Until very recently, clinical research in the psychopathologies typically focused upon one or two diagnostic groups at a time. An almost universal research strategy was to select for study only those individuals who nicely "fit" into one diagnostic category or another. Multiple disordered patients were usually excluded, especially in those research projects which sought outside funding support. Schizophrenics who drank heavily or abused drugs were rarely included in studies of schizophrenia; alcoholics who persistently hallucinated in the absence of acute intoxication and/or withdrawal were rarely included in studies of alcoholism. Indeed, when we examined the research literature prior to 1980, we found very few externally supported research projects which focused on individuals suffering from a chemical dependency problem as well as another psychiatric disorder. In the last several years, this situation has changed and is likely to change even more in the future, especially as the country becomes more aware of the needs of the nation's homeless. Just as the term "dual diagnosis" has achieved a certain prominence recently in the substance abuse field, so has the term "co-morbidity" become increasingly used in the mental health field. The terms "co-morbidity" or "co-occurrence" are used to describe individuals who satisfy definitional diagnostic standards for two or more mental disorders, such as depression and anorexia nervosa or panic attack disorder and agoraphobia. The concept of dual diagnosis, when applied to the chemically dependent, resembles closely the concept of "co-morbidity" used in the mental health field. As true within the substance abuse field until very recently, patients seeking help for two or more *NON*-substance abuse mental disorders were often overlooked or ignored or shuffled back and forth from one specialist to another by professionals within the mental health field. The non-substance abuse "dual diagnosis" patients also rarely became the focus of large, well funded research projects. Despite the similarities, the neglect of dual diagnosis or "co-morbidity" among the chemically dependent was historically unique and especially harmful. In part, it has resulted from the very successes achieved long ago by those who vigorously sought to overcome the public and professional stigma attached to the excessive use of alcohol. The independence and solidarity of the substance abuse treatment field, which is one of its great strengths, has at the same time tended to discourage "new" ways of looking at "old" problems. This book, with its many chapters, is intended to stimulate interest in a group of chemically dependent individuals who have not always been well served by the health care system and who certainly deserve better.

II. IMPORTANCE OF DUAL DIAGNOSIS

It is a general truism that as diagnostic accuracy improves, the care and management of patients is also likely to improve. This basic assumption has stimulated many in the substance abuse field to focus on dual diagnosis. At this point in time, however, it is important to keep in mind how little we know about dual diagnosis and its implications for patient care. The ratio of what *is* known to what *is not* known about dual diagnosis unfortunately weighs heavily in favor of the unknown. A large number of very fundamental issues and questions remain unanswered. Skeptics can and do argue that the recent interest in "dual diagnosis" among the chemically dependent is "nothing new," simply representing "another fad" which periodically seems to sweep across the field. Perhaps this is true. It is certainly true that reliance upon anecdotal case vignettes such as those which began this chapter are no substitute for carefully researched facts and systematic, shared clinical experiences. It is also true that the case vignettes we presented implied that each of those three individuals would have been "better off" if properly treated for their dual diagnosis. We really don't know. We hope so. But there is little empirical evidence to support this assumption. Nevertheless, we have to start somewhere, especially the clinician or service provider who often does not have the luxury of waiting until all the questions have been fully answered to everyone's satisfaction. We know that there are many chemically dependent people who do not benefit from traditional approaches. We have to find something "better" for them.

We propose that the recognition of "dual diagnosis" is important even though it is not clear at the present time how such individuals can be helped best. The recognition of dual diagnosis is necessary for the growth and development of the field, even if it turns out to represent a "blind alley." At least it would be one more "blind alley" that could be eliminated in our search to better understand and treat the substance abuser.

It has been recognized for decades, of course, that individuals who abuse substances differ greatly from one another. Nevertheless, this diversity has not been fully appreciated or well documented until recently. In fact, descriptions of "the" alcoholic or "the" drug abuser in the popular literature, in training guides and in educational materials for patients and their families have become increasingly stereotyped over time just as the "treatment" of these individuals has become more inflexible and doctrinaire. The creation of stereotypes and doctrinaire beliefs is not, in itself, necessarily harmful. It allows a field to define itself and its work more precisely. However, when stereotypes interfere with seeing what is there and doctrinaire beliefs prevent our trying out new ideas, they become obstructions to progress. Recent research indicates that alcoholics as a group, and drug abusers as a group, are extremely *heterogeneous.* These findings challenge a "unitary" concept of alcoholism or drug abuse (Pattison, 1985; Miller and Heather, 1986). Family history, age of onset, clinical course, medical and psychosocial sequellae as well as outcomes, both long and short, are now known to vary remarkably among those who are identified by others, as well as by themselves, as an "alcoholic" or a "drug abuser" (Vaillant, 1983; Prugh, 1986). Equally important is the heterogeneity associated with treatment results. Some people who come to us do well; some do not after treatment. Just as some do well and some do not, without any formal treatment. Controlled studies of treatment efficacy, unfortunately, have not been very encouraging (Miller and Hester, 1986a, 1986b; Holden, 1987). Pretreatment characteristics (including the severity of abuse) and correlary social influences (such as social support systems) seem to influence "how well" someone is going to do in a program more than the treatment activities themselves (Polich et al., 1981; Moos and Finney, 1983). Recent research has confronted us with two challenges: First, that there is enormous clinical diversity among people who share the common problem of psychoactive substance abuse and, second, our existing methods of treatment are not very good compared to time alone. The interest in dual diagnosis emerged from this growing appreciation of the complexities which surround substance abuse and its treatment. It was reasoned that perhaps some people do poorly, despite our best efforts, because they also require assistance with "other problems" that we have failed to recognize.

As we shall see in the next section, when "new" diagnostic criteria are systematically applied to groups of substance abusers, a very large number are found to satisfy psychiatric definitional standards for other non-substance abuse mental disorders as well. Such findings led some to assume that the striking clinical diversity among the chemically dependent was due, in part, to the co-existence or co-occurrence of additional mental disorders (Powell et al., 1983; Penick et al., 1984). They also led to the proposal that some substance abusers might benefit from treatments originally developed for other types of mental disorder (e.g., Klein et al., 1974). This conclusion was supported by the experiences of some clinicians who pointed out that many individuals diagnosed and treated only for a non-substance abuse mental disorder clearly also needed assistance for alcohol and/or drug problems when their clinical histories were examined more carefully (Gottheil, McLellan and Druley, 1980).

Recognition of dual diagnoses is important to both the patient and his/her family for several reasons. The most obvious reason, of course, is the possibility of receiving additional forms of treatment which may reduce suffering and enhance personal efficiency, thereby decreasing the "need" to use substances of abuse. This presumption is unchallenged when applied to the many medical complications which often accompany substance abuse. It is less well accepted with respect to possible co-occurring mental disorders. Nevertheless, many believe that symptoms of anxiety, depression, restlessness or confused thinking can interfere with the individual's ability to effectively "work a program" and may directly trigger a relapse (Marlatt, 1985; Gorsky and Miller, 1986). From this prospective, the combination of substance abuse treatment with other therapeutic strategies is thought to provide greater overall benefit to some dual diagnosis patients. Recognition of dual diagnosis is potentially important even in instances where a consensus has *not* been formed in the professional community about how the co-existing disorder should best be treated; for example, treatment of many of the personality disorders. Despite the absence of "proven" treatments, the patient and his/her family can often acquire a much greater understanding about "what is going on" if provided with information about another disorder which is co-existing with the substance abuse. A basic component of most substance abuse treatment programs is education about the "illness," another pioneering contribution of the chemical dependency field which only recently has begun to find its way into other areas of mental health. This very practical and focused educational approach can be quite helpful when applied to non-substance abuse types of mental disorders such as phobia, or panic attack or mood disorder. It is reasonable to assume that patient/family education about the substance abuse problem when combined with educational efforts about other co-existing disorders should prove especially helpful. For example, patients whose alcoholism is complicated by episodes of major depression or panic attacks may experience significant marital and job-related problems even when sober. Education about these disorders and the initiation of treatment for these disorders frequently can result in a lessening of symptoms, decreased self doubt and greater acceptance and support from others.

Awareness of "dual diagnoses" by the health care provider is equally important. Recognition of co-existing disorders can increase the number of treatment options and provide patients and their families with useful information and "management tips" about a variety of interrelated problems. The result is a truly "individualized," longterm treatment plan where the elimination of substance abuse continues as a major goal. A less obvious benefit that goes along with the recognition of dual diagnosis concerns the morale among health care providers. High rates of relapse and/or the failure of abstinence to produce "normally" happy and successful human beings can promote "burn out," self depreciation or, worse, a tendency to "blame" the patient if he/she is not doing well. This is true for those providers who mostly work with substance abusers as well as those who mostly work in mental health where the addition of substance abuse to another psychiatric disorder can prove particularly discouraging. Increased risk for relapse and less than optimal functioning during periods of abstinence is thought to characterize dual diagnosis patients, especially if their co-existing disorder is overlooked or ignored. Recognition of dual diagnosis can prevent the service provider from "getting down" on him/herself and their patients. It can also lead to a renewed sense of optimism and a more discriminating appraisal of what is or is not realistically possible from their efforts alone.

Program developers and program administrators need to become more cognizant of the issues surrounding dual diagnosis in order to overcome the legacies of the past that promoted the unfortunate schisms between the substance abuse and mental health fields (Caragonne and Emery, 1987). Without their understanding and support, very little progress is likely to be made. Admission criteria, evaluation procedures, staffing patterns, program formats, referral policies and aftercare plans will have to be re-examined if the dual diagnosis patient is to find an adequate place in our health care system. This is not to say that all programs should be "all things" to every dual diagnosis patient. Such an approach would be unnecessary, unworkable and excessively expensive. Nevertheless, many substance abuse personnel are likely to require additional training in the identification of, and screening for, co-occurring mental disorders. Many could also benefit from exposure to forms of therapy that are often used in caring for individuals with these nonsubstance abuse disorders in order to maintain their role as full partners in the treatment endeavor. In a like manner, many mental health personnel would benefit from more varied and intense training experiences in the shortterm and longterm management of chemically dependent individuals. These training experiences might include: exposure to the rich variety of educational materials that have been developed by the substance abuse field for patients and their families; close supervision in different approaches that have been used to "motivate" patients to relinquish their dependency; and, guided experiences in ways of trying to prevent a "relapse" or minimizing the consequences of a relapse when it occurs. Just as important, programs representing the substance abuse and mental health fields will need to acknowledge that simply combining two widely used and well regarded treatments *may not* be the answer for many dual diagnosis patients. For example, Harrison et al. (1985) believe that the confrontational approaches often used with good success in drug and alcohol abuse rehabilitation programs are particularly counterproductive when applied to substance abusers who also suffer from a schizophrenic or schizoaffective disorder. Entirely original forms of treatment may need to be created and tested. Established substance abuse and mental health programs are in a unique position to lead the way in discovering more effective ways of caring for dual diagnosis patients, especially if both are willing to learn from each other and both are willing to eliminate some of the rigid separatist beliefs and practices that have divided them for so long. However, change will not come about easily or cheaply. Thus, recognition of dual diagnosis patients is important for those who control and allocate funds. Hopefully, private boards, legislators and public interest groups will learn from the mistakes of the past. Certainly what is *not* needed is a third parallel system of care, exclusively dedicated to dual diagnosis patients, which is distinct from and in competition with ongoing substance abuse and mental health programs.

Finally, it is essential for the research communities and those who support them to focus more clearly on the problem of dual diagnosis. Large, systematic, longterm followup and family studies are badly needed to gain a greater understanding of these conditions (Caragonne and Emery, 1987). We need to know more about the genetic and psychosocial backgrounds of dual diagnosis patients and more about the interplay between co-occurring disorders with the substance abuse disorders over time. Equally important, carefully controlled clinical trials are needed to document the short and longterm efficacy of various forms of treatment with dual diagnosis patients. The service providers cannot manage these tasks alone; the research community must help out.

III. WHAT RESEARCH TELLS US ABOUT DUAL (REALLY PLURAL) DIAGNOSIS

Those working closely with chemically dependent individuals have recognized for decades that *signs and symptoms* associated with other nonsubstance abuse mental disorders are common manifestations. This is especially true of signs and symptoms that are associated with the various mood disorders, psychotic states, organic neurological conditions and personality disorders. The question has been and continues to be: what *do* these signs and symptoms mean? Are they just the direct and indirect consequences of the chemical abuse itself? Are they causally related or partially responsible for the abusive behaviors? Should one consider these signs and symptoms in order to form an independent diagnosis which is separate from the complications known to be associated with chronic abuse? And, most important, should one use these signs and symptoms to form an independent diagnosis for the purpose of treatment? There are no definitive answers to these questions at the present time (Frances and Allen, 1986; Allen and Frances, 1986). A basic assumption which weaves its way through the chapters of this book is that the identification and recognition of co-existing signs and symptoms representative of other types of mental disorders is, first of all, possible and second, potentially meaningful and useful to both the clinician and the patient. The reader who would like to quickly get an overview of this field would probably find it helpful to survey the following books in the order that they were published: *Alcoholism and Affective Disorders* (Goodwin and Erickson, 1979); *Substance Abuse and Psychiatric Illness* (Gottheil, McLellan, Druley, 1980); *Alcoholism and Clinical Psychiatry* (Solomon, 1982); *Substance Abuse and Psychopathology* (Mirin, 1984); *Substance Abuse and Psychopathology* (Alterman, 1985); and, *Psychopathology and Addictive Disorders* (Meyer, 1986a). These edited books discuss a wide range of issues and practical questions associated with "dual diagnosis"; they represent the "state of the art" at the close of the 1980s.

Until recently, a very large obstacle which stood in the way of recognizing and understanding "dual diagnosis" was the lack of clear and straight-forward diagnostic standards in the mental health field. Although not without problems of their own, the creation of DSM-III in 1980 and its revision, DSM-III-R in 1987, essentially resolved this problem for the time being.[3] The Task Force responsible for the DSM-IIIs deliberately adopted a descriptive, "atheoretical," categorical approach to diagnosis (Spitzer and Klein, 1978). They attempted to provide explicit standards or criteria that could be easily applied by representatives of different professions to identify and diagnose mental disorders—also referred to as syndromes—which included the substance abuse disorders. When possible, the DSM-III Task Force tried to provide standards or diagnostic criteria that previous research had shown to be both reliable and valid. The Task Force realized that individual patients often manifest signs and symptoms of more than one mental disorder. The first DSM-III tried to help the clinician formulate a diagnostic judgment about these dual and multiple syndrome patients by providing a series of "decision trees" based upon a "partial" ordering or heirarchy of the various mental disorders. This effort was not very successful (Boyd et al., 1984). Thus, the revised DSM-III adopts a more "hierarchy-free" approach to dual or multiple diagnosis patients, encouraging clinicians to list all identified syndromes in their diagnostic formulations.

What has been found when these modern diagnostic standards are applied, without bias, to groups of substance abusers? The results have been remarkably consistent overall, although details may vary from study to study. Beginning with the early studies by Winokur and his colleagues at Washington University in St. Louis (Winokur et al., 1970, 1971; Cadoret and Winokur, 1974), investigators have found that a substantial proportion of individuals seeking help for a chemical dependency problem will also satisfy inclusive diagnostic criteria for one or more additional mental disorders. These findings have been replicated in clinical studies as well as large-scale community studies which do not begin with individuals who are requesting help from a specialist. For example, Weissman et al., (1980) using the Schedule for Affective Disorders and Schizophrenia (SADS), reported that approximately 70 percent of the identified community alcoholics also met criteria for another major psychiatric syndrome, with depression being the most prevalent co-existing disorder. An important recent community study reported by Helzer and Pryzbeck (1988) administered the Diagnostic Interview Schedule (DIS) to thousands of residents throughout the United States. The authors identified all community participants who fulfilled rigorously defined, lifetime diagnostic criteria for alcoholism and then looked at what other psychiatric disorders they also had. As noted by Helzer and Pryzbeck: "every one of the psychiatric disorders we examined was more likely to occur in alcoholics than nonalcoholics" (1988, p 219. See also Deykin et al., 1987, for a community study of adolescents and Weissman, 1988, for community studies of the co-occurrence of alcoholism and anxiety disorders.) Table 1 presents some data we collected in two studies of 928 male VA patients admitted for alcoholism treatment. Using the Psychiatric Diagnostic Interview (PDI, Othmer et al., 1981), we found that 38 percent of the men satisfied inclusive diagnostic criteria for alcoholism only; 62 percent met diagnostic criteria for one or more additional psychiatric syndromes. Thirty percent fulfilled criteria for one additional syndrome; 16 percent met diagnostic criteria for two additional syndromes; 12 percent satisfied criteria for three additional syndromes; while 4 percent met criteria for four or more co-existing disorders. The average number of positive syndromes, out of a possible 15, was 2.2 (SD = 1.12) which included alcoholism. The second column of this table presents the lifetime prevalence figures or base rates for the various syndromes reviewed independently by the PDI for this large group of alcoholic males. As can be seen, depression, antisocial personality and drug abuse were the most frequently identified co-occurring syndromes. This table also shows how these additional syndromes were related to each other. Thus, if one starts with the 159 alcoholic men who were also positive for drug abuse, one can see that 55 percent of these also fulfilled diagnostic criteria for antisocial personality. Conversely, if one starts with the 223 alcoholic men who met criteria for antisocial personality, one can see that only 39 percent also satisfied diagnostic criteria for drug abuse. The starred Odds Ratios show those syndrome combinations which exceeded expectation (e.g., the association between mania and depression is nine times greater than expected). These findings indicated that the majority of alcoholic patients had an additional psychiatric disorder and that a substantial number had two or more additional disorders, (over 50 percent of the alcoholics with one additional psychiatric disorder, also had at least one more). Furthermore, these findings indicated that certain disorders seem to co-occur in combinations beyond that expected by chance alone.

Other investigators who have utilized modern contemporary diagnostic standards have reported similar results among: *alcoholic* samples (e.g., Fowler et al., 1977; Mullaney and Trippet, 1979; Powell et al., 1983; Meyer and Hesselbrock, 1984; Hesselbrock, Meyer, Keener, 1985; Chambess et al., 1987; Mendelson et al., 1986); *opiate abuse* samples (e.g., Croughan et al., 1982; Rounsaville et al., 1982, 1985; Dackis and Gold, 1984; Khantzian and Treece, 1985); *cocaine abuse* samples (e.g., Weiss and Mirin, 1984; Gawin and Kleber, 1986) and, *marijuana abuse* samples (e.g., Halikas, 1974; Weller and Halikas, 1985). We are aware of no study of substance abusers that used modern diagnostic criteria, where the rate of dual diagnosis or multiple psychiatric syndromes fell appreciably below one third. Thus, at a minimum, one out of three men and women who seek help for a chemical dependency problem are likely to satisfy diagnostic standards for another psychiatric disorder. Recent studies suggest that the figure should be greater; that is, at least one half will probably satisfy definitional standards for a co-occurring psychiatric disorder, with rates for co-morbidity probably ranging higher among narcotic abusers. As procedures created to implement DSM-III-R criteria for personality disorders improve, the co-morbidity rates among substance abusers are likely to rise even more. An additional factor which probably will also influence the incidence of dual diagnoses or multiple psychiatric syndromes in the future is the substantial increase, over the last two decades, of the combined abuse of alcohol and other drugs (Clayton, 1986; Norton and Noble, 1987; Ross et al., 1988).

There is a flip side to clinical data for dual diagnosis. In the clinical studies cited above, the investigators began with identified substance abuse groups and found high rates of other additional psychiatric disorder. The flip side is to begin with samples of patients who are assigned some *other* psychiatric diagnosis or patients who represent diagnostically heterogeneous psychiatric populations, such as inpatients, and then determine the rates of substance

TABLE 1. Co-Occurrence of Psychiatric Syndromes in a Large Sample of Male Alcoholics Administered the Psychiatric Diagnostic Interview (N = 928)

Lifetime Prevalence[1]

N	%	Syndrome	OBS	Drug	Mania	Dep
17	1.8	OBS	--- ---	6 (1) 0.3	41 (7) 3.6*	65 (11) 3.3*
159	17.1	Drug	1 (1) 0.3	--- ---	23 (36) 1.6	44 (70) 1.5
154	16.6	Mania	4 (7) 3.6*	23 (36) 1.6	--- ---	79 (121) 9.4*
338	36.4	Dep	3 (11) 3.3*	21 (70) 1.5	36 (121) 9.4*	--- ---
30	3.2	Schiz	3 (1) 1.9	33 (10) 2.5*	53 (16) 6.3*	90 (27) 16.9*
223	24.0	ASP	1 (3) 0.7	39 (88) 5.8*	23 (51) 1.7*	44 (99) 1.6
6	0.1	Briquet	0 (0)	17 (1) 0.9	67 (4) 10.3*	83 (5) 8.8
80	8.6	O-C	4 (3) 2.3	31 (25) 2.4*	42 (34) 4.5*	77 (62) 7.1*
62	6.7	Phobia	3 (2) 1.9	23 (14) 1.5	43 (27) 4.5*	68 (42) 4.0*
88	9.5	Panic	6 (5) 4.2*	25 (22) 1.7	48 (42) 5.9*	70 (62) 4.9*
7	0.8	MR	29 (2) 24.2*	0 (0)	57 (4) 6.9*	71 (5) 4.4
10	1.1	Homo	0 (0)	30 (3) 2.1	30 (3) 2.2	60 (6) 2.6

1. The precentages do not add up to 100 because an alcoholic subject could satisfy criteria for more than one additonal psychiatric disorder.

2. In each cell of the matrix, the first line indicates the percent, in bold, of those patients positive for the syndrome shown in the far left column who were *also* positive for the co-occurring syndromes shown in the right matrix. The first

Co-Occurring Psychiatric Syndromes

Schiz	ASP	Briquet	O-C	Phob	Panic	MR	Homo
6 (1) 1.9	18 (3) 0.7	0 (0)	18 (3) 2.3	12 (2) 1.9	29 (5) 4.2*	12 (2) 24.2*	0 (0)
6 (10) 2.5*	55 (88) 5.8*	1 (1) 0.9	16 (25) 2.4*	9 (14) 1.5	14 (22) 1.7	0 (0)	2 (3) 2.1
10 (16) 6.3*	33 (51) 1.7*	3 (4) 10.3*	22 (34) 4.5*	17 (27) 4.5*	27 (42) 5.9*	3 (4) 6.9*	2 (3) 2.2
8 (27) 16.9*	29 (99) 1.6	1 (5) 8.8	18 (62) 7.1*	12 (42) 4.0*	18 (62) 4.9*	1 (5) 4.4	2 (6) 2.6
--- ---	43 (13) 2.5*	0 (0)	43 (13) 9.5*	43 (13) 13.3*	50 (15) 11.3*	3 (1) 5.1	7 (2) 7.9*
6 (13) 2.5*	--- ---	4 (1) 0.6	18 (40) 3.6*	9 (21) 1.7	13 (28) 1.5	1 (3) 2.4	1 (3) 1.4
0 (0)	17 (1) 0.6	--- ---	33 (2) 5.4	33 (2) 7.2*	67 (4) 19.9*	17 (1) 30.5*	0 (0)
16 (13) 9.5*	50 (40) 3.6*	2 (2) 5.4	--- ---	27 (22) 7.7*	36 (29) 7.6*	2 (2) 4.3	2 (2) 2.7
21 (13) 13.3*	34 (21) 1.7	3 (2) 7.2*	35 (22) 7.7*	--- ---	43 (27) 10.2*	6 (4) 19.8*	0 (0)
17 (15) 11.3*	32 (28) 1.5	4 (4) 19.9*	33 (29) 7.6*	31 (27) 10.2*	--- ---	4 (4) 13.3*	1 (1) 1.1
14 (1) 5.1	43 (3) 2.4	14 (1) 30.5*	29 (2) 4.3	57 (4) 19.8*	57 (4) 13.3*	--- ---	0 (0)
20 (2) 7.9*	30 (3) 1.4	0 (0)	20 (2) 2.7	0 (0)	10 (1) 1.1	0 (0)	--- ---

line also provides the absolute number, in parentheses, of alcoholic cases with both disorders. The second line in each cell shows the Odds Ratio derived from LOGIT; the starred Odds Ratios indicate that the ratio exceeds that expected at a 95 percent confidence level.

abuse among these groups. Again, the results are impressively consistent although the details vary from investigator to investigator. Patients associated with mental health systems who carry a *non*-substance abuse diagnosis also tend to be at higher risk for a co-existing chemical dependency problem compared to the general population (e.g., Crowley, 1973; Fowler et al., 1977; Robins et al., 1977; Mezzich et al., 1982; Alterman, 1985c; Koenigsberg et al., 1985; Allen and Frances, 1986; Frances and Allen, 1986). Increased rates of substance abuse have been reported for patients diagnosed as: *schizophrenic* (Alterman et al., 1980); *manic-depressive* (Dunner et al., 1979); *depressed* (O'Sullivan et al., 1979); *dysthymic* (Markowitz, Kocsis and Frances, 1988); *phobic anxiety* (Quitkin et al., 1972; Mullaney and Trippett; 1979), *agoraphobia with panic attacks* (Brier et al., 1986); *bulimic* (Mitchell et al., 1985); *somatization disorder* (Katon, 1984); *antisocial personality* (Robins, 1986); *post traumatic stress disorder* (Davidson, 1985); and, *borderline personality disorder* (Dahl, 1985).

Despite the impressive consistency of modern research which indicates that dual diagnoses or plural diagnoses are fairly common among substance abusers, some clinicians remain skeptical. They fear a premature and uncritical "bandwagon mentality" that may result in the application of inappropriate and potentially harmful treatments which could subvert the main goal of therapy which is, of course, to assist the individual to overcome his or her pathological dependency on chemical substances. Meyer (1986b) refers to this as the "chicken and egg" problem. There are two major, interrelated problems about the idea of dual diagnosis that remain unclear (Huey, 1978; Keeler et al., 1979; Petty and Nasrallah, 1981; Schuckit, 1983a, 1983b, 1985, 1986; Alterman, 1985b; Mayfield, 1985; Cummings et al., 1985; Allen and Frances, 1986; Bean-Bayog, 1986, 1988; Brown and Schuckit, 1988). The first concerns the widely acknowledged fact that social, emotional and cognitive *consequences* of chronic drug abuse can fully "mimic" the signs and symptoms associated with other mental disorders, including those associated with many personality disorders. As the substance abuse improves, many of these signs and symptoms also disappear or resolve spontaneously, suggesting that they are little more than transient epiphenomena rather than "true" indicators of a separate disease or disorder. The second problem surrounding dual diagnosis is the primary-secondary question where the words "primary" and "secondary" are used only to indicate the sequence in time a disorder or condition first occurs, not causal relationships. Many authors feel that the primary-secondary distinction is critical in understanding the clinical implications of dual diagnosis although accurate dating of the onset of substance abuse and other chronic psychiatric disorders is very difficult (Penick et al., 1982; Parrella and Filstead, 1988). Such authors would argue, for example, that depressions which are secondary or begin after abusive drinking should be regarded quite differently than depressions which precede and are primary to alcoholism. Similarly, antisocial activities which precede and are primary to drug abuse should be regarded differently, in a diagnostic sense, than anti-social acts which accompany or follow drug abuse (Schuckit, 1983b, 1986). At this point in time, these unresolved problems surrounding the issue of dual diagnosis involve complex research methodological problems that would be of little interest to most readers but which continue to create an air of controversy about this subject.

When we first became interested in studying the co-occurrence of additional psychiatric syndromes among male alcoholics, we were repeatedly told: "You CAN'T make another psychiatric diagnosis with alcoholics until they have been dry for at least 6 months" . . . or "The only SURE way to know if an alcoholic has another psychiatric disorder is to prove that the other disorder started well before the drinking problems started." We were also repeatedly asked: "How do you know the alcoholic depression is a REAL depression? How do you know alcoholics have TRUE panic attacks? Alcohol makes some people anti-social, how do you know that they REALLY have an antisocial personality?" The answer was, and still is, that we have no way of knowing if these co-occurring conditions are "real" or "true" disorders because the mental health field has no definitive markers or laboratory tests that could be used to answer such questions. We simply know that certain clusters of signs and symptoms occur among many substance abusers and that these clusters of signs and symptoms resemble those used to identify or diagnose other disorders in the mental health field. The etiology or cause of most psychiatric disorders is unknown just as the pathophysiology or underlying mechanisms which produce the signs and symptoms of substance abuse are also not understood (Goodwin and Guze, 1984). When the etiology and pathophysiology of *major* clinical syndromes are unknown, indirect study methods have been used to establish the clinical validity or clinical relevance of definitional criteria created to diagnose them (Guze, 1970). We have suggested that a similar strategy would be helpful in examining the significance of meaningfulness of co-morbid or co-occurring syndromes among substance abuse groups (Penick et al., 1984). Table 2 provides a conceptual model of validation for substance abuse subtypes which is derived from a clinical medicine. In this model we recognize that many approaches have been proposed to reduce the enormous clinical diversity which exists among individuals who receive the diagnosis of substance use disorder. These approaches essentially represent different ways of classifying or subtyping the chemical dependencies and result in

TABLE 2. Methods to Establish the Clinical Validity of Substance Abuse Subtypes

---

To fully demonstrate the clinical validity (i.e., practical relevance and usefulness) of substance abuse subtypes, it is necessary to show that:

1. THE PROCEDURES OF SUBTYPING ARE RELIABLE (i.e., shortterm reliability and consistency).

2. THE SUBTYPYES ARE STABLE OVER TIME (i.e., longterm reliability and consistency).

3. THE NATURAL COURSE AND MORBIDITY VARY AS A FUNCTION OF SUBTYPE (i.e., age of onset, medical and social sequelae, patterns of drinking, mortality, spontaneous remissions differ across subtypes).

4. THE PROGNOSIS OF THE SUBTYPES DIFFER OVER TIME (i.e., the subtypes serve as differential predictors of outcome).

5. THE SUBTYPES ARE DISTINGUISHED BY FAMILY HISTORY OF SUBSTANCE ABUSE AND OTHER PSYCHIATRIC DISORDER (i.e., the prevalance of psychiatric disorder among biological relatives differ by subtype).

6. CERTAIN TREATMENT MODALITIES ARE MORE EFFECTIVE WITH CERTAIN SUBTYPES THAN OTHERS (i.e., differential response to treatment).

7. BIOLOGICAL VARIABLES ARE DIFFERENTIALLY CORRELATED WITH THE SUBTYPES (e.g., cell metabolism, neurotransmitter levels, biological markers, etc.).

typologies of substance abuse (Babor and Meyer, 1986; Babor and Lauerman, 1986). The concept of dual diagnosis is one approach that has been proposed to classify or subtype substance abusers (Penick et al., 1984). That is, substance abusers who manifest signs and symptoms of *other* psychiatric disorders are regarded differently and placed in different subclasses than those who do not.

But is this approach to subtyping substance abusers useful, meaningful and clinically valid? Are the skeptics correct when they suggest that most of the signs and symptoms associated with other psychiatric disorders are little more than transient correlates of suffering and secondary manifestations of the substance abuse itself? When asked questions about the "reality" or "trueness" of clinical symptoms which *seem* to reflect additional or co-occurring psychiatric disorders, we refer to the model shown in Table 2. We suggest that these are important questions. We also suggest that such questions can be addressed empirically by applying the validation model outlined in Table 2. For example, take alcoholics who also fulfill modern diagnostic criteria for schizophrenia, depression or antisocial personality and then compare them to alcoholics who do not satisfy these diagnostic criteria. If these alcoholic subgroups did not differ among themselves in any way, according to any of the features listed in Table 2, then one would have to conclude that these dual diagnosis subtypes are lacking clinical validity, are largely meaningless, and are unlikely to be useful or helpful. But these groups do appear to differ from each other. And, it is such differences that support the idea of dual diagnosis. It is such differences that provide some validation for classifying substance abusers according to the presence or absence of co-occurring psychiatric disorder.

IV. CLINICAL CHARACTERISTICS OF DUALLY DIAGNOSED SUBSTANCE ABUSERS

If the blueprint in Table 2 is used to survey what is known about the clinical validity of dual diagnosis subtypes, large gaps in our knowledge become immediately apparent. The supportive rhetoric that currently surrounds the concept of dual diagnosis clearly exceeds the "facts" as we know them today. We do know that the diagnosis of substance use disorder is among the most consistent, reliable and valid within the mental health field (Goodwin and Guze, 1984; Williams and Spitzer, 1980). We do not, however, know very much about the diagnostic reliability or consistency of *co-occurring* mental disorders among chemically dependent groups. This is such a basic question that it is often overlooked or simply taken for granted by proponents of dual diagnosis. The essential question is whether different clinicians, using the same definitional criteria, will agree with each other and themselves over time about the existence of one or more additional mental disorders among individuals who *also* satisfy diagnostic criteria for a substance abuse disorder. If the diagnoses of additional mental disorders are not reliable or reasonably consistent, then the whole idea of dual diagnosis becomes suspect. We know of only two studies that specifically addressed this question using contemporary diagnostic criteria. Rounsaville and his colleagues examined the short and long-term consistency of additional psychiatric diagnoses among opiate abusers (e.g., Rounsaville and Kleber, 1984). Using the SADS and lifetime criteria, good test-retest agreement was found for most of the additional psychiatric diagnoses up to a period of six months. However, after 2 1/2 years, the test-retest agreements declined substantially even though the additional diagnosis of depression, assigned initially at intake, was significantly associated with poorer outcomes (Rounsaville and Kleber, 1986b; Kosten, Rounsaville, Kleber, 1986). We gave the Psychiatric Diagnostic Interview (PDI) to a group of males hospitalized for alcoholism treatment and repeated the interview approximately one year later (Penick et al., 1988). We found that the 12-month test-retest agreements for "dual diagnoses" was relatively poor for the anxiety disorders and mania while they were more acceptable for drug abuse, depression and antisocial personality. We do not know why the agreements were not uniformly high across all disorders, especially since we applied lifetime definitional criteria. We do know that the few "new cases" which developed during the followup period could not explain the disagreements. We also know that most disagreements did not occur in alcoholics who denied *all* symptoms of another psychiatric disorder on one occasion the interview was given while admitting to many symptoms on a second occasion. Instead, it appeared that the number and intensity of symptoms decreased over time, tending to fall below the diagnostic *thresholds* used to define the various disorders. More research is obviously needed before any definite conclusions can be drawn about the reliability and consistency of dual diagnosis. Nevertheless, these studies suggest that a certain amount of caution is needed before the concept of dual diagnosis is uncritically embraced by clinical practitioners.

Returning to the outline in Table 2, we ask whether different dual diagnosis subtypes differ in terms of family history, age of onset, social-demographic characteristics, social effectiveness, clinical severity and outcome? The short answer is: "yes, probably." The more accurate answer is that this area of research is so vast and unsystematic at the present time that it is possible to find studies which both support and do not support the clinical validity of dual diagnosis subtypes according to these parameters. The research is impressively consistent in demonstrating that a large number of people who abuse substances will also satisfy diagnostic criteria for one or more additional mental disorders. And, that the frequency of these co-occurring disorders generally exceeds rates found in the general population. Nevertheless, we know little about how the co-occurring disorders are distributed among men and women substance abusers of different ages, different ethnic groups, different social-class backgrounds and different geographic regions. Equally important, we do not know much about these additional disorders among individuals who abuse different classes of drugs, within the social composites listed above. For example, it is now fairly well established that antisocial personality disorder occurs more often among male substance abusers while depressive disorders occur more frequently among female substance abusers (e.g., Rounsaville et al., 1982; Hesselbrock et al., 1985; Helzer and Pryzbeck, 1988). But this is also true among male and female *non*substance abusers as well (Regier et al., 1988). In reviewing the available data, it would appear to us that while the *absolute frequency* of other mental disorders is increased among chemically dependent groups, the *relative frequencies* of these disorders pretty much follow the rates established for socially comparable groups of nonsubstance abusers. For example, in our study of the prevalence of additional psychiatric disorders among male alcoholics (Powell et al., 1983), the *relative* rankings of the co-occurring disorders closely resembled the rankings found among men psychiatric patients and male non-patients without a drug or alcohol problem. Clearly, we need to know much more about the epidemiology of the different dual diagnoses in order to better allocate resources for prevention, formulate new approaches to treatment and facilitate basic research (Meyer and Kranzler, 1988).

We have discussed dual diagnosis in a global manner. What about the validity of specific dual diagnosis subtypes, such as substance abuse combined with depression or personality disorder? How well do these subtypes hold up against the parameters of clinical validation outlined in Table 2? Again, the short answer is: "pretty well" for all but the last two guidelines in Table 2. The more accurate answer, again, is that the research is extremely recent and unfocused. A broadly representative summary statement covering all possible dual diagnosis subtypes is not feasible at present. The authors of the chapters which follow will provide the reader with more details about specific clinical features which characterize and differentiate the various dual diagnosis subtypes. We will only comment generally about a study reported several years ago (Penick et al., 1984) which has recently been replicated with men alcoholics (Powell et al., 1989). We concluded that the *mono*syndromatic male alcoholic who satisfied modern diagnostic criteria for alcoholism *only*, differed in many striking ways from the *multi*syndromatic alcoholic who met criteria for one or more additional lifetime psychiatric disorders. In particular, the men with alcoholism-only tended to have a later onset of sustained problem drinking, fewer alcohol-related problems, somewhat greater social stability and more satisfying 12-month outcomes. They also acknowledged fewer biological relatives with an alcoholism problem and fewer biological relatives suffering from symptoms of other psychiatric disturbances. In a sense, the alcoholism-only group was older, less sick or impaired when we first met them, reported less genetic vulnerability in their families and tended to do better over time when compared to men alcoholics with major depression, manic-depressive disorder or antisocial personality disorder. The younger, antisocial personality disorder alcoholic subtype appeared most impaired, relatively speaking, whereas the depressed alcoholic subtype most closely resembled the alcoholism-only group according to age, course, severity and outcome of their abusive drinking. The distinctions noted above have generally been supported by the research of other investigators who have studied different substance abuse groups and other diagnostic subtypes (Croughan et al., 1982; O'Sullivan et al., 1983; Merikangas et al., 1984; Rounsaville et al., 1984, 1986, 1987; Hesselbrock et al., 1984, 1985, 1986; Mirin et al., 1984; Schuckit, 1985; Perkins, Simpson, Tsuang, 1986; Stabenau and Hesselbrock, 1984; Kostin et al., 1986, 1987: Lewis et al., 1987; Gawin and Kleber, 1986; Hasin, Endicott, Keller, 1988; Weissman, 1988). There have been some inconsistencies, however. In an early study by Schuckit and Winokur (1972), women alcoholics with primary depression did slightly better after three years than women with primary alcoholism. Hesselbrock et al. (1986) reported that only antisocial personality disorder, but not depression, was associated with an early onset and more virulent course of alcoholism in both men and women. Rounsaville et al. (1987) noted better clinical outcomes for women alcoholics who were depressed while depression was associated with poorer outcomes in men alcoholics. The same researchers found poorer outcomes associated with depression for both male and female opiate abusers (Rounsaville et al., 1986b). Thus, one cannot say that dual and multiple diagnoses among chemically dependent groups are always associated with an earlier onset of abusive behavior, greater clinical severity, poorer outcomes and increased psychopathology among biological relatives. But so far, these differentiating features seem to generally hold, especially for the antisocial substance abuse subtype which has been most extensively studied (Kay, 1985; Hesselbrock, 1986b). Clearly, more systematic comparative studies are needed.

There are four general issues in need of clarification before the concept of dual diagnosis can be widely adopted with confidence. The first is the primary-secondary issue mentioned previously. Schuckit (1983b, 1985, 1986) has argued persuasively that an understanding of this distinction is crucial, although studies supporting his emphasis are not always convincing (O'Sullivan et al., 1983; Powell et al., 1987; Rounsaville et al., 1987). Some consensus must be reached about the precise definition of "onset" so that studies can be conducted to examine the suggested importance of this temporal factor in dual diagnosis. As perceived by Schuckit and those who agree with him, other co-occurring mental disorders among substance abusers are clinically important only when they clearly started before the onset of the chemical abuse; i.e., when they are primary.

The second issue in need of clarification concerns the genetic factors possibly associated with dual diagnosis subtypes, (Stabenau, 1986). There is considerable controversy surrounding this technically complex area of research. Nevertheless, it appears fairly certain that the family pedigrees of substance abusers with and without another mental disorder differ from one another. Furthermore, the presence of an additional psychiatric disorder appears to increase the likelihood of that same disorder among biological relatives (Merikangas, 1984, 1985; Mirin et al., 1984a, 1984b; Penick et al., 1984; Hesselbrock, 1985, 1986a; Weissman, 1984, 1988; Crowe, 1985). How specific and direct the genetic influence is, remains an unanswered question. That is, do dual diagnosis subtypes "breed true?" No one is sure. Hesselbrock et al. (1984), have raised another intriguing issue regarding the genetic correlates of dual diagnosis. They suggest that individuals with certain dual diagnoses are more likely to marry and/or mate with others who also suffer from similar kinds of co-occurring mental disorder (i.e., assortative mating). If true, the question of genetic influence becomes tremendously more complicated.

Although we did not find striking genetic specificity in a recent family study of dual diagnosis subtypes, we did report a significant relationship between psychiatric heterogeneity among male alcoholics, as measured simply by the number of additional co-occurring syndromes, and the psychiatric heterogeneity of their family members, as measured by the number of different mental disorders reported among first degree relatives (Penick et al., 1984, 1987). Thus, the greater the psychiatric diversity in our male alcoholic patients, the greater the likelihood of increased psychopathology in their families. While this finding needs to be replicated by others, it suggests that both specific and nonspecific genetic factors may distinguish dual diagnosis subtypes from one another. Presently of greater theoretical interest than practical interest, the family genetic studies of dual and multiple diagnosis substance abusers are important and could be quite meaningful in the future. Such studies not only help to clinically validate the various dual diagnosis subtypes, they also are likely to prove helpful in clarifying the sociobehavioral precursors and natural histories of certain substance abuse groups. This information might be extremely useful in constructing more effective early identification and prevention strategies (Vaillant, 1983; Francis et al., 1984; Goodwin, 1984; Tarter et al., 1985; Cloninger, 1987). Such information might be equally useful in facilitating the search for biological "markers" of substance abuse disorders (Hill et al., 1986) which could ultimately result in a better understanding of the etiology and pathogenesis of the chemical dependencies.

Clinicians accustomed to treating heterogeneous substance abuse groups are quickly convinced by experience that enormous differences *do* exist between various kinds of dual diagnosis subtypes (Caragonne and Emery, 1987). The polydrug schizophrenic patient with a history of early antisocial behavior presents an entirely different set of problems to the clinician than the alcoholic who also happens to suffer from an abnormal fear of heights which he has usually managed to successfully avoid with few negative consequences. For example, Tsuang et al. (1982) reported that drug abusers with long-duration psychoses (i.e., greater than 6 months) most closely resembled "atypical" schizophrenic *non-drug* abusers with regard to their family histories, premorbid personality problems and clinical courses. Drug abusers with shorter duration psychoses (i.e., less than 6 months) most closely resembled drug abusers who had never experienced a frank psychosis. Thus, drug abusers who also appeared schizophrenic showed greater dysfunction and had unusually high rates of schizophrenia and affective disorder among their biological relatives. While this research involved a hospital chart review and the patients were not directly examined from a dual diagnosis perspective, it is one of the few studies that has examined the longterm course of substance abusers with a severe mental illness. Systematic comparative studies of substance abusers with the more severe forms of co-occurring mental disorders are virtually nonexistent: a third area in which needed information is lacking (Alterman, 1985b). One reason for this neglect is that most dual diagnosis researchers are associated with programs that specialize in substance abuse treatment. Because of the "schisms" from the past that we spoke of earlier, the more severely mentally ill patients usually do not end up in such programs and, as a result, do not end up in the researchers' study samples. It is not very satisfying to simply state that dual diagnosis subtypes seem to differ in their family histories, onsets, natural courses and outcomes. The more substantial question is not only how they differ but also by how much? And, for how long? More dual diagnosis subtypes need to be included in our studies and directly compared to each other before generalizations can be made. We need more information about the possible interactions between specific drugs of abuse and the additive influence of co-occurring psychiatric disorders. Finally, more attention needs to be given to those chemically dependent individuals who fulfill modern diagnostic criteria for *two or more* additional co-occurring mental disorders. Such individuals are not rare (Powell et al., 1983) and only now are beginning to be looked at more closely (Powell et al., 1986). The issue of multiple co-occurring disorders could assume special importance in the future. For example, Woody and his colleagues (1985) suggest that drug abusers with antisocial personality disorder *and* depression responded somewhat better to psychotherapy and methadone maintenance than antisocial drug abusers who were not depressed.

The last issue in need of clarification is the association between different *kinds* of outcomes and different dual diagnosis subtypes. Very little is known about the relationship between outcome and dual diagnosis subtypes despite the fact that followup studies have been considered one of the most powerful ways to establish the validity of clinical syndromes. Practitioners in the field tend to equate a "good" outcome with total abstinence although every experienced practitioner knows of abstinent patients who are miserable and function very poorly. Many different ways have been used to assess the clinical outcomes of substance abusers, besides continued consumption. These include: death from natural causes; the presence of other medical conditions; continued need for treatment, including medication; social and occupational functioning; legal difficulties; life stress events; performances on tests of cognitive ability; measures of personality; ratings of life satisfaction; evaluations by significant others; and, dimensions of emotional distress, such as anxiety and depression. Unfortunately, these different ways of defining outcome are not perfectly correlated with each other or with the individual's substance abuse status at followup. Furthermore, the relationships among such outcome measures can change as the duration of followup lengthens (Polich et al., 1981). In an important recent paper, Babor and colleagues (1988) examined the correlations among different outcome measures in a one-year followup study of alcoholics. They found support for both the unitary and multidimensional models of treatment outcome, recommending the continued use of multiple measures until there is a better understanding of what these measures really signify in the lives of individual substance abusers.

In a recently completed 12-month, "naturalistic" followup study of 319 men alcoholics (Powell et al., 1989), we were surprised by our findings. Initially, we had classified these male inpatients into four subtypes according to the co-occurrence of additional psychiatric syndromes: (1) alcoholism-only; (2) alcoholism plus affective and/or anxiety disorder; (3) alcoholism plus drug abuse and/or antisocial personality; and (4) a mixed group with alcoholism plus drug abuse/antisocial personality as well as affective and/or anxiety disorder. Our decision to combine drug abuse with antisocial personality and affective disorder with anxiety disorder was based upon the results of a discriminant function analysis which indicated that the clinical histories of such individuals resembled each other. At the beginning of the study, these four dual diagnosis subtypes were found to differ markedly along multiple dimensions which included alcoholism severity, social functioning, indices of psychopathology and the use of mental health treatments. After one year, to our surprise, the four subtypes *did not* differ on most measures of drinking behavior. Although the patient group as a whole, and each subtype, had significantly improved during this time, the alcoholism severity scores, reflecting the 12-month followup period, had begun to converge. The drinking outcomes of the four subtypes were no longer significantly different. We examined a variety of drinking outcomes, such as total abstinence from alcohol, and found the same thing. Drinking behaviors and problems associated with drinking no longer strongly distinguished the four dual diagnosis subgroups at the end of the study. However, this lack of distinction was not true for other outcome measures that we used. The four groups continued to differ after one year on measures of psychopathology, current emotional distress and social effectiveness. If we had focused exclusively on drinking and its effects, we would have had to conclude that the dual diagnosis subtypes did not predict outcome. Actually, our findings showed that subtyping by co-occurring psychiatric syndromes predicts some outcomes better than others. We suspect this is also probably true for many dual diagnosis subtypes. Rounsaville et al., (1986a, 1986b) reported a similar result in a 2.5-year followup of opiate abusers where certain initial co-occurring mental disorders predicted current functioning and psychosocial adjustment at outcome but not substance use impairment. Using 22 measures to assess 7-month outcomes in a sample of opiate abusers, Woody et al. (1985), also found that the type of co-occurring psychiatric disorder influenced the various outcomes in different ways, with no direct effect of diagnosis on drug use although the opiate-abuse-only subtype showed the least amount of improvement on the drug use factor but was also least impaired initially. In contrast to the results of our recent study described above, Rounsaville et al. (1987) *did* find a significant relationship between co-occurring psychiatric disorders and the one-year drinking outcomes of alcoholics, with different effects for men and women. They too noted that the various methods of assessing outcome produced somewhat different results depending upon which co-occurring disorders were compared. Considering the above, it is apparent that research designed to examine the outcomes of dual diagnosis subtypes is still in its infancy. The question now is not whether dual diagnosis subtypes differ in outcome; they very probably do. The question now is how the various outcome measures differ by subtype and how stable and meaningful such differences are over time. The ability to predict different outcomes is certainly not a trivial pursuit. Suicide, violent deaths, traffic accidents and a reduced life span have all been associated with substance abuse and may be more highly related to some dual diagnosis subtypes than others (Helzer et al., 1985; Tsuang et al., 1985; Murphy, 1988).

We suspect that most practitioners interested in dual diagnosis have particular questions about the sixth method of establishing the validity of clinical syndromes outlined in Table 2: namely, differential responsiveness to treatment. Do the different dual diagnosis subtypes respond better or worse to different kinds of treatment? The experiences of many skilled clinicians suggest that they do. Research-based support for this assertion is, unfortunately, not very convincing at the present time. It is the treatment issue, probably more than any other, where the rhetoric of hope substantially exceeds the knowledge which has accumulated. For example, Alterman (1985b) realistically notes . . . "there is little known about how patients with conjoint diagnoses respond to treatment, although the limited available evidence suggests that they fare more poorly than do patients without . . ." (p. 133). A somewhat more hopeful conclusion was drawn by Francis and Allen (1986) who wrote:

> Patients who present with substance abuse and psychopathology have a poorer prognosis than those who have a single substance disorder without accompanying psychiatric disorders; however, they respond to treatment better when the multiple problems are addressed in a treatment tailored to their needs. *It is better to cut the shoes to fit the feet rather than the other way around.* [authors' emphasis, p. 436]

It is widely believed that dual diagnosis patients *generally* do not comply with, or respond well to, traditional substance abuse treatments compared to those patients who suffer from a chemical dependency problem alone (Carragonne and Emery, 1987). It is also widely believed that attempts to treat the co-occurring mental disorder among substance abusers are *generally* much less successful than attempts to treat the same disorder in nonsubstance abuser patients. Difficulties encountered in treating dual diagnosis patients is clearly not limited to the field of substance abuse alone. It is also true for the mental health field as a whole. For example, Grunhaus (1988) described a group of dual diagnosis patients who "respond less well to conventional . . ." treatment (p. 1214). He was not referring to substance abusers, however, but to patients who suffer from both major depression and panic attack disorder! Similarly, nonsubstance abuse patients who suffer from manic-depressive illness as well as a sustained psychosis (i.e., schizoaffective disorder) are notoriously difficult to treat successfully (Levitt and Tsuang, 1988).

Controlled, treatment evaluation studies of dual diagnostic subtypes are few in number, relatively recent and often methodologically poor, even when pharmacotherapy methods have been used (Ciccone, O'Brien, Khatami, 1980; Jaffe, 1984; Jaffe and Ciraulo, 1986; Liskow and Goodwin, 1987). Furthermore, the results of different studies often do not always agree (Kleber, 1983). Anecdotal descriptions of the treatment of dual-diagnosis patients are interesting but do not address the issue of *differential* therapeutic efficacy (e.g., see Gottheil and Weinstein, 1980; Harrison et al., 1985; Kofoed et al., 1986, 1988; Hellerstein and Meehan, 1987; Gallant, 1986, 1988).

Although psychotropic drugs are successfully used in the withdrawal phase of detoxification, the clinical usefulness of these medications in the extended care of dual diagnosis subtypes has not been shown (Liskow and Goodwin, 1987). At this time, there is no systematic evidence to support the longterm *differential efficacy* of psychotropic medications with dual diagnosis subtypes, despite the early enthusiasm for lithium, antidepressants and antianxiety agents. Part of the problem in evaluating the effectiveness of psychotropic drugs with dual diagnosis subtypes is the very poor compliance with medication regimes (Fawcett et al., 1984; Powell et al., 1985a). Other problems are: the definition of dual diagnosis subtypes, including the primary-secondary issue; the failure to include individuals with severe forms of additional mental illness in the clinical trials; insufficient monitoring of serum levels; and the pervasive research design problems which continue to plague the treatment evaluation field as a whole (Moos and Finney, 1983; Emrick and Hansen, 1983; Jaffe and Ciraulo, 1986; Miller and Heather, 1986; Holden, 1987; Longabaugh and Lewis, 1988). Similar difficulties can be found in attempts to study the effectiveness of psychosocial interventions, such as counseling and psychotherapy, with dual diagnosis subtypes. Currently, we do not definitely know if dual diagnosis substance abuse subtypes respond differently, in clinically significant ways, to various pharmacotherapies. We also do not definitely know whether the combination of pharmacotherapy with "standard" psychosocial interventions work "better" with some dual diagnosis subtypes than others. Finally, we do not definitely know if certain types of psychosocial treatment interventions are more or less helpful with specific dual diagnosis subtypes. Obviously, many experienced clinicians have come up with different ways, pharmacologic as well as psychosocial, to treat dual diagnosis subtypes (e.g., Gallant, 1988). The research community now needs to help the clinician sort out those treatment regimens which are most effective for different dual diagnosis subtypes. There are hints from research but few facts that have been replicated.

The extremely productive group in Pennsylvania has provided some of these hints (Woody et al., 1983, 1984, 1985, 1986; McLellan et al., 1980, 1983a, 1983b, 1986). These researchers found that a global measure of "psychiatric severity" best predicted the outcomes of alcohol and drug abusing patients (not the severity of substance abuse initially). They also found that the different treatment programs did not seem to influence the outcomes of substance abusers in the "low" and "high" ranges of psychiatric severity but did exert a differential influence on the treatment outcomes of those patients in the "middle" range of psychiatric severity. Later, in a prospective study, patients were "matched" to treatment programs which earlier research had suggested would be most beneficial for them and it was found that "matched" patients had more favorable outcomes than "unmatched" patients. These authors also showed, in a controlled study, that psychotherapy added to methadone maintenance benefited an opiate dependent group more than drug counseling alone and that depressed opiate abusers seemed to benefit most from the methadone-psychotherapy combination, followed by opiate-abusers only and opiate abusers with antisocial personality. Although antisocial opiate abusers showed the poorest outcomes, opiate abusers with antisocial personality disorder plus depression responded better than those with antisocial personality disorder alone.

The equally productive Connecticut group came to a somewhat different conclusion although they, too, have been interested in examining the influence of co-occurring psychiatric disorders among substance abusers (Rounsaville et al., 1982a, 1982b, 1984, 1985a, 1985b, 1986a, 1986b; Kosten et al., 1986, 1987; Kleber and Gawin, 1986; Gawin and Kleber, 1986). Like others, these researchers reported that the prevalence of co-occurring psychiatric disorders was high among alcohol and drug abusers and that the co-occurring psychiatric disorders predicted treatment outcomes. Furthermore, they reported different outcome effects for different therapeutic modalities on some measures of outcome. However, unlike the Pennsylvania group, they did not find that the dual-diagnosis-opiate-abuse subtypes were affected differently by the various treatment modalities; i.e., there was little interaction between diagnosis and treatment at outcome. They did report two intriguing results which may assume special importance in the future development of treatments for dual diagnosis subtypes. First, Kosten et al. (1986, 1987) in a 2 1/2 year followup study of treated opioid abusers reported that depression was associated with a continued or increased use of cocaine which, in turn, was associated with a poorer response to methadone maintenance treatment. They also noted that both depression and recent life crises were correlated with each other and that both predicted less favorable outcomes. Even more striking was the fact the combination of depression and recent life crises appeared to operate in an additive fashion; patients with both seemed to do even more poorly. These findings suggest complex causal relationships between co-occurring disorders, subsequent maladaptive behaviors, environmental influences and the effects of various forms of treatment.

Because the authors of the following chapters will provide greater detail about therapeutic approaches with specific dual diagnosis subtypes, we wish only to comment generally about two treatment issues. First, in many respects, the demonstration of differential responsiveness to various forms of treatment is one of the *weakest* methods to test the clinical validity of diagnostic classifications. This is true because most treatments in the mental health field, even psychotrophic medications, are quite nonspecific. Thus, the fact that two or more dual diagnosis subtypes respond equally well or equally poorly to the same treatment does not necessarily mean that they have the same etiologies and pathogeneses in common. Equating treatment response to responsible causes can only serve to block the discovery of unique precursors which must be known before rational treatment strategies can successfully evolve.

Our second comment centers on the "matching patients to treatment hypothesis'' (Gottheil et al., 1981; Pattison, 1985; Miller and Hester, 1986). This extremely seductive and apparently sensible idea is actually enormously difficult to implement in real life. It assumes that we have a clear idea about what outcomes are most important, over what period of time, and that we agree how they should be measured. As we noted earlier, this is not true. It also assumes that we have a clear idea about what features of the individual are important for matching purposes. Age? Age of onset? Sex? Ethnic background? Early childhood? Family history? Duration and pattern of abuse? Social functioning? Employment status? Indices of personality? Cognitive deficits? Or what? All of these have been suggested as ways of differentiating chemically dependent patients for specialized treatments. Defining subgroups of substance abusers according to the presence or absence of certain co-occurring psychiatric disorders – the dual diagnosis approach – is only one method that has been proposed for ''matching'' patients to treatment (Penick et al., 1984). As we have seen, it is too early to decide whether the dual diagnosis subtyping strategy will really ''pay off'' and help maximize our treatment efforts.

The ''matching hypothesis'' also assumes that the domain of currently available treatments is inclusive and exhaustive. It is this assumption that is most worrisome about the ''matching hypothesis.'' More specifically, the assumption is often made that we *have already created* good and effective treatment strategies; the only remaining problem is to find ways of selecting the ''right'' treatments for the ''right'' patients. An examination of the large body of research on treatment effectiveness with substance abuse casts doubt on this assumption (Emrick and Hansen, 1983; Powell et al., 1985b; Miller and Hester, 1986c). Just as there are many different ways of defining outcome and many different ways of defining patient characteristics for the purpose of ''matching,'' the word ''treatment'' has come to have many different meanings as well (Longabaugh and Lewis, 1988). Some think of treatment in terms of the facility in which it is offered such as inpatient versus outpatient. Others think of treatment in terms of who provides the service, such as professional versus nonprofessional or medical versus nonmedical. Still others define treatments by the goals of therapy (e.g., education vs. insight-oriented) or the specific procedures that are used (e.g., behavioral vs. dynamic). In the instance of dual diagnosis, it is frequently assumed that one need only add treatments for certain nonsubstance abuse mental disorders. This simplistic approach may prove to be correct; we really do not know. It should be tried. However, if our efforts to treat dual diagnosis patients by simply piling "conventional" treatments on top of each other do not work, the effort should not be abandoned as a failure of the "matching hypothesis." Instead, more creative and original ways of caring for these patients will need to be developed and tested.

The astute reader will note that we have not addressed the seventh or final method of validating dual diagnosis subtypes outlined in Table 2. This is because virtually nothing is known about the biological correlates of substance abusers classified according to co-occurring mental disorders. Jaffe and Ciraulo (1986) point out that while endocrine function tests, such as Dexomethasone Suppression Test for depressive conditions, may prove useful in differentiating dual diagnosis subtypes in the future, much more work needs to be done before such procedures have any practical value.

V. SUMMARY AND CONCLUSIONS

In this broad overview of dual diagnosis, we attempted to show how theoretical and professional "schisms" of the past and present have prevented a greater understanding of chemically dependent individuals who also suffer from one or more additional mental disorders. We argued that the recognition and treatment of such conditions was important to the continued growth and development of both the substance abuse and mental health fields where the merging of interests has become more common. We suggested that an increased focus on dual diagnosis was likely to benefit our patients and their families as well as those of us who serve them. The need for greater cooperation and collaboration at all levels, across many disciplines, was emphasized. Society becomes the "winner" if more effective ways of treating the dual diagnosis patient can be found.

Controversies surrounding the concept of dual diagnosis were reviewed; it was noted that many are skeptical of the importance of this idea. Nevertheless, when modern diagnostic criteria are used, a very large proportion of substance abusers will satisfy the definitional standards for another mental disorder. The paucity of systematic information about dual diagnoses subtypes was noted repeatedly; clearly, much more research needs to be done. Employing a model of clinical validity, we concluded that dual diagnosis patients seem to differ in many significant ways from their chemically dependent counterparts who do not experience signs and symptoms of other mental disorders. Many dual diagnosis subtypes appear to suffer from substance abuse problems at an earlier age and become more dysfunctional over time. Greater psychopathology seems to exist in their families of origin and they are less likely to respond well to conventional forms of treatment. However, not enough is known at this time to characterize differences among the various dual diagnosis subtypes or their specific treatment needs. The work in this field has hardly begun.

ENDNOTES

1. In 1986, the NCA changed its name to the National Council on Alcoholism and Drug Abuse (NCADA).
2. Longtime supporters of substance abuse treatment often caustically note that the professionals' interest in this problem was awakened by the 'smell of money.' This statement is true as far as it goes. The availability of public and private funds on a large scale signaled growing public support and a sense of responsibility for a problem no longer perceived as simply a human weakness. The "old timers" can take much of the credit for this change in public sentiment.
3. *Diagnostic and Statistical Manual of Mental Disorder*. Washington, DC, American Psychiatric Press.

REFERENCES

Report to the U.S. Congress on Alcohol and Health (1972, 1974). U.S. Govt. Printing Office, Washington, DC.

Allen, M. H., & Frances, R. J. (1986). Varieties of psychopathology found in patients with addictive disorders: A review. In R. E. Meyer (Ed.), Psychopathology and Addictive Disorders. New York: Guilford Press.

Alterman, A. I. (1985a). Substance Abuse and Psychopathology. New York: Plenum Press.

Alterman, A. I. (1985b). Relationships between substance abuse and psychopathology: Overview. In A. I. Alterman (Ed.), Substance Abuse and Psychopathology. New York: Plenum Press.

Alterman, A. I. (1985c). Substance abuse in psychiatric patients: Etiological, developmental, and treatment considerations. In A. I. Alterman (Ed.), Substance Abuse and Psychopathology. New York: Plenum Press.

Alterman, A. I., Erdlen, F. R., & McLellan, A. T. (1980). Problem drinking in a psychiatric hospital: Alcoholic schizophrenics. In E. Gottheil, A. T. McLellan, & K. A. Druley (Ed.), Substance Abuse and Psychiatric Illness. New York: Pergamon Press.

Babor, T. F., & Lauerman. (1986). Classification and forms of inebriety: Historical antecedents of alcoholism typologies. In E. M. Galanter (Ed.), Recent Developments in Alcoholism. New York: Plenum Press.

Babor, T. F., & Meyer, R. E. (1986). Typologies of alcoholics. In E. M. Galanter (Ed.), Recent Developments in Alcoholism. New York: Plenum Press.

Babor, T. F., Dolinsky, Z., Rounsaville, B. J., & Jaffe, J. (1988). Unitary versus multidimensional models of alcoholism treatment outcome: An empirical study. Journal of Studies on Alcohol, 49, 167-177.

Bean-Bayog, M. (1986). Psychopathology produced by alcoholism. In R. E. Meyer (Ed.), Psychopathology and Addictive Disorders. New York: Guilford Press.

Bean-Bayog, M. (1988). Alcoholism as a cause of psychopathology. Hospital and Community Psychiatry, 39, 352-354.

Boyd, J. H., Burke, J. D., Greenberg, E., Holzer, C. E., Rae, D. S., George, L. K., Karno, M., Stoltzman, R., & McEvoy, L. (1984). The exclusion criteria of DSM-III: A study of the co-occurrence of heirarchy-free syndromes. Archives of General Psychiatry, 41, 983-989.

Brier, A., Charney, D. S., & Heninger, G. R. (1986). Agoraphobia with panic attacks. Archives of General Psychiatry, 43, 1029-1036.

Brown, S. (1985). Treating the Alcoholic: A Developmental Model of Recovery. New York: John Wiley & Sons.

Brown, S. A., & Schuckit, M. A. (1988). Changes in depression among abstinent alcoholics. Journal of Studies on Alcohol, 49, 412-417.

Cadoret, R., & Winokur, G. (1974). Depression in alcoholism. Annals of The New York Academy of Science, 233, 34-39.

Caragonne, P. & Emery, B. (1987). Mental Illness and Substance Abuse: The Dually Diagnosed Client. 12300 Twinbrook Parkway, Suite 320, Rockville, Maryland: National Council of Community Mental Health Centers.

Chambless, D. L., Cherney, J., Caputo, G. C., & Rheinstein, B. J. G. (1987). Anxiety disorders and alcoholism: A study with inpatient alcoholics. Journal of Anxiety Disorders, 1, 29-40.

Ciccone, P. E., O'Brien, C. P., & Khatami, M. (1980). Psychotropic agents in opiate addiction: A brief review. International Journal of Addictions, 15, 449-513.

Clayton, R. R. (1986). Multiple Drug Use: Epidemiology, correlates, and consequences. In M. Galanter (Ed.), Recent Developments in Alcoholism. New York: Plenum Press.

Cloninger, C. R. (1987). Neurogenetic adaptive mechanisms in alcoholism. Science, 236, 410-416.

Croughan, J. L., Miller, J. P., Wagelin, D., & Whitman, B. Y. (1982). Psychiatric illness in male and female narcotic addicts. Journal of Clinical Psychiatry, 436(6), 225-228.

Crowe, R.R. (1985). The genetics of panic disorder and agoraphobia. Psychiatric Developments, 2, 171-186.

Crowley, T. J., Chesluk, D., Dilts, S., & Hart, R. (1973). Drug and alcohol abuse among psychiatric admissions. Archives of General Psychiatry, 30, 13-20.

Cummings, C. P., Prokop, C. K., & Cosgrove, R. (1985). Dysphoria: The cause or the result of addiction? The Psychiatric Hospital, 16, 131-134.

Dackis, C. A., & Gold, M. S. (1984). Depression in opiate addicts. In S. M. Mirin (Ed.), Substance Abuse and Psychopathology. Washington, DC: American Psychiatric Press.

Dahl, A.A. (1985). Borderline disorders: The validity of the diagnostic concept. Psychiatric Developments, 2, 109-152.

Daley, D. C., Moss, H., & Campbell, F. (1987). Dual Disorders: Counseling Clients with Chemical Dependency and Mental Illness. Hazeldon Foundation, Center City, MN.

Davidson, J., Swartz, M., Storck, M., Krishman, R. R., & Hammet, E. (1985). A Diagnostic and family study of posttraumatic stress disorder. American Journal of Psychiatry, 142(1), 90-93.

Deykin, E. Y., Levy, J. C., & Wells, V. (1987). Adolescent depression, alcohol and drug abuse. American Journal of Public Health, 77(2), 178-182.

Dunner, D. L., Hensel, B. M., & Fieve, R. R. (1979). Bipolar illness: Factors in drinking behavior. American Journal of Psychiatry, 136, 583-585.

Emrick, C. D., & Hansen, J. (1983). Assertions regarding effectiveness of treatment for alcoholism: Fact or fantasy? American Psychologist, 38, 1078-1088.

Fawcett, J., Clark, D. C., Gibbons, R. D., Aagesen, C. A., Pisani, V. D., Tilkin, J. M., Sellers, D., & Stutzman, D. (1984). Evaluation of Lithium therapy for alcoholism. Journal of Clinical Psychiatry, 45, 494-499.

Fingarette, H. (1988). Heavy Drinking: The Myth of Alcohol as a Disease. Berkeley, California: University of California Press.

Fowler, R. C., Liskow, B. I., Tanna, V. L., & Van Valkenburg, C. (1977). Psychiatric illness and alcoholism. Alcoholism: Clinical and Experimental Research, 1(2), 125-128.

Frances, R. J. (1988). Update on alcohol and drug disorder treatment. Journal of Clinical Psychiatry, 49, 13-17.

Frances, R. J., Bucky, S., & Alexopoulous, G. S. (1984). Outcome study of familial and nonfamilial alcoholism. American Journal of Psychiatry, 141, 1469-1471.

Frances, R. J., & Allen, M. H. (1986). The interaction of substance-use disorders with nonpsychotic psychiatric disorders. In R. Michels, & J. O. Cavenar Jr. (Ed.), Psychiatry (Vol. I). New York: Basic Books.

Freed, E. X. (1970). Alcoholism and manic depressive disorders: Some perspectives. Quarterly Journal of Studies on Alcohol, 31, 62-89.

Freed, E. X. (1973). Drug abuse by alcoholics: A review. International Journal of the Addictions, 8, 451-473.

Freed, E. X. (1975). Alcoholism and schizophrenia: The search for a perspective. Journal of Studies on Alcohol, 36, 853-881.

Gallant, D. M. (1986). The use of psychotrophic medications in alcoholism. Substance Abuse, 7, 35-47.

Gallant, D. M. (1988). Diagnosis and treatment of the depressed alcoholic patient. Substance Abuse, 9, 147-156.

Gawin, F. H., & Kleber, H. D. (1986). Abstinence symptomatology and psychiatric diagnosis in cocaine abusers. Archives of General Psychiatry, 43, 107-113.

Gorski, T. T., & Miller, M. (1986). Staying Sober: A Guide for Relapse Prevention. Independence, Missouri: Independence Press.

Goodwin, D. W. (1981). Alcoholism: The Facts. New York: Oxford University Press.

Goodwin, D. W. (1984). Studies of familial alcoholism: A growth industry. In D. W. Goodwin, K. T. Van Dusen, & S. A. Mednick (Ed.), Longitudinal Research in Alcoholism. Boston: Kluwer-Nijhoff.

Goodwin, D. W. & Erickson, C. K. (1979). Alcoholism and Affective Disorder. Jamaica, New York: Spectrum Publications.

Goodwin, D. W., & Guze, S. B. (1984). Psychiatric Diagnosis. New York: Oxford University Press.

Gottheil, E., & Weinstein, S. P. (1980). A coordinated program for treating combined mental health and substance abuse problems. In E. Gottheil, A. T. McLellan, & K. A. Druley (Ed.), Substance Abuse and Psychiatric Illness. New York: Pergamon Press.

Gottheil, E., McLellan, A. T., & Druley, K. A. (1980). Substance Abuse and Psychiatric Illness. New York: Pergamon Press.

Gottheil, E., McLellan, A. T., & Druley, K. A. (1981). Matching Patient Needs and Treatment Methods in Alcoholism and Drug Abuse. Springfield, Ill.: Charles C. Thomas.

Grunhaus, L. (1988). Clinical and psychobiological characteristics of simultaneous panic disorder and major depression. American Journal of Psychiatry, 145, 1214-1221.

Guze, S. B. (1970). The need for toughmindedness in psychiatric thinking. Southern Medical Journal, 63, 662-671.

Halikas, J. A., Goodwin, D. W., & Guze, S. B. (1972). Marijuana use and psychiatric illness. Archives of General Psychiatry, 27, 162-165.

Harrison, P. A., Martin, J. A., Tuason, V. B., & Hoffman, N. G. (1985). Conjoint treatment of dual disorders. In A. I. Alterman (Ed.), Substance Abuse and Psychopathology. New York: Plenum Press.

Hasin, D. S., Endicott, J., & Keller, M. B. (1988). RDC alcoholism in patients with major affective symptoms: 2 year course. American Journal of Psychiatry, in press.

Hellerstein, D. J., & Meehan, B. (1987). Outpatient group therapy for schizophrenic substance abusers. American Journal of Psychiatry, 144, 1337-1339.

Helzer, J.E., Robins, L.N., Taylor, J.R., Carey, K., Miller, R.H., Combs-Orme, T., & Farmer, A. (1985). The extent of long-term moderate drinking among alcoholics discharged from medical and psychiatric treatment facilities. New England Journal of Medicine, 312, 1678-1682.

Helzer, J. E., & Pryzbeck, T. M. (1988). The co-occurrence of alcoholism with other psychiatric disorders in the general population and its impact on treatment. Journal of Studies on Alcohol, 49(3), 219-224.

Hesselbrock, M. N., Hesselbrock, V. M., Babor, T. F., Stabenau, J. R., Meyer, R. E., & Weidenman, M. A. (1984). Antisocial behavior, psychopathology and problem drinking in the natural history of alcoholism. In D. W. Goodwin, K. T. Van Drusen, & S. A. Mednick (Ed.), Longitudinal Research in Alcoholism. Boston: Kluwer-Nijhoff.

Hesselbrock, M. N., Meyer, R. E., & Keener, J. (1985). Psychopathology in hospitalized alcoholics. Archives of General Psychiatry, 42, 1050-1055.

Hesselbrock, V. M., Stabenau, J. R., & Hesselbrock, M. N. (1985). Subtyping of alcoholism in male patients by family history and antisocial personality. Journal of Studies on Alcohol, 49, 89-98.

Hesselbrock, M. N. (1986a). Family history of psychopathology in alcoholics: A review and issues. In R. E. Meyer (Ed.), Psychopathology and Addictive Disorders. New York: Guilford Press.

Hesselbrock, M. N. (1986b). Childhood behavior problems and adult antisocial personality disorder in alcoholism. In R. E. Meyer (Ed.), Psychopathology and Addictive Disorders. New York: Guilford Press.

Hesselbrock, V. M., Hesselbrock, M. N., & Workman-Daniels, K. L. (1986c). Effect of major depression and antisocial personality on alcoholism: Course and motivational patterns. Journal of Studies on Alcohol, 47, 207-212.

Hill, S. M., Steinhauer, S. R., & Zubin, J. (1986). Biological Markers for Alcoholism: A Vulnerability Model Conceptualization. Lincoln, Nebraska: University of Nebraska Press.

Holden, C. (1987). Is alcoholism treatment effective? Science, 236, 20-22.

Huey, L. Y. (1978). Psychiatric problems of alcoholics. Postgraduate Medicine, 64, 123-128.

Jaffe, J. H. (1984). Alcoholism and affective disturbance: Current drugs and current shortcomings. In G. Edwards, & J. Littleton (Ed.), Pharmacological Treatments for Alcoholism. New York: Methuen, Inc.

Jaffe, J. H., & Ciraulo, K. A. (1986). Alcoholism and depression. In R. E. Meyer (Ed.), Psychopathology and Addictive Disorders. New York: Guilford Press.

Jellinek, E. M. (1960). The Disease Concept of Alcoholism. New Brunswick, New Jersey: Hillhouse Press.

Kalb, M., & Propper, M. S. (1976). The future of alcohology: Craft or science? American Journal of Psychiatry, 133, 641-645.

Katon, W. (1984). Panic disorder and somatization. The American Journal of Medicine, 77, 101-106.

Kay, D. C. (1985). Substance abuse in psychopathic states and sociopathic individuals. In A. I. Alterman (Ed.), Substance Abuse and Psychopathology. New York: Plenum Press.

Keeler, M. H., Taylor, C. I., & Miller, W. C. (1979). Are all recently detoxified alcoholics depressed? American Journal of Psychiatry, 136, 586-588.

Khantzian, E. J., & Treece, C. (1985). DSM-III Psychiatric diagnosis of narcotic addicts. Archives of General Psychiatry, 42, 1967-1971.

Kleber, H., & Gawin, F. (1986). Psychopharmacological trials in cocaine abuse. American Journal of Drug and Alcohol Abuse, 12, 235-246.

Kleber, H.D., Weissman, M.M., Rounsaville, B.J., Wilber, C.H., Prusoff, B.A. & Riordan, C.E. (1983). Imipramine as treatment for depression in addicts. Archives of General Psychiatry, 40, 649-653.

Klein, N. S., & Cooper, T. B. (1979). Lithium therapy in alcoholism. In D. W. Goodwin & C. K. Erickson (Ed.), Alcoholism and Affective Disorder. Jamaica, New York: Spectrum Publications.

Knight, R. P. (1937). The dynamic and treatment of chronic alcohol addiction. Bulletin of the Menninger Clinic, 1, 233-237.

Koenigsberg, H.W., Kaplan, R.D., Gilmore, M.M. & Cooper, A.M. (1985). The relationship between syndrome and personality disorder in DSM-III; Experience with 2,462 patients. American Journal of Psychiatry, 142, 207-212.

Kofoed, L., Kania, J., Walsh, T., & Atkinson, R. M. (1986). Outpatient treatment of patients with substance abuse and coexisting psychiatric disorders. American Journal of Psychiatry, 143, 867-872.

Kofoed, L., & Keys, A. (1988). Using group therapy to persuade dual-diagnosis patients to seek substance abuse treatment. Hospital and Community Psychiatry, 39, 1209-1211.

Kosten, T. R., Rounsaville, B. J., & Kleber, H. D. (1986). A 2.5 year follow-up of depression, life crises, and treatment effects on abstinence among opioid addicts. Archives of General Psychiatry, 43, 733-738.

Kosten, T. R., Rounsaville, B. J., & Kleber, H. D. (1987). A 2.5 year follow-up of cocaine use among treated opioid addicts. Archives of General Psychiatry, 44, 281-284.

Levitt, J. J., & Tsuang, M. T. (1988). The heterogeneity of schizoaffective disorder: Implications for treatment. American Journal of Psychiatry, 145, 926-936.

Lewis, C. E., Rice, J., Andreasen, N., Endicott, J., & Rochberg, N. (1987). The antisocial and the nonantisocial alcoholic: Clinical distinctions in men with major unipolar depression. Alcoholism: Clinical and Experimental Research, 11, 176-182.

Lewis, J.S. (1988). Congressional rites of passage for the rights of alcoholics. Alcohol Health and Research World, 12, 240-251.

Liskow, B. I., & Goodwin, D. W. (1987). Pharmacological treatment of alcohol intoxication, withdrawal and dependence: A critical review. Journal of Studies on Alcohol, 48, 356-370.

Longabaugh, R., & Lewis, D. C. (1988). Key issues in treatment outcome studies. Alcohol Health and Research World, 12, 168-175.

Markowitz, J. C., Kocsis, J. H., & Frances, A. J. (1988). Comorbidity and prevalence of dysthymic disorder. Montreal: American Psychiatric Association.

Marlatt, G. A., & Gordon, J. R. (1985). Relapse Prevention. New York: Guilford Press.

Mayfield, D. (1985). Substance abuse in the affective disorders. In A. I. Alterman (Ed.), Substance Abuse and Psychopathology. New York: Plenum Press.

McLellan, A. T., MacGahan, J. A., & Druley, K. A. (1980). Psychopathology and substance abuse. In E. Gottheil, A. K. McLellan, & K. A. Druley (Ed.), Substance Abuse and Psychiatric Illness. New York: Pergamon Press.

McLellan, A. T., Woody, G. E., Luborsky, L., O'Brien, C. P., & Druley, K. A. (1983a). Increased effectiveness of substance abuse treatment: A prospective study of patient-treatment "matching." Journal of Nervous and Mental Disease, 171, 597-605.

McLellan, A. T., Luborsky, L., Woody, G. E., O'Brien, C. P., & Druley, K. A. (1983b). Predicting response to alcohol and drug treatments. Archives of General Psychiatry, 40, 620-625.

McLellan, A. T., Childress, A. R., & Woody, G. E. (1985). Drug abuse and psychiatric disorders. In A. I. Alterman (Ed.), Substance Abuse and Psychopathology. New York: Plenum Press.

McLellan, A. T. (1986). "Psychiatric severity" as a predictor of outcome from substance abuse treatments. In R. E. Meyer (Ed.), Psychopathology and Addictive Disorders. New York: Guilford Press.

Mendelson, J. H., Babor, T. F., Mello, N. K., & Pratt, H. (1986). Alcoholism and prevalence of medical and psychiatric disorders. Journal of Studies on Alcohol, 47(5), 361-366.

Merikangas, K. R., Leckman, J. F., Prusoff, B. A., Pauls, D. L., & Weissman, M. M. (1984). Familial transmission of depression and alcoholism. Archives of General Psychiatry, 42, 367-372.

Merikangas, K. R., Weissman, M. M., Prusoff, B. A., Pauls, D. L., & Leckman, J. F. (1985). Depressives with secondary alcoholism: Psychiatric disorders in offspring. Journal of Studies on Alcohol, 46, 199-204.

Meyer, R. E. (1986a). Psychopathology and Addictive Disorders. New York: Guilford Press.

Meyer, R. E. (1986b). How to understand the relationship between psychopathology and addictive disorders: Another example of the chicken and the egg. In R. E. Meyer (Ed.), Psychopathology and Addictive Disorders. New York: Guilford Press.

Meyer, R. E., & Hesselbrock, M. N. (1984). Psychopathology and addictive disorders revisited. In S. M. Mirin (Ed.), Substance Abuse and Psychopathology. Washington, D.C.: American Psychiatric Press.

Meyer, R. E., & Kranzler, H. R. (1988). Alcoholism: Clinical implications of recent research. Journal of Clinical Psychiatry, 49(9), 8-12.

Mezzich, J. E., Coffman, G. A., & Goodpaster, S. A. (1982). A format for DSM-III diagnostic formulation: Experience with 1,111 consecutive patients. American Journal of Psychiatry, 139, 591-596.

Miller, W. R., & Heather, N. (1986). Treating Addictive Behaviors: Processes of Change. New York: Plenum Press.

Miller, W. R., & Hester, R. K. (1986a). The effectiveness of alcoholism treatment: What research reveals. In W. R. Miller, & N. Heather (Ed.), Treating Addictive Behaviors: Processes of Change. New York: Plenum Press.

Miller, W. R., & Hester, R. K. (1986b). Inpatient alcoholism treatment: Who benefits. American Psychologist, 41, 784-805.

Miller, W. R., & Hester, R. K. (1986c). Matching problem drinkers with optimal treatments. In W. R. Miller, & N. Heather (Ed.), Treating Addictive Behaviors. New York: Plenum Press.

Mirin, S. M. (1984). Substance Abuse and Psychopathology. Washington, DC: American Psychiatric Press.

Mirin, S. M., Weiss, R. D., Sollogub, A., & Michael, J. (1984a). Family pedigree of psychopathology in substance abusers. In R. E. Meyer (Ed.), Psychopathology and Addictive Disorders. New York: Guilford Press.

Mirin, S. M., Weiss, R. D., Sollogub, A., & Michael, J. (1984b). Psychopathology in the families of drug abusers. In S. M. Mirin (Ed.), Substance Abuse and Psychopathology. Washington, D.C.: American Psychiatric Press.

Mirin, S. M., Weiss, R. D., Sollogub, A., & Michael, J. (1987). Affective illness in substance abusers. In S. M. Mirin (Ed.), Substance Abuse and Psychopathology. Washington, D.C.: American Psychiatric Press.

Mitchell, J. E., Hatsukami, D., Eckert, E. D., & Pyle, R. L. (1985). Characteristics of 275 patients with bulimia. American Journal of Psychiatry, 142(4), 482-485.

Moos, R. H., & Finney, J. W. (1983). The expanding scope of alcoholism treatment evaluation. American Psychologist, 38, 1036-1044.

Mullaney, J. A., & Trippet, C. J. (1979). Alcohol dependence and phobias: Clinical description and relevance. British Journal of Psychiatry, 135, 565-573.

Murphy, G. E. (1988). Suicide and substance abuse. Archives of General Psychiatry, 45, 593-594.

Norton, R., & Noble, J. (1987). Combined alcohol and other drug use and abuse: A status report. Alcohol Health and Research World, Summer, 78-80.

Othmer E., Penick, E. C., & Powell, B. J. (1981). The Psychiatric Diagnostic Interview. Los Angeles: Western Psychological Services.

O'Sullivan, K. B., Daly, M. M., Carroll, B. M., Clare, A. W., & Cooney, J. G. (1979). Alcoholism and affective disorder among patients in a Dublin hospital. Journal of Studies on Alcohol, 40(11), 1014-1022.

O'Sullivan, K. O., Whillans, P., Daly, M., Carroll, B., Clare, A., & Cooney, J.

(1983). A comparison of alcoholics with and without coexisting affective disorder. British Journal of Psychiatry, 143, 133-138.

Parrella, D. P., & Filstead, W. J. (1988). Definition of onset in the development of onset-based alcoholism typologies. Journal of Studies on Alcohol, 49, 85-92.

Pattison, E. M. (1985). The selection of treatment modalities for the alcoholic patient. In J. H. Mendelson, & N. K. Mello (Ed.), The Diagnosis and Treatment of Alcoholism (2nd ed.). New York: McGraw-Hill.

Penick, E. C., Powell, B. J., & Othmer, E. (1982). The importance of drug use histories in a series of alcoholics: Letter to the editor. Journal of Clinical Psychiatry, 43, 42.

Penick, E. C., Powell, B. J., Othmer, E., Bingham, S. F., Rice, A. S., & Liese, B. S. (1984). Subtyping alcoholics by coexisting psychiatric syndromes: Course, family history, outcome. In D. W. Goodwin, K. T. Van Dusen, & S. A. Mednick (Ed.), Longitudinal Research in Alcoholism. Boston: Kluwer-Nijhoff Publishing.

Penick, E.C., Powell, B.J., Bingham, S.F., Liskow, B.I., Miller, N.S. and Read, M.R. (1987). A comparative study of familial alcoholism. Journal of Studies on Alcohol, 48, 136-146.

Penick, E. C., Powell, B. J., Liskow, B. I., Jackson, J. O., & Nickel, E. J. (1988). The stability of coexisting psychiatric syndromes in alcoholic men after one year. Journal of Studies on Alcohol, 49, 395-405.

Perkins, K. A., Simpson, J. C., & Tsuang, M. T. (1986). Ten-year followup of drug abusers with acute or chronic psychosis. Hospital and Community Psychiatry, 37, 481-484.

Petty, F., & Nasrallah, H. A. (1981). Secondary depression in alcoholism: Implications for future research. Comprehensive Psychiatry, 22, 587-595.

Polich, J. M., Armor, D. J., & Braiker, H. B. (1981). The Course of Alcoholism. New York: Wiley and Sons.

Powell, B. J., Penick, E. C., Othmer, E., Bingham, S. F., & Rice, A. S. (1983). Prevalence of additional psychiatric syndromes among male alcoholics. Journal of Clinical Psychiatry, 43, 404-407.

Powell, B. J., Penick, E. C., Liskow, B. I., Rice, A. S., & McKnelly, W. (1985a). Lithium compliance in alcoholic males: A six-month followup study. Addictive Behaviors, 11, 135-140.

Powell, B. J., Penick, E. C., Read, M. R., & Ludwig, A. M. (1985b). Comparison of three outpatient treatment interventions: A twelve-month followup of men alcoholics. Journal of Studies on Alcohol, 46, 309-312.

Powell, B. J., Rice, A. S., Liskow, B. I., & Penick, E. C. (1986). Additional psychopathology and MMPI T-score elevations in alcoholics. Washington, DC: Paper presented at the 94th Annual Meeting of the American Psychological Association.

Powell, B. J., Read, M. R., Penick, E. C., Miller, N. S., & Bingham, S. F. (1987). Primary-secondary depression in alcoholic men: An important distinction? Journal of Clinical Psychiatry, 48, 98-101.

Powell, B. J., Penick, E. C., Nickel, E. J., Liskow, B., Hassanein, R. E. S., Campbell, J., & Brown, E. (1988). Classification of men alcoholics by number and type of co-existing psychiatric disorder. Unpublished manuscript.

Prugh, T. (1986). Recovery without treatment. Alcohol Health and Research World, 12, 24.

Quitkin, F. M., Rifkin, A., Kaplan, J., & Klein, D. F. (1972). Phobic anxiety syndrome complicated by drug dependence and addiction. Archives of General Psychiatry, 27, 159-162.

Regier, D. A., Boyd, J. H., Burke, J. D., Rae, D. S., Myers, J. K., Kramer, M., Robins, L. N., George, L. K., Karno, M., & Locke, B. Z. (1988). One-month prevalence of mental disorders in the United States. Archives of General Psychiatry, 45, 977-986.

Robins, L. N. (1986). Epidemiology of antisocial personality. In R. Michaels, & J. O. Cavenar (Ed.), Psychiatry (Vol I). New York: Basic Books.

Robins, E., Gentry, K. A., Munoz, R. A., & Martin, S. (1977). A contrast of the three more common illnesses with the ten less common in a study and 18-month followup of 314 psychiatric emergency room patients. Archives of General Psychiatry, 34, 285-291.

Ross, H. E., Glaser, F. B., & Germanson, T. (1988). The prevalence of psychiatric disorders in patients with alcohol and other drug problems. Archives of General Psychiatry, 45, 1023-1031.

Rounsaville, B. J., Weissman, M. M., Kleber, H. D., & Wilber, C. (1982). Heterogeneity of psychiatric diagnosis in treated opiate addicts. Archives of General Psychiatry, 39, 161-166.

Rounsaville, B. J., & Kleber, H. D. (1984). Psychiatric disorders and course of opiate addiction: Preliminary findings on predictive significance and diagnostic stability. In S. M. Mirin (Ed.), Substance Abuse and Psychopathology. Washington, D.C.: American Psychiatric Press.

Rounsaville, B. J., & Kleber, H. D. (1985a). Psychotherapy/counseling for opiate addicts: Strategies for use in different treatment settings. International Journal of the Addictions, 20, 869-896.

Rounsaville, B. J., & Kleber, H. D. (1985b). Untreated opiate addicts: How do they differ from those seeking treatment? Archives of General Psychiatry, 42, 1072-1077.

Rounsaville, B. J., Kosten, T. R., Weissman, M. M., & Kleber, H. D. (1986a). Prognostic significance of psychopathology in treated opiate addicts. Archives of General Psychiatry, 43, 739-745.

Rounsaville, B. J., & Kleber, H. D. (1986b). Psychiatric disorders in opiate addicts: Preliminary findings on the course and interaction with program type. In R. E. Meyer (Ed.), Psychopathology and Addictive Disorders. New York: Guilford Press.

Rounsaville, B. J., Dolinsky, Z. S., Babor, T. F., & Meyer, R. E. (1987). Psychopathology as a predictor of treatment outcome in alcoholics. Archives of General Psychiatry, 44, 505-513.

Schuckit, M. A. (1973). Alcoholism and sociopathy: Diagnostic confusion. Quarterly Journal of Studies on Alcohol, 34, 157-164.

Schuckit, M. A. (1983a). Alcoholic patients with secondary depression. American Journal of Psychiatry, 140, 711-714.

Schuckit, M. A. (1983b). Alcoholism and other psychiatric disorders. Hospital and Community Psychiatry, 34, 1022-1027.

Schuckit, M. A. (1985). The clinical implications of primary diagnostic groups among alcoholics. Archives of General Psychiatry, 42, 1043-1049.

Schuckit, M.A. (1986). Genetic and clinical implications of alcoholism and affective disorder. American Journal of Psychiatry, 143, 140-147.

Schuckit, M. A., & Winokur, G. (1972). A short term followup of women alcoholics. Diseases of the Nervous System, 33, 672-678.

Siegler, M., & Osmond, H. (1974). Models of Madness, Models of Medicine. New York: Harper & Row.

Solomon, J. (1982). Alcoholism and Clinical Psychiatry. New York: Plenum Press.

Spitzer, R. L., & Klein, D. F. (1978). Critical Issues in Psychiatric Diagnosis. New York: Raven Press.

Stabenau, J. R. (1986). Genetic factors and human reactions to alcohol. In J. L. Fuller (Ed.), Perspectives in Behavior Genetics. New York: Erlbaum Press.

Stabenau, J. R., & Hesselbrock, V. M. (1984). Psychopathology in alcoholics and their families and vulnerability to alcoholism: A review and new findings. In S. M. Mirin (Ed.), Substance Abuse and Psychopathology. Washington, DC: American Psychiatric Press.

Tarter, R. E., Alterman, A. I., & Edwards, K. L. (1985). Vulnerability to alcoholism in men: A behavior-genetic perspective. Journal of Studies on Alcohol, 46, 329-356.

Tsuang, M.T., Simpson, J.C. & Kronfol, Z. (1982). Subtypes of drug abuse with psychosis. Archives of General Psychiatry, 39, 141-147.

Tsuang, M.T., Boor, M. & Fleming, J.A. (1985). Psychiatric aspects of traffic accidents. American Journal of Psychiatry, 142, 538-546.

Vaillant, G. E. (1983). The Natural History of Alcoholism. Cambridge, MA: Harvard University Press.

Wallace, J. (1986). The other problems of alcoholics. Journal of Substance Abuse Treatment, 3, 163-169.

Weiss, R., & Mirin, S. M. (1984). Drug, host, and environmental factors in the development of chronic cocaine abuse. In S. M. Mirin (Ed.), Substance Abuse and Psychopathology. Washington, DC: American Psychiatric Press.

Weissman, M. M. (1984). Familial transmission of depression and alcoholism. Archives of General Psychiatry, 42, 367-372.

Weissman, M. M. (1988). Anxiety and alcoholism. Journal of Clinical Psychiatry, 49(10), 17-19.

Weissman, M. M., Meyers, J. K., & Harding, P. S. (1980). Prevalence and psychiatric heterogeneity of alcoholism in a United States urban community. Journal of Studies on Alcohol, 41, 672-681.

Weller, R. A., & Halikas, J. A. (1985). Marijuana use and psychiatric illness: A followup study. American Journal of Psychiatry, 142(7), 848-850.

Williams, J. B. W., & Spitzer, R. L. (1980). DSM-III field trials. Diagnostic and Statistical Manual of Mental Disorders (third edition). Washington, DC: American Psychiatric Press.

Winokur, G., Reich, T., Rimmer, J., & Pitts, F. N. (1970). Alcoholism III: Diagnosis and familial psychiatric illness in 259 alcoholic probands. Archives of General Psychiatry, 23, 104-111.

Winokur, G., Rimmer, J., & Reich, T. (1971). Alcoholism IV. Is there more than one type of alcoholism? British Journal of Psychiatry, 118, 525-532.

Woody, G. E., Luborsky, L., McLellan, A. T., O'Brien, C. P., Beck, A. T., Blaine, J., Herman, I., & Hole, A. (1983). Psychotherapy for opiate addicts: Does it help? Archives of General Psychiatry, 40, 639-645.

Woody, G. E., McLellan, A. T., Luborsky, L., O'Brien, C. P., Blaine, J., Fox, S., Herman, T., & Beck, A. T. (1984). Severity of psychiatric symptoms as a predictor of benefits from psychotherapy: The Veteran's Administration-Penn study. American Journal of Psychiatry, 141, 1172-1177.

Woody, G. E., McLellan, A. T., Luborsky, L., & O'Brien, C. P. (1985). Sociopathy and psychotherapy outcome. Archives of General Psychiatry, 42, 1081-1086.

Woody, G. E., Luborsky, L., McLellan, A. T., & O'Brien, C. P. (1986). Psychotherapy as an adjunct to methadone treatment. In R. E. Meyer (Ed.), Psychopathology and Addictive Disorders. New York: Guilford Press.

Psychopathology and Substance Abuse:
A Psychoanalytic Perspective

Russell Smith, MA

Psychoanalysis offers a highly deterministic vision of behavior. For analysts, the child is father of the man. The personality core is thought to evolve from infantile and childhood experiences during crucial, inevitable, developmental phases. The infant's relationship with the mother is considered to be of singular importance while somewhat later the relationship with the parent of the opposite sex is viewed as paramount. The perceptions, drives, attitudes, emotions, etc. of an adult are derived from—though not completely governed by the events of childhood. The degree of self-determination or free will of an individual is dependent on maturity and ego strength. The ego (the central, organizing or executive agency in the personality) flourishes if, in the early years, a healthy balance between nurturance and frustration is established. On the other hand, the ego can be enfeebled by childhood trauma. If trauma occurs after the ego has formed a solid foundation, after the age of three or four. the ego may end up fighting internal wars against the id (the repository of survivalistic and hedonistic instincts) and/or the superego (conscience) in an effort to maintain psychic homeostasis or equilibrium while also dealing with external reality. If the infant or very young child is subjected to an environment that seems to threaten its very existence either by deprivation, rejection, abandonment, physical harm or perceived annihilation, the development of the ego may be arrested and its ability to deal with the internal or external world severely handicapped. Such conditions may dispose

Russell Smith is Clinical Psychologist and Supervisor of Psychological Services, Eastern Diagnostic Center, Pennsylvania Department of Corrections.
NOTE: A glossary of terms is provided at the end of this article.

the person toward psychosis or the erection of drastic defensive measures against the disintegration of the ego. The type of psychopathology arising out of later childhood distress would likely be characterized by neurotic symptoms. In some cases, depending on the stage of fixation and the nature of the defenses employed, the person may manifest symptoms of a character disorder such as a borderline or narcissistic personality. These disturbances are characterized by unstable, chaotic interpersonal relationships, identity problems and an intense need for external distraction or stimulation ("stimulus hunger") among other symptoms. Persons whose behavior is primarily unlawful, immoral, or exploitive are thought to have deficient superegos and diagnosed with the roughly synonomous terms psychopath, sociopath, anti-social personality, or impulse disorder. Analysts generally view drug abuse as an expression of a personality disorder (though many see more utility in a psychodynamic description than a diagnostic classification). That the personality disturbance often encompasses some anti-social features is not surprising since most substance abuse is illegal and all substance abuse is socially condemned though there are many cultural inconsistencies and double standards in this regard.

Early analytic descriptions of drug dependence were framed in terms of libidinal theory and erogenous zones. Freud, (1950 A) who used cocaine himself for a while early in his career, for example, believed at one time that addiction was a form or derivative of masturbation. That notion which gained little acceptance then or now, and which Freud in later writings made little reference to, seems like a relic of ante-diluvian analytic thought. However, whether or not drug abuse and masturbation are apposite, there are points of comparison, the most obvious being that both are sources of intense, self-indulgent pleasure; in addition, some users of drugs that induce a "rush" describe this experience as orgasmic.

Until relatively recently few analysts seemed interested in drug dependence; certainly not because there haven't been prior epidemics in the western world. The lack of attention may have been because it was identified as more of a social problem than a reflection of intrapsychic processes and thus wasn't treated by analytic therapists. A few eminent psychoanalysts did offer some theoretical comments. For example, Abraham (1960) and Rado (1933) believed that hedonism was central to drug use. As Rado (1963) put it: "The patient doesn't suffer from his illness, he enjoys it." They viewed addiction as a regressive phenomenon, a reversion to infantile forms of gratification. Glover, in 1932 (1956) used libidinal theory in his formulation but departed from his contemporaries with his belief that drug use could be a "defense" against aggressive, destructive urges. This view of addiction as having an internal regulative and adaptive function anticipated later ego-psychological thought. In the pantheon of contemporary analytic writers on the subject several emerge as most influential. These authors such as Edward Khantzian, Leon Wurmser, and Henry Krystal owe a debt to classical or neo-orthodox theorists such as Anna Freud, Margaret Mahler, Heinz Hartmann, Otto Kernberg, Melanie Klein, and Heinz Kohut.

Khantzian, Wurmser and Krystal all believe that substance abusers suffer from defects in personality development, structure, and organization that renders them vulnerable to powerful, painful, and destructive emotions (affects). They are inadequately defended against affects such as rage, fear of abandonment, helplessness, and shame. Because of primitive ego development, sometimes their experience of these emotions is not well differentiated and therefore not comprehended or even acknowledged. These three analysts also generally agree that the personality impairment found in drug abusers is due to the lack of opportunity in the formative years to identify with (introject) a nurturant, benevolent parent. This may lead to a narcissistic insult — an injury to the persons fundamental sense of worth, competence, and identity. Khantzian (1977, p. 93) states that as a result "... drug-dependents may not "want" control of appropriate self functions" (original emphasis). He goes on to say that drug users "wall-off" the maternal image (presumably because of rejection or neglect) and are then unable to adopt for themselves the caring functions of the mother. These functions find external embodiment in the form of drugs which provide comfort, support, emotional analgesia, and a symbolic fusion with a fantasized benevolent mother personified by the drug.

Frosch and Milkman (1977) express a similar idea stating "... self esteem is dependent on supplies of food and warmth; the drug represents these supplies" (p. 152).

Otto Kernberg discusses the same phenomenon in terms of object relations theory which deals with this process of an internalized and permanent psychic representation of a nurturant parent(s). The word "object" here refers to a perception of the mother as an entity having material existence above and beyond the infant's need for her. Kernberg asserts that if a mother is perceived as threatening the psychic image of her will be divided into two representations, the good mother which is the one needed for survival, and the feared, hated bad mother. He postulates that this division, called "ego-splitting," will not attain internal, symbolic status in the ego because this risks destruction of the good by the more powerful bad. These manicheistic perceptions remain externalized, incarnated and reincarnated repeatedly in the form of persons with whom the so called "borderline personality" becomes closely involved. The borderline comes to perceive others as sometimes all good and sometimes all bad when they can't live up to the perfection required of the former. The relationships become tumultuous, conflict-ridden, and usually short lived. The "borderline," who already suffers from a psychic void and intense feelings of loneliness, creates nothing but misery and havoc in these relationships. As Woody (1977) reports, Kernberg believes that they turn to euphoria producing drugs to relieve the emptiness they experience. The drugs also provide an illusion of being loved and a sense of being whole and real. The abuser's narcissism is thus bolstered. Some drug users also experience a feeling of magical control over the environment during the intoxicated state.

Both Kohut (1977) and Krystal (1977), in the context of object relations theory, express the belief that drug use is a symbolic attempt at merging with a love object, the phantom of the good mother longed for in infancy. Kohut states that the user is soothed by the drug but that since no developmental progress or growth in the "self" results the solution is transitory, at best.

Khantzian (1977) notes another aspect of the failure to internalize the function of self-care (Khantzian's equivalent the good mothering); this is the addict's seeming obliviousness to risk and danger. He indicates that the addict's lack of concern for his welfare especially applies to the drug use itself ". . . where despite obvious deterioration and imminent danger as a result of their drug use, there is little evidence of fear, anxiety, or realistic assessment about their substance involvement" (1977, p. 108). He is not referring here to the addict who is primarily self-destructive or who may seek out danger in order to prevail over their fears (the counter-phobic addict). Rather, he is discussing the addict who lacks what Freud (1926) called "signal" or "real" anxiety. Khantzian says that this insouciance or recklessness poses one of the most serious problems in trying to treat the addict who continues playing with fire seemingly unaware that he is being scorched.

Based on behavioral and psychodynamic considerations, the analysts reviewed in this article would diagnose drug abusers as borderline personalities who rely on drugs as a means of establishing or shoring up psychological defenses. Krystal believes that addicts and alcoholics try to subdue their aggression (resulting from frustration of the need for love) and/or their grief (over the perceived loss of a loving parent) by the use of narcotizing substances. He states that if users abstain—while in therapy, for example—they will invariably go through a depressive phase as their emotions surface. Greenspan (1977) would concur, stating: "The substance abuse . . . is a defense against separation anxiety and its accompanying depression" (p. 78). Greenspan also notes that drugs may serve an adaptive purpose by promoting a psychic/emotional equilibrium not attained in childhood because of trauma.

Hartmann (1969) also views underlying depression and a need to counteract painful feelings arising from deprivation of affection as causal elements in drug abuse. Like Kohut, he sees dependence on drugs as palliative in the short-term but ultimately highly maladaptive and contributory to arrested character development.

Hartmann, however, in his study of adolescent drug abusers, could not identify any unique developmental events or clinical syndromes that predisposed adolescents to drug abuse rather than some other behavioral or psychological abnormality. Furthermore, he believes that object relations problems, low frustration tolerance, and other psychic turbulence are found in all adolescents and therefore are not predictive of drug abuse.

Wurmser (1974, 1977), on the other hand, after years of studying compulsive drug users from an analytic perspective, concluded that severe psychopathology characterized by regressive tendencies and defective regulation of powerful emotions is an antecedent of substance dependence. He postulates that the most disturbing emotions that overwhelm potential drug abusers are rage, shame, alienation, and disappointment – all the result of "narcissistic frustration" (unfulfilled needs). Overcome with psychic pain, tortured and sickened by their emotions, they are reduced to a state of terror and despair before turning to drugs. Wurmser believes, as do other writers (Frosch, 1970; Milkman and Frosch, 1973, 1977) that various drugs are used for their differential abilities to alleviate certain emotional states as well as for their ability to satisfy needs arising from developmental fixation. Thus, according to Wurmser (1977): depressants help deny rage and shame; hallucinogens counteract emptiness, anomie, boredom; stimulants relieve depression and promote feelings of mastery, control and power; alcohol helps overcome shyness, facilitates the release of anger, and blunts loneliness.

Wurmser (1974) indicates that without drugs the needs, primitive drives, and psychopathology of the user will be revealed. The narcotics addict will become violent; the stimulant user depressed; the psychodelic user apathetic and existentially sad.

Wurmser (1977) states that the addict often does not experience emotions in a well defined way but rather in the form of diffuse tension. Many clinicians who treat addicts are similarly aware of their inability to articulate their feelings.

To capsulize his position, Wurmser views drug use as a form of self-medication, an exogenous, chemical defense that amplifies or establishes defenses of denial, dissociation ("ego-splitting"), acting-out of internal conflict – and the related defense of externalization which involves projection of symbolic, infantile emotions and needs. Narcotics and alcohol serve the purposes of denial; hallucinogens induce dissociation; stimulants release aggression.

Wurmser (1977) focuses much attention on the defenses of splitting and externalization which he believes are fundamental to the psychic operations and behavior of the drug user. His notion of splitting is consistent with Kernberg's (1975) described above. Splitting results in a dichotomized view of others as all good (perfect) or all bad (punitive, rejecting, destructive). Splitting has a pervasive effect on perceptions and attitudes. Continua such as mind-body, past-present, moral-immoral, hate-love, become rigidly compartmentalized. An oft observed symptom of splitting is the verbalization of contradictory thoughts in a narrow space of time. For example, an intense interest in reaching a certain goal might be expressed (e.g., get a certain job, obtain a diploma, start a family, quit drugs) while a few statements or minutes later the person will indicate no interest whatsoever in that goal. In the borderline personality Wurmser and Kernberg write about this is not a manifestation of ambivalence or indecisiveness but rather a reflection of ego fragmentation. A listener trying to follow such unpredictable and contradictory thoughts — whether it is a psychotherapist or acquaintance — often feels he is dealing with a sort of multiple personality though the ego structure and psychic processes involved are quite different.

Wurmser says that splitting leads to experiences of depersonalization and derealization. He states: "Drug abuse thus seems like an artificial depersonalization coupled with . . . externalization, which is so characteristic for 'sociopaths'" (1977, p. 55).

By externalization Wurmser means the acting-out of an unconscious conflict or problem. Things or other persons come to represent some aspect of or solution to the internal, dynamic source of the distress. In this way drugs are viewed as magical and omnipotent cures for an ongoing psychological difficulty. Similarly, authoritarian institutions or persons (parents, police, teachers, therapists) may become avatars for the individual's conscience. Through externalization a concrete enemy is established and can be struggled against or submitted to as the case may be. In addiction — and here Wurmser extends the concept to compulsive behavior such as T.V. watching, gambling, and overeating — the addictive substance or compulsive ritual represents an illusory means of control over externalized forces. He summarizes the nature of this mechanism he considers so basic to the drug user stating: ". . . an external conflict situation and action ward the internal conflict and the archaic overwhelming affects stemming from it" (1977, p. 58).

Kernberg (1975) indicates that these same two mechanisms — ego-splitting and externalization — are crucial to the functioning of the borderline personality (although he uses the term "projective identification" instead of externalization).

Wurmser (1977) concludes by categorically stating that all of the drug dependent patients whom he has examined fit the diagnosis of borderline personality.

COMMENTS

In 1895 Freud wrote a manuscript entitled, "Project for a Scientific Psychology" (1953) in which he proposed the objective investigation of mental and emotional processes in an effort to elevate psychology to the realm of the natural sciences. In that paper, Freud, being a neurologist, emphasized the neuronal basis of the psychic functions. As time went on he saw less need for neurological explanations of behavior. Instead, he developed a model of the mind as composed of various structures (id, ego, superego) which interact in very complex ways. The nature of these structures and their interaction form the personality which, to a great extent, is determined by a sequence of developmental experiences occurring in the first few years of life.

Freud collected his data using idiographic methods; that is, he studied the individual. In his clinical practice he attempted to reconstruct the life experiences of his patients from which he drew conclusions about the pathogenesis of psychological disorders, mainly neuroses. He relied on inductive reasoning whereby broad principles are derived from the particular. He thought of himself as a scientist though he spurned the scientific method of experimentation believing it was neither relevant to nor necessary for his work.

Freud's approach to the study of psychology established precedents which are quite evident in modern psychoanalysis. Behavior, motivation, emotion, psychopathology are conceptualized in metapsychological terms also known as psychodynamics. Freud's language drawn from literature and mythology, is still used in describing warring psychological and social forces. The main drives are the Darwinian notion of survival and procreation embodied in the libido, and the aggressive instinct.

The writers reviewed in this article have clearly been influenced by Freud and other psychoanalytic theorists. They view drug use as footprints in the sand, the behavioral manifestation of psychic imbalance arising from frustration, deprivation, emotional pain. Drug use is also thought to be purposeful and, in the short term, adaptive. The user generally feels better when intoxicated.

The observations analysts submit on drug taking are humanistic and well integrated within a comprehensive theory of psychology. Their writings are literate and imaginative, eloquent and forceful.

Their method of collecting and interpreting data, however, is not a paragon of science. Neither is their terminology which is often esoteric and lacking standardization. For example, even Wurmser who engages in some very cryptic metapsychology, writing about the formulations of certain other analysts complains that their ". . . theoretical expositions are very abstract and difficult to understand" (1977, p. 54).

There is also the same implicit disdain for controlled studies that Freud had. In this context, Hartmann's (1969) comment that drug using adolescents do not seem very different psychologically from other adolescents is a noteworthy exception since the non-drug users would constitute a control group in a formal study. No other author reviewed in this article seems very concerned with this type of comparison.

Direct laboratory experimentation with humans taking addictive drugs, while it has been done (Fischman and Schuster, 1982; Griffiths, Bigelow & Liebson, 1979; Henningfield et al., 1986; Johnson & Uhlenhuth, 1978; Mello & Mendelson, 1980; Schuster, 1982; Wilkler, 1952) poses obvious problems of ethics and liability. Those who do conduct such studies are either behaviorists or pharmacologists and rarely are naive subjects (those having no history of drug dependence) used. So analysts cannot be faulted for not giving heroin to borderlines and non-borderlines to find out who is more addiction prone. However, the utter disregard for a comparison group and for statistics — for all of its pitfalls and misuses — seems inexcusable. In this vein, Wurmser's assertion that every drug addict he had ever examined was a borderline personality smacks of self-selection or some other form of bias. Numerous psychological studies (Gilbert and Lombardi, 1967; Hill Haertzen and Glaser, 1960; Ling et al., 1973; McDonald, 1965; Messinger & Zitrin, 1965; Mirin, Meyer, and McNamee, 1976; Olsen, 1964; Sheppard et al., 1972; Stefanis et al., 1976; Sutken, Allain, and Cohen, 1974) refute his contention while others (Gay et al., 1972; Gerard & Kometsky, 1955; Halikas, Goodwin, and Guze, 1972; Kaufman, 1974; Monroe, Ross, and Bergins, 1971; Robbins, 1974; Senay, Dorus, and Meyer, 1976; Sheppard et al., 1973) offer some support or at least find some form of severe psychopathology in drug users.

Animal studies, though of debatable relevance to human motivation, do provide examples of controlled experimentation. Some of these studies (Deneau et al., 1969; Johanson & Schuster, 1981; Pickens, Meisch, and Thompson, 1978; Schuster & Thompson, 1969) clearly indicate that exposure to certain drugs such as amphetamine, barbiturates, morphine, diazepam (Valium) "not" psychopathology—is all that is required to produce continued self-administration (the animal equivalent of dependence).

Furthermore, some researchers (Boyarth and Wise, 1985; Deneau et al., 1969; Dwrokin, Gorders, Grabowski and Smith, 1986; Johanson et al., 1976) have found that given unlimited access to cocaine animals will continue taking this drug until it proves fatal while Winger & Woods (1973) reported the same thing with unlimited access to ethanol (alcohol). There is a striking congruity between drugs animals seem to be attracted to and those humans seek. At face value, then, this would seek to argue for some biologically reinforcing mechanism involved in drug use. If so, it renders concepts such as "ego splitting" or "narcissistic impairment" less important though not necessarily irrelevant to human use.

There are analysts and analytically oriented investigators who are not doctrinaire. Zinberg and Schaffer (1985), for example, believe that sociological processes have an influence on drug use and state that to the extent that drugs become more available and normative ". . . there is less likelihood that users who have disturbed personalities will predominate" among the universe of users (p. 70). Zinberg (1984) in a highly illuminating study comparing heroin addicts with occasional opiate users found that addicts were more prone to distort reality and that a much greater number of addicts used opiates to relieve depression and satisfy a need for risk-taking. More occasional users indulged in opiates for social purposes, recreation, and enjoyment of the "high." Zinberg found no significant differences in history of trauma, pre-drug use maladjustment, or social class. Zinberg does believe that personality variables (the "set") are important factors in who uses opiates and how often but he indicates that the social circumstances of use (the "setting") are at least of equal importance. Thus he found that chronic users were much more likely to use opiates in the company of other chronic users whereas most occasional users (67%) when partaking of opiates, kept to the company of other non-addicted users. Zinberg further found that occasional users were much more likely to have ritualistic rules governing when and where they used than the addicted subjects. He concludes: "Setting variables were found to be a major, if not the primary, element in determining degree of control" (1984, p. 81).

In most of the investigations done by analysts, however, there is rarely an attempt to isolate variables by comparing one group of subjects with another. To the contrary, their inferences are almost always based on subjects in treatment which, in terms of science, is chasing one's tail.

Wurmser (1977) does note many of the problems for the psychoanalytic exploration of drug abuse including distortion of personal history by the patient, resistance to long-term treatment, the influence of cultural and familial processes, and the rareness of a well defined transference (reenactment of the past) in therapy. In view of all of these serious obstacles Wurmser should feel obliged to explain how he learned so much about the psyches of drug abusers.

That analysts will win no prizes for methodological rigor is hardly a novel opinion. This does not mean that psychoanalysis should be consigned to the scientific garbage heap with astrology, phrenology, and numerology. Psychology is not physics which, in turn, is not pure mathematics. Psychoanalysis, like the study of history, is based on reconstruction of events. As such, the comments of the Greek historian, Herodotus, sometimes apply. He said few things happen at the right time; the rest never happens at all. It is the duty of the historian to correct these defects of his subject.

GLOSSARY

Acting-Out — The behavioral expression or discharge of a drive, psychological conflict, or tension derived from much earlier trauma. It often denotes the conversion of the psychic (memory, thoughts, needs) into the motoric either as a defense against recognition of the drive or because of affective flooding.

Affect — An emotion derived from an instinct. Sometimes: Manifest mood which may or may not correspond with the actual feeling reported.

Borderline Personality — A disorder originally thought of as a form of schizophrenia but which in the last 20 years has been widely described as a primitive personality disturbance characterized by grossly unstable social and psychological functioning, severe identity problems, self-destructive behavior, rapidly shifting or contradictory perceptions and attitudes.

Defense — A mechanism in service to the ego to protect against unpleasant emotions or dangerous impulses. Denial, repression, reaction formation, projection, sublimation, are some examples.

Depersonalization — A feeling, often accompanied by anxiety and confusion, that one has changed. The feeling may be a vague bodily sensation or pertain to personal/social identity.

Derealization — The feeling that ones immediate environment has changed and is thus rendered unfamiliar or unreal.

Dissociation — A process by which psychological material is detached from the ego such as amnesia; or, the fragmentation of the ego into disharmonious elements. Is sometimes used interchangeably with "ego-splitting" (q.v.).

Ego — In psychoanalysis, that agency of the personality that functions as a mediator between biological urges (the id) and conscience (superego) or the demands of society and the real world. One of the primary tasks of the ego is reality testing. Adaptation, affect regulation, cognition, identity, are other important ego processes.

Ego Psychology — A modern movement with psychoanalysis that stresses the importance of ego functioning to behavior over that of libido. The manner in which the ego maintains psychic equilibrium through the use of defenses is considered of special interest in understanding normal as well as pathological conditions.

Ego-Splitting — The division of the ego into unintegrated parts or sub-systems. Splitting often results in dichotomized perceptions of everything in terms of good and bad as well as erratic fluctuations in the experience of love-hate, trust-mistrust, dependence-autontomy, etc. Splitting is viewed by some as a defense, by others as a non-adaptive defect in personality integration.

Externalization — Usually, the displacement of a psychological conflict onto things or persons in the outer world that symbolically come to represent aspects of the conflict. The defense of projection is often involved and is sometimes used synonomously with externalization.

Id — The part of the personality encompassing the biological drives or instincts. It operates according to the pleasure principle which dictates immediate gratification of needs either in the real world or in fantasy.

Incorporation — The process by which things external to the ego become part of the ego through a kind of psychic ingestion. Identification and introjection are often used interchangeably with incorporation though some writers draw fine distinctions among these terms.

Libido — Broadly speaking, the basic life force or energy. The libido becomes attached to specific erogenous zones during critical developmental stages.

Narcissism — The focusing (cathexis) of libidinal energy on the self. In normal early development this is a healthy process that later in life is manifested by a sense of worth, competence, and desirability as a love object. Narcissism that is damaged or insulted may lead to a defective sense of self, while excessive narcissism might engender feelings of omnipotence, superiority, entitlement. Paradoxically, either condition can produce the same demanding, egocentric behavior. For the person with deficient narcissism the behavior is compensatory. In the person with excessive narcissism the behavior represents infantile fixation and self-love.

Object Relations — The "object" is a reference to the nurturant mother especially as she is perceived by the infant/child to have existence separate from its needs. Object relations generally refers to the mature and reciprocal relationships a psychologically healthy person is capable of and enters into because of love, fondness, or other emotional investment.

Psychodynamics — The personality forces that arise from the interaction of the psychic structures (id, ego, superego). The study of these forces is called metapsychology.

Separation Anxiety — Dread of or distress from being separated from the mother. As a morbid condition the separation is construed by the infant/child as abandonment or death.

Superego — Conscience. Societal standards and values. Often punitive, the superego is considered to be the source of guilt feelings.

REFERENCES

Abraham, K., (1960). The psychological relation between sexuality and alcoholism. *Selected Papers of Karl Abraham*. New York: Basic Books.

Bozarth, M. A., & Wise, R. A., (1985). Toxicity associated with long-term intravenous heroin and cocaine self-administration in the rat. *Journal of the American Medical Association*, 253, pp. 81-83.

Deneau, G., Yanagita, T., & Seevers, M. H., (1969). Self-administration of psychoactive substances by the monkey. *Psychopharmacologia*, 16, pp. 30-48.

Dworkin, S. I., Geoders, N. E., Grabowski, J., and Smith, J. E., (1987). In Harris, L. S., ed. *Problems of Drug Dependence 1986*. National Institute on Drug Abuse Research Monograph 76. DHHS no. (ADM) 87-1508. Washington, D.C.: U.S. Government Printing Office. pp. 221-225.

Fischman, W. M., & Schuster, G. R. (1982). Cocaine self-administration in humans. *Federation Proceedings*, 41, pp. 241-246.

Freud, S., (1953). *The Standard Edition of the Complete Psychological Works*. Vol. I. Strachey, J. ed. London: Hogarth Press.

Freud, S. (1959). Inhibitions, Symptoms, and Anxiety (1926). *The Standard Edition of the Complete Psychological Works*. Vol. XX. Strachey, J. ed. London: Hogarth Press. pp. 75-174.

Frosch, W. A., (1970). Psychoanalytic evaluation of addiction and habituation. *Journal of the American Psychoanalytic Association*. 18: pp. 209-218.

Frosch, W. A., & Milkman, H., (1977). Ego functions in drug users. In Blaine, J. D. & Julius, D. A. eds. *Psychodynamics of Drug Dependence*. National Institute on Drug Abuse Research Monograph 12. DHEW no. ADM 77-470. Washington, D.C.: U.S. Government Printing Office. pp. 142-156.

Gay, G. R., Wellisch, D. K., Wesson, D. R., & Smith, D. E., (1972). *The Psychotic Junkie*. New York: Insight Publishing Company.

Gerard, D. I., and Kronetsky, C., (1955). Adolescent opiate addiction: A study of control and addict subjects. *Psychiatric Quarterly*, 29, pp. 457-486.

Gilbert, J. G., & Lombarde, D. N., (1967). Personality characteristics of young male narcotic addicts. *Journal of Consulting Psychology*, 31 (5), pp. 536-538.

Glover, E. (1932). On the aetiology of drug addiction. *International Journal of Psychoanalysis*, 13, pp. 298-328.

Greenspan, S. I., (1977). Substance abuse: An understanding from psychoanalytic developmental and learning perspectives. In Blaine, J. D., and Julius, D. A. eds., *Psychodynamics of Drug Dependence*. National Institute on Drug Abuse Research Monograph 12. DHEW no. (ADM) 77-470. Washington, D.C.: U.S. Government Printing Office. pp. 73-87.

Griffiths, R. R., Bradford, L. D., & Brady, J. V. (1979). Predicting the abuse liability of drugs with animal drug self-administration procedures: Psychomotor stimulants and hallucinogens. In Thompson, T., & Dews, P. B. eds., *Advances in Behavioral Pharmacology*. Vol. 2. pp. 163-208. New York: Academic Press.

Halikas, J. A., Goodwin, Donald W., and Guze, S. B., (1972). Marijuana use and psychiatric illness. In: Miller, L., ed. *Marijuana: Effects on Human Behavior*. New York: Academic Press, Inc., pp. 265-302.

Hartmann, D., (1969). A study of drug-taking adolescents. *Psychoanalytic Study of the Child*, 24, pp. 384-398.

Henningfield, J. E., Kenneth-Coslett, R., Katz, J. L., & Goldbert, S. R., (1987). Intravenous cocaine self-administration by human volunteers: Second—order schedules of reinforcement. In Harris, L. S., ed. *Problem of Drug Dependence 1986*. National Institute on Drug Abuse Research Monograph 76. DHHS no. (ADM) 87-1508. Washington, D.C.: U.S. Government Printing Office. pp. 266-273.

Hill, H. E., Haertzen, C. A., and Glaser, R., (1960). Personality characteristics of narcotic addicts as indicated by the MMPI. *Journal of General Psychology*, 62, pp. 127-139.

Johnson, C. E., Balster, R. L., & Bonese, K., (1976). Self-administration of psychomotor stimulant drugs: The effects of unlimited access. *Pharmacology Biochemistry and Behavior*, 4, pp. 45-51.

Johnson, C. E., & Schuster, C. R., (1981). Animal models of drug self-administration. In Mello, N. K., ed. *Advances in Substance Abuse: Behavioral and Biological Research*. Vol. 2. pp. 219-297. Greenwich, CT. IAI Press.

Kaufman, E. (1974). The psychodynamics of opiate dependence: A New Look. *American Journal of Drug and Alcohol Abuse*, 1 (3), 349-370.

Kernberg, O. F., (1975). *Borderline Conditions and Pathological Narcissism*. New York: Jason Aronson.

Khantzian, E. J., (1977). The ego, the self, and opiate addiction: Theoretical and treatment considerations. In Blaine, J. D., & Julius, D. A., eds. *Psychodynamics of Drug Dependence*. National Institute on Drug Abuse Research Monograph 12. DHEW no. ADM 77-470. Washington, D.C.: U.S. Government Printing Office. pp. 101-117.

Kohut, H., (1977), Preface to: Blaine, J. D., & Julius, D. A., eds. *Psychodynamics of Drug Dependence*. National Institute on Drug Abuse Research Monograph 12. DHEW no. ADM 77-470. Washington, D.C.: U.S. Government Printing Office. pp. vii-ix.

Ling, W., Holmes, E. D., Post, G. R., & Litaker, M. B. (1973). A systematic psychiatric study of the heroin addicts. In: National Association for the Prevention of Addiction to Narcotics. *Proceedings of the Fifth National Conference on Methadone Treatment*. Vol. 1. New York: The Association. pp. 429-432.

Mello, N. K., & Mendelson, J. H., (1980). Buprenorphine suppresses heroin use by heroin addicts. *Science*, 207, pp. 657-659.

Messinger, E., and Zitrin, A., (1965). A statistical study of criminal drug addicts. *Crime and Delinquency*, 11(3), pp. 283-292.

Milkman, H., and Frosch, W. A., (1973). On the preferential abuse of heroin and amphetamine. *Journal of Nervous and Mental Disease*. 156(4), pp. 242-248.

Mirin, S. M., Meyer, R. E., and McRamee, H. B., (1976). Psychopathology, craving, and mood during heroin acquisition: An experimental study. *International Journal of the Addictions*, 11 (3), pp. 525-544.

Monroe, J. J., Ross, W. F., and Bergins, J. I., (1971). The decline of the addict as "psychopath": Implications for community care. *International Journal of the Addictions*, 6 (4), pp. 601-608.

Olson, R. W., (1964). MMPI sex differences in narcotics addicts. *Journal of General Psychology*, 71, pp. 257-266.

Pickens, R., Meisch, R. A., & Thompson, T., (1978). Drug Self-administration: An analysis of the reinforcing effects of drugs. In Iversen, L. I., Iversen, S. D., & Snyder, S. H., eds., *Handbook of Psychopharmacology*, Vol. 12. pp. 1-37. New York: Plenum Press.

Rado, S., (1933). The psychoanalysis of pharmacothymia. *Psychoanalytic Quarterly*, 2, pp. 1-23.

Robbins, P. R., (1974). Depression and drug addiction. *Psychiatric Quarterly*, 48 (3), pp. 374-386.

Schuster, C. R., & Thompson, T., (1969). Self-administration of and behavioral dependence on drugs. *Annual Review of Pharmacology*, 9, pp. 483-502.

Sheppard, C., Fracchia, J., Ricca, E. & Merlis, S., (1972). Indications of psy-

chopathology in male narcotic abusers, their effects and relation to treatment
effectiveness. *Journal of Psychology*, 8 (12), pp. 351-360.

Sheppard, C., Ricca, E., Fracchia, J., and Merlis, S., (1973). Indications of
psychopathology in applicants to a county methadone maintenance program.
Psychological Reports, 33, pp. 535-540.

Stefanis, C., Liakas, A., Boulougouris, J., Fink, M., and Freeman, A., (1976).
Chronic hashish use and mental disorder. *American Journal of Psychiatry*, 133
(2), pp. 225-227.

Sutker, P. B., Allain, A. N., & Cohen, G. H., (1974). MMPI indices of personality change following short-term and long-term hospitalization of heroin addicts. *Psychological Reports*, 34, pp. 495-500.

Wikler, A., (1952). A psychodynamic study of a patient during self-regulated
readdiction to morphine. *Psychiatric Quarterly*, 26, pp. 270-293.

Winger, G. D. & Woods, J. H., (1973). The reinforcing property of ethanol in the
rhesus monkey: Initiation, maintenance, and termination of intravenous ethanol — reinforced responding. *Annals of the New York Academy of Sciences*.
215, pp. 162-175.

Woody, G. E., (1977). Psychiatric aspects of opiate dependence: Diagnostic and
therapeutic research issues. In Blaine, J. D., and Julius, D. A., eds. *Psychodynamics of Drug Dependence*. National Institute on Drug Abuse Research Monograph 12. DHEW no. ADM 77-470. Washington, D.C.: U.S. Government
Printing Office. pp. 157-178.

Wurmser, L., (1977). Mr. Pecksniff's Horse? (Psychodynamics in compulsive
drug use). In Blaine, J. D., and Julius, D. A., eds. *Psychodynamics of Drug
Dependence*. National Institute on Drug Abuse Research Monograph 12.
DHEW no. ADM 77-470. Washington, D.C.: U.S. Government Printing Office. pp. 36-72.

Zinberg, N. E., (1984). *Drug, Set, and Setting*: The basis for controlled intoxicant
use. New Haven: Yale University Press.

Zinberg, N. R. and Shaffer, H. J., (1985). The social psychology of intoxicant
use: The interaction of personality and social setting. In Milkman, H. B., and
Shaffer, H. J., eds. *The Addictions: Multidisciplinary Perspectives and Treatments*. Lexington, Mass.: D.C. Heath and Company.

A Guide to the Assessment
of Psychiatric Symptoms
in the Addictions Treatment Setting

Barbara S. Woolf-Reeve, MD

SUMMARY. Large numbers of patients in substance abuse programs have symptoms of serious mental illness. Effective treatment and/or referral of these individuals involves accurate and timely evaluation of behaviors or symptoms which may interfere with the patient's ability to make use of addictions treatment. This guide offers a 'current symptom' focused assessment tool to be used by the clinician in the addictions setting in making the initial evaluation of psychiatric symptoms and behaviors. It is through the objective evaluation of the problems, symptoms and treatment needs of these complex patients that effective treatment approaches will be developed.

INTRODUCTION: CURRENT SYMPTOMS
AND BEHAVIORS AS A GUIDE
TO ADDICTIONS TREATMENT PLANNING

A large number of clients in chemical dependency treatment programs are being found to have serious mental illnesses in addition to problems with drugs and/or alcohol (Balcerzak & Hoffmann, 1985). While existing treatment approaches for addictions in the absence of mental illness can claim relative success, the presence of psychiatric symptoms has been associated with poor treatment response and, no doubt, has limited the overall success rate of otherwise effective treatment programs (McClellan, Luborsky, Woody,

Barbara S. Woolf-Reeve is Director, Alcohol and Drug Abuse Program, W. P. Carter Community Mental Health Center and Clinical Assistant Professor, Department of Psychiatry, University of Maryland School of Medicine.

O'Brien & Druley, 1983; Rounsaville, Dolinsky, Babor & Meyer, 1987). An understanding of psychiatric symptoms can help the addictions counselor (1) to form realistic treatment plans, (2) to make appropriate referrals to specialized treatment programs, (3) to identify the need for psychiatric consultation, (4) to know when to request psychological testing and (5) to help the patient get the most from the available treatments.

A popular belief holds that it is necessary to determine which illness is considered to be the *primary* condition in order to appropriately treat the individual with both mental illness and substance abuse (Ewing, 1980; Powell, Read, Penick, Miller & Bingham, 1987). In the author's experience, the focus on this "chicken and egg" dilemma has served more often to *prevent* the individual from receiving appropriate treatment. Individuals are often shuttled back and forth between addictions programs and mental health programs without receiving adequate treatment for either problem. It is true that certain conditions need to be addressed before others may be accurately diagnosed or effectively treated. For example, it is known that most patients entering alcohol treatment centers meet the criteria for major depression and 80% of these resolve within 2 weeks without any specific treatment other than abstinence (Dackis, Gold, Pottash & Sweeney, 1986). From this it is clear that a diagnosis of major depression cannot be made within the first few weeks of treatment for alcoholism. Many of the depressive symptoms seen in drinking alcoholics are caused by the direct effects of alcohol; however, little is gained by speculating at the time of admission which came first. Whether the depression or the alcoholism occurred first, the initial treatment is the same: abstinence.

The essential purpose of DIAGNOSIS is to form the basis for TREATMENT planning; the diagnosis provides a tool for determining the appropriate treatment(s). The diagnosis should be made with available data but should be considered tentative (working diagnosis) and be revised when additional data (history, clinical observations, treatment response) are available (Lieberman & Baker, 1985).

What follows is a "Decision Tree" to be used by addictions or mental health professionals in a variety of settings, including emergency rooms, outpatient treatment and residential treatment programs. A "current symptom" focus will assist the evaluation of patients seeking, or currently in, treatment for chemical dependency and will provide a way of identifying special treatment needs and defining treatment priorities. Special attention will be given to situations in which psychiatric symptoms prevent the patient from making use of available treatments.

A DECISION TREE FOR ASSESSING PSYCHIATRIC SYMPTOMS IN THE CHEMICALLY DEPENDENT INDIVIDUAL

Assessing the Potential for Violence

One of the most alarming situations for any clinician is one in which the patient indicates, by his words or actions, that he may be physically dangerous to himself or others. These types of situations arise in almost any context: in emergency treatment centers where the patient may be seen following suicide attempts, during individual counseling where the client may confide thoughts of homicide or suicide, or in residential treatment centers where persons may express threats of violence. It is important for the clinician to keep in mind that any and all such expressions must be treated with the utmost seriousness. Suicidal, homicidal or other violent ideation is not a joking matter. Laws exist in each state which permit the practitioner to isolate an individual who is believed to be at risk of hurting himself or of hurting others (Slovenko, 1985; Tancredi, Lieb & Slaby, 1975). Usually, this involves certification to involuntary hospitalization by more than one professional (e.g., psychologist or physician) licensed to perform such a function. The addictions counselor should familiarize himself with the laws in his area and with the mechanisms (such as the law enforcement agencies or emergency services) by which an individual believed to be dangerous may be detained or isolated.

Evaluation of Violent Expressions in an Acutely Intoxicated Individual

In this, as in many of the situations to follow, an accurate mental status examination cannot be performed while the patient is intoxicated; however, there is a great deal of assessment that *can* be done while the patient is intoxicated. If an actual act of violence has taken place (this includes any form of suicide attempt such as overdose, or any assaultive behavior toward others), a secure holding environment is needed until the acute intoxication has passed and a more accurate mental status examination may be performed. If, however, such violent ideation is being verbalized but has not yet been acted upon, other indicators can be used to determine the potential risk (Patterson, Dohn, Bird & Patterson, 1983). In general, if any doubt exists on the part of the practitioner, a careful, complete and rapid evaluation should be conducted by a professional capable of hospitalizing and/or medicating the patient. The following provide a guide for gathering information to be used in such an evaluation:

Symptoms indicating poor reality testing or poor impulse control. Symptoms such as command HALLUCINATIONS (these are often described as "voices telling me to kill myself") or DELUSIONS (e.g., a belief that a neighbor is a Nazi and must be annihilated) indicate that an acute psychotic process, such as PCP psychosis or schizophrenic illness, may be going on and most certainly are indicators that the individual is out of touch with reality. Regardless of the presumed cause of such symptoms, the temptation to dismiss them on the basis of recent drug or alcohol ingestion must be resisted. The expression of violent intent in the context of altered reality calls for a complete and rapid evaluation in a secure area. Most suicides occur while the individual is under the influence of drugs or alcohol (Fowler, Rich & Young, 1986).

History of violence. A prior history of violence increases the risk of violent ideation being acted upon (Kreitman, 1986). Again, the temptation must be resisted to dismiss current suicidal or other violent ideation on the basis of prior similar events, "He always says things like this," is not sufficient reason to take such expressions less seriously.

History of mental illness. A history of mental illness or treatment consistent with major depression or psychotic illness should be noted in an unbiased manner. An individual's actions must not be dismissed on the basis of "He's just crazy." On the other hand, it is useful to keep in mind that a psychiatric diagnosis is not to be feared. Mental illnesses can result in unusual or upsetting behaviors but they *are* illnesses which can be treated. In addition, it is important to consider all prior diagnoses as tentative until a new clinical evaluation with complete history and mental status examination confirms or establishes the diagnosis. An example of potential unhappy consequences comes from a case in the general hospital:

CASE A

> A psychiatric consultation was requested by the nursing staff on a surgical ward. The request was to "evaluate and medicate this 67 year old schizophrenic woman who is incontinent following surgery to stabilize an arm with multiple fractures." The "diagnosis" was given in the consult request: schizophrenia. This diagnosis was considered tentative and a careful chart review and examination was done. No history or symptoms of schizophrenia were found. What *was* found was an elderly woman with fluctuating level of awareness, with an irritable temper and without orientation for place or time. This lady was experiencing a post-surgical delirium as a result of sedatives received during and following surgery. (A more complete discussion of delirium will follow in the section on Medical Danger.) The "diagnosis" of schizophrenia was given by the nursing student who was frustrated with the constant demands being made by this confusing patient and her symptoms. If the consultant had accepted the "diagnosis" of schizophrenia, without conducting a complete evaluation, the sedatives may have been continued and the "schizophrenia" remain a problem.

This case illustrates the problems of using diagnostic labels to describe behavior. An accurate description of observable symptoms and behaviors and any known response of these symptoms to prior treatments (medications) is usually more helpful than a diagnostic label.

Secondary gain. It may be useful to consider whether the patient has something to gain by expressing violent ideas. For example, does he need a place to spend the night and know that hospital admission often follows suicidal expressions? The issue of secondary gain is another which can lead the practitioner into taking violent expressions less seriously. Intoxication impairs judgement sufficiently to lead some manipulative patients to act on violent thoughts to "get back at" those who turn him away. Again, a cautious attitude is recommended.

Available support system. Are family or friends available who can provide physical protection until a sober state is achieved and a more complete evaluation can be made? It is important to respect any fears that family may express about their own safety. Limited resources for the referral of the potentially violent patient often result in "the system" pushing the patient onto the family for protection when the family may not be equipped to provide the necessary structure. Before you release an individual into the care of family or friends, inquire about details of the environment. For example, are there any weapons? or will someone be available around the clock to transport the patient to emergency services if the situation should worsen?

Evaluation of Violence After a Detoxification or Sobering Up

It is possible that the violent ideation will subside and the patient will express regret or amnesia for these thoughts or gestures. In these cases, it is important to use firm confrontation emphasizing (1) the need to prevent recurrence of this type of situation and (2) the patient's responsibility for his actions while under the influence. "I didn't mean it; I was just drunk," *is not* a sufficient response. One must wonder how many of the 8,000 suicides committed in this country each year by persons under the influence of psychoactive substances were "unintended" (Miles, 1977).

Evaluation of Violence in Non-Intoxicated Individuals

The same principles apply in this situation as in the evaluation of intoxicated individuals; however, a more accurate mental status examination can be conducted and the evaluation can take place with the full participation of the patient.

Symptoms indicating poor reality testing. As in the case of intoxicated individuals, the presence of symptoms which would indicate a loss of touch with reality or an inability to control ones actions must be considered. Hallucinations and delusions as mentioned above are this type of indicator. Other symptoms of serious concern include the belief or experience of having thoughts inserted into one's mind (thought insertion). This can range from a delusional belief that "Martians have implanted a radio receiver in my head" to a sense or feeling that thoughts of suicide or death are intruding when unwanted and cannot be pushed aside. It is important to inquire openly about these symptoms; the avoidance of such material can add to the patient's perception that these thoughts themselves are powerful or controlling. A direct, matter-of-fact approach can elicit the needed information and, in some cases, can be reassuring to the patient.

Seriousness of intent. It is important to distinguish between general violent ideation and clear intent. Most individuals who find themselves in a treatment setting talking about such ideas *do* want help. It is reasonable to assume that they will talk about any plans or means which they may have to act on violent impulses; so ask about these. It is also important to have a frank discussion of the risks involved in attempting to block out such ideas by resuming drug or alcohol use. Remember, most suicide attempts take place while the individual is intoxicated.

History of violence. It is important to obtain a history of any prior violence. In the non-intoxicated individual additional information may be obtained including: his feelings and reactions to prior episodes, any similarities to the current situational factors, any unpleasant consequences which may have resulted, or insights she may have gained. These can be used to assess the individual's current ability to control his impulses.

CASE B

T.W. is a 26 year old man with a 10 year history of alcohol and sedative abuse. He has had 5 hospital admissions for suicide attempts in the past. All of these hospitalizations were brief and he has never taken medication for depression. T.W. has been attending a weekly outpatient alcohol treatment group for the past year in addition to attending Alcoholics

Anonymous (AA) several time per week. He is proud of the 9 months of sobriety he has achieved.

Mr. W. just learned that he is being laid off from his job because of "general cutbacks." His employer was careful to explain his work record for the past 6 months was good but he had the least seniority and he had to be let go. Mr. W. reported to his group that he feels worthless and that "it is useless to work so hard to do good." He said life is "too hard" and he "may as well be dead." The group leader, recalling Mr. W's history of suicide attempts, responded promptly:

LEADER: T., I see you are really discouraged by all this; but do you think you really want to die?

T.W.: I don't know. It all seems so hopeless.

LEADER: Have you thought about what you would do if you decided you really did want to give up?

T.W.: Oh, I don't have to think about it; I've done it plenty of times. First, I would buy a bottle.

LEADER: A bottle?

T.W.: Yeah, when I felt like this before, I would get drunk, then somehow I would find a way to overdose.

LEADER: Then what?

T.W.: Well, I guess the next thing I'd know, I would be in some emergency room having my stomach emptied.

The group joined in and gave T.W. their view of his situation. Some members agreed he had a right to feel down, some shared that they had had similar experiences. None thought it was a good idea for T. to take his life over this.

During the session, T. realized that he did not want to die; he also realized that he *did* want to take a drink. With the support of the group, T. decided to attend two AA meetings daily and to make an appointment with the clinic doctor to request Antabuse. He also made an agreement with the group that, if he felt like he could not resist the urge to drink, he would call someone in AA or the 24-hour emergency hotline. T. had identified a key factor (alcohol) in the feelings-thoughts-actions cycle. He had learned that, for him, discouraged feelings can lead to suicidal thoughts and that he can prevent these thoughts from being translated into action by removing the alcohol "link."

This case provides an example of how an expanded history of prior violence can (1) help the clinician to assess risk and (2) lead the patient into more self awareness.

History of mental illness. In addition to eliciting a history of prior violent events, it is important to obtain a good history of prior treatment for major illnesses which may indicate the need for medication. Suicide has been associated with a number of major mental illnesses including major depression, bipolar illness (manic-depressive illness), and schizophrenia. If a client mentions medications which are unfamiliar, record the names of these as accurately as possible, but more importantly, record a description of the symptoms the medications were intended to help. The patient's assessment of how helpful these medications were, as well as any adverse effects experienced are all valuable information. This can be passed on to another professional who is knowledgeable about medications and illnesses and can be useful in arriving at a decision about the current need for medication.

Situational factors. Life situation is important to consider when assessing the potential for violence. The individual may need help in identifying recent events which may have contributed to his current thoughts and feelings. For example, it may have "slipped" his "mind" that an old friend walked past him on the street without speaking or he may consider it unimportant that his mother locked him out of the house last night because he came home late. If the patient is agreeable to a dialogue, it may be helpful to spend some time attempting to identify precipitating events and to help the patient to identify solutions to the situation other than violence. As in the case of the intoxicated individual, a supportive family can provide needed structure and protection until the crisis passes. Other community supports include friends, AA, Narcotics Anonymous (NA) or other self-help groups. However, bear in mind that mere attendance at groups may not provide sufficient support. Some individuals attend many meetings but obtain a minimal amount of support because of little interpersonal interaction.

Treatment context. Treatment context is another life situation which deserves separate attention. Every residential rehabilitation, detox, or group home program has rules of conduct and these can be used as a guide to determine appropriate action in any individual case. For example, some programs consider verbal threats of violence toward another individual so disruptive that the consequences are the same as actual physical violence: discharge. The underlying message is: "If you cannot control your verbal expressions, then we cannot trust you to control your actions." Of course, this is clearly explained in the orientation to the program and written in the rules.

It may be useful to review with the patient the details of his "contract" and to make certain he clearly understands the potential consequences of his actions. Helping the individual to see the potential consequences of his actions may be especially useful in the context of individual or group counseling. In the case of T.W., he was able to recall the unpleasant consequences of prior suicide attempts ("woke up in the emergency room") and to resolve to avoid repeating these (or less reversible) consequences. An effort can be made to determine what the patient is "really saying," and to help him gain a broader perspective on his situation, but if the patient is unable to understand these connections and, as a consequence, to control his actions, the need for external controls continues.

Assessing the Risk of Medical Danger

In the patient with major mental illness and alcohol or drug abuse, the signs and symptoms of intoxication, overdose, or withdrawal can be difficult to evaluate. DELIRIUM is an alteration of mental functioning resulting from injury or metabolic insult to the central nervous system. Delirium can result from drug overdose, drug or alcohol withdrawal, head trauma or infections such as HIV encephalitis. Delirium tremens (alcohol withdrawal) is a serious medical illness and, untreated, may result in death (Behnke, 1976). It is important to distinguish between life threatening syndromes (such as delirium tremens or drug overdose) and simple intoxication. The practitioner needs to know when to make rapid referral to medical emergency services and gather any important information which may be useful in the medical assessment.

Signs and Symptoms of Delirium

Elevated pulse rate, blood pressure, temperature (vital signs) or profuse sweating. While intoxication with some stimulants may cause some rapid pulse and elevated blood pressure, the above symptoms in conjunction with a history of recent abstinence generally indicate the autonomic nervous system hyperactivity found in alcohol or sedative withdrawal (Leroy, 1979). These are often seen in conjunction with confusion and hallucinations in the full delirium tremens syndrome. However the absence of confusion or hallucinations should not delay immediate medical attention. Remember, total abstinence is not required for withdrawal; an individual may reduce his alcohol intake significantly but continue to drink and experience withdrawal. Elevated vital signs may be the only way to distinguish a withdrawal delirium from intoxication or functional psychosis.

Disorientation. Confusion or disorientation for time, place or person is an indicator of serious metabolic, traumatic or other injury to the central nervous system such as acute intoxication, withdrawal or head trauma. Functional mental illness without physical origins (e.g., schizophrenia) seldom results in the inability to orient oneself; however, symptoms such as hallucinations or delusions may interfere with the examiner's ability to obtain an accurate assessment of orientation. Another potentially misleading feature of delirium is that it involves a *fluctuating course*. In delirium it is possible to be oriented and coherent at one time and disoriented a short time later. The less experienced practitioner often misconstrues this mixed picture to indicate a volitional component on the part of the patient and therefore does not treat this symptom with the seriousness which it deserves. Disorientation or changing mental status, whether or not it is in the company of metabolic signs, always needs medical assessment.

Alterations in perception. Perceptual distortions, illusions and hallucinations are associated with acute intoxication with hallucinogens (PCP, LSD, marijuana), cocaine, amphetamine and occasionally alcohol; they are also found in withdrawal delirium. Drug or alcohol intoxication or withdrawal can occur in individuals with serious mental illnesses; these illnesses can also have hallucinations as symptoms. In general, visual or tactile (involving the sense of touch) hallucinations are rarely found in functional mental illness; rather these types of hallucinations are considered indicators of an organic involvement such as delirium or intoxication. The visual hallucinations of delirium tremens often are rather simple in nature and rarely elicit an emotional response. On the other hand, hallucinations accompanied by elaborate delusional ideation are more often found in functional illnesses. (See Hallucinations below.)

Tremors and physical agitation. These classic signs of early delirium tremens can be evident in a number of other illnesses. In general, early withdrawal from any addictive substance may result in tremor, agitation and/or sleeplessness. These symptoms may accompany intoxication with stimulants or functional psychiatric illnesses such as bipolar illness, attention deficit disorder, or anxiety disorders. Again, careful assessment of other symptoms is needed to determine the need for medical intervention.

History of Recent Events

In assessing the potential for medical danger due to overdose, withdrawal, or head trauma, a complete history of recent events is of key importance. In many cases a great deal of detail may not be available; however, any information regarding recent activities may be helpful to the clinician in making an evaluation. Family, friends or acquaintances may be able to provide useful information about drug, alcohol, or medication ingestion including time of last drink. Keep in mind that some over-the-counter preparations taken in excess or in combination with alcohol can result in metabolic disturbance (Gardner & Hall, 1982). It is also important to record any information which may indicate recent head trauma (e.g., "found at road side unconscious"). Past history of delirium tremens is important to know about but it does not confirm the diagnosis; a complete medical evaluation is needed. In a similar manner, a history of serious mental illness may be helpful to know but, as mentioned above, does not explain confusion or metabolic signs if they are present.

Assessing Symptoms Which May Interfere with the Patient's Ability to Participate in Treatment for Addictions

Situations often arise in the treatment of drug or alcohol abuse in which the patient does not seem to be getting the benefit of the treatment being offered. We often consider lack of progress as an indicator that "the client is not ready for change" or "he has not reached bottom." Lack of sufficient motivation to enter into and to follow through with treatment is certainly the most common reason for lack of progress in treatment among substance abusers without other mental illness. However, serious mental illness introduces a number of additional factors which may impact on the individual's suitability for a given type of treatment and his ability to make use of available treatments. In addition, the effects of long term substance abuse (especially alcohol) result in impaired cognition including difficulty in learning new facts and in organizing them in ways which can be applied to life situations.

Isolation, Withdrawal or Difficulty Relating to Others

These symptoms, in the extreme, can keep an individual homebound. Withdrawal from interpersonal interactions can have at its basis many factors including: paranoia, anxiety, depression or personality traits. Conditions which can be involved include paranoid disorder, schizophrenia, bipolar disorder, social phobia, agoraphobia, major depression, post traumatic stress disorder and personality disorder. If an individual has engaged in some form of treatment and is observed to become withdrawn during the course of treatment, it is unlikely that this is due to a personality disorder or paranoid disorder. The symptoms of these conditions are stable and relatively unchanging (Hoffmann, 1971; Hoy, 1969). In the case of an observed change in behavior, it is important to inquire about reasons rather than to assume it is due to "avoidance" or "denial."

In the case of depression, the patient may only be able to describe low energy, disinterest, or hopelessness; he may even refer to himself as "lazy" for lack of a better explanation. Inquire about the specific symptoms of depression including change in sleep or appetite, tearfulness, irritability, hopelessness, worthlessness, ruminations on themes of death, or suicidal ideation. Some of these symptoms are common during withdrawal from chemicals and the early recovery process; however, if they persist past 2 or 3 weeks or if they develop during the course of active treatment for addictions, they should be more fully evaluated. Eighty percent of patients who enter alcoholism treatment with symptoms of depression improve within 2 weeks. Conversely, 20% have depressive symptoms which do not spontaneously resolve, and therefore, may have major depressions in need of treatment with medication.

Isolation or withdrawal may also occur during an active psychotic illness. Usually, other symptoms will be present which will indicate the need for psychiatric evaluation; however, this is not always the case. In the cases where delusions and/or hallucinations lead to social withdrawal, direct inquiry may or may not yield an explanation. For example, if a paranoid schizophrenic has begun isolating himself because he fears his family is trying to poison him, he may or may not reveal this to his counselor depending on whether or not the counselor has been included in the delusional thinking. He may remark, "If I tell you what is going on, you will tell my parents." It is important to be direct with the patient about the way his behavior (e.g., withdrawal) is interfering with his treatment and to try to have him explore this with you. An individual with impaired reality testing may be surprisingly frank when asked about his symptoms and provide the counselor with sufficient information to allow for appropriate referral.

Social isolation associated with anxiety specific to going into public places is a characteristic of social phobia, when scrutiny by others is feared, or agoraphobia, when impeded escape is feared. Post traumatic stress disorder is another condition which may lead to social isolation. Individuals may avoid situations which remind them of the traumatic event. Emotional blunting, increased startle response and flashbacks or bad dreams are characteristic of this condition. Usually the individual with these conditions is genuinely distressed by his symptoms and is willing to be referred for specialized help. On the other hand, some anxiety about participating in the treatment process is almost universal. Every individual feels some anxiety about talking in groups until these skills are repeatedly practiced.

In the case of individuals who have not yet engaged in the active treatment process, evaluation of the symptom of isolation or withdrawal is not so straightforward. An example would be someone who was detoxified after a motor vehicle accident and transferred to a residential treatment facility for the first time. Again the approach needs to be a direct one: ask for an explanation. If a direct inquiry does not provide an adequate explanation, it is possible that a thought disorder is present but remaining undetected. Psychological testing may be useful in uncovering serious pathology about which the patient is unable or unwilling to talk. If psychological testing is unavailable or if no thought disorder is found, it is useful to assume the patient is not aware of the problem his behavior causes to others and to his recovery process. He should be given an opportunity to correct his behavior. Explain the nature of the therapeutic/recovery process as one which necessitates interaction with others. If he is unable to correct his behavior with education, support and limits, look at this behavior in the context of the whole individual: does he show the ability to interact appropriately? Are his interactions provocative? Does he have a history of poor relationships? If his patterns of interactions have been unsatisfactory in the past, a personality disorder is likely. The methods of presenting clear, consistent limits with carefully defined consequences are well known to addictions counselors. These methods provide the individual with character pathology, the structure necessary to be able to tolerate the formation of positive relationships in the therapeutic environment (Zarcone, 1978).

Extremes of Mood, Mood Swings, Labile Mood

It is well known to the addictions counselor that depression, irritability and sleeplessness are common among drinking alcoholics and barbiturate users and are often a part of the "crash" following cocaine use (Gawin & Kleber, 1986). The patient who first presents for treatment, is actively using drugs or alcohol, and is depressed should be advised to undergo a detox first. Accurate assessment of mood symptoms cannot be made while the individual is still using substances. (Violent or suicidal ideation should be handled in the manner outlined in the above sections.)

When depression and related symptoms occur during the early addiction recovery process, the patient is usually guided through this phase by reassurance about the time-limited nature of these symptoms and by the support of others in recovery who have had similar symptoms and found them to decrease in frequency and intensity as the length of abstinence increases. Most severe symptoms of mood disturbance pass after about two weeks of abstinence but many milder symptoms may persist for several weeks or months. For patients with major depression, sleeplessness, sadness, low energy, lack of interest in activities, or poor attention span may continue for several weeks to the extent that they interfere with daily activities, such as the ability to go to meetings, or to work, or the ability to read or concentrate on an interesting television program. In these cases, a referral should be considered for a psychiatric evaluation to assess the usefulness of medication in controlling these symptoms. Other factors which would suggest the likelihood of a major depression are a history of severe depression prior to drug or alcohol use, a history of significantly improved symptoms with prior treatment with antidepressants or the presence of depression or of manic depressive illness in a close relative.

Increased physical activity, impulsiveness, euphoria, and rapid thoughts are all symptoms of cocaine or amphetamine abuse. However, mood swings or the emergence of an extremely irritable or euphoric mood with prolonged abstinence may be due to mental illness requiring medication. The symptoms of attention deficit disorder (ADD, a childhood disorder which can persist into adulthood) and of bipolar disorder may resemble stimulant intoxication (Cocores, Patel, Gold & Pottash, 1987). As with depression, if these symptoms persist or worsen after several weeks of abstinence and interfere with normal functioning, a psychiatric evaluation should be conducted to determine the usefulness of medication. A history of similar symptoms prior to any drug or alcohol use or a positive family history will be helpful in the evaluation.

Finally, a brief mention will be made regarding LABILE AFFECT. Mood swings are common in early recovery; however, labile affect is a particular kind of mood swing in which, quite rapidly and often for no apparent reason, the mood may switch from elation to tearfulness or from euthymia (normal mood) to irritability. Several moods may be observed during a single conversation and often the patient is not aware of his own inconsistency. This labile mood is most often associated with an organic disturbance such as intoxication, but when it persists beyond detoxification, other organic etiologies should be considered. In these cases, the labile mood is often accompanied by deficits in cognition and may be the result of permanent neurologic damage. A full discussion of these conditions is found in the sections to follow.

Hallucinations

Disordered perception has been discussed in the above sections about violence and delirium. However, this discussion will help to put this symptom into a broader perspective. As noted above, disordered perception may occur with auditory, visual or tactile senses. The conditions in which hallucinations are found are numerous and include intoxication, withdrawal delirium, delirium of other etiologies, schizophrenia, bipolar illness, and major depression. Visual and tactile hallucinations are most often indicators of an organic process (for example, the snakes on the wall or the bugs on the skin reported in delirium tremens). Auditory hallucinations are more often associated with functional (i.e., psychiatric without clear organic origin) illness. One exception to this is the frequently reported experience of persons in withdrawal or early recovery to believe they have heard their named called. In fact, this is such a common and relatively unalarming symptom that even the reader may recall such experiences especially when tired or distracted.

The best way to find out about hallucinations is to ask. If an individual is having difficulty concentrating on educational material presented as part of his treatment, or if he is having difficulty joining in with the activities around him, or if he seems easily distracted from conversation by nothing in particular, or if he has difficulty expressing his thoughts in a coherent, goal directed manner, it can be useful to ask if thoughts or other experiences are making it difficult to concentrate. The interviewer may find it helpful to suggest that some people who have trouble concentrating may hear voices inside or outside their head or see distracting things around them. In these cases, as in the case of unexplained isolation or social withdrawal, psychological testing may be useful to identify disturbance in thought or perception which is difficult for the patient to report directly. Any report of hallucinations should be referred for more complete evaluation. Again, it is helpful to find out if there is a history of similar experiences. If there has been prior treatment, ask what medications were used and if they helped. In addition, inquire about other family members who may have similar symptoms and any known diagnosed illnesses in the family and/or treatments.

Delusions

To the student of psychopathology, delusions are the most bizarre and fascinating symptoms of altered mental status. As with many of the symptoms previously discussed here, delusions may stem from a number of conditions. Delusions may occur in any condition which has altered reality testing: schizophrenia, bipolar illness, major depression, paranoid disorder, toxic psychosis (cocaine, PCP, LSD), delirium, or dementia. In general, delusions are beliefs held by an individual which are inconsistent with external reality. Delusions may be quite organized and elaborate; such as: "the neighbors are beaming x-rays into the house and any attempt to block these rays results in feedback to the neighbors and they increase the intensity of the rays." Or, they may be disconnected beliefs about being "bad" or of the police watching, or "my brain is melting."

Some delusions, referred to as secondary delusions, are developed to "explain" perceptual distortions (hallucinations) resulting from a delirium. An example would be the belief that "the little man behind the door is spying on me," developed in response to a visual hallucination induced by medication overdose. In secondary delusions, the patient is usually willing to listen to reason. Such is not the case with most other types of delusions. DO NOT waste your time trying to talk someone out of a delusional belief (Wallen & Weiner, 1988), at the same time do not allow them to think you share their belief. When delusional material emerges during the course of treatment, encourage discussion only as far as necessary to determine the degree of organization of the belief system. In addition, try to determine how long the delusion has been active and any other symptoms or experiences which may accompany (e.g., "I know there is a radio receiver in my head because I hear the voices").

Ideas of reference are another type of delusion. In this case, usual environmental cues are misinterpreted in a personal way. An example would be: an individual sees a group of people talking and assumes that they are talking about him. In general, ideas of reference are less firmly held and interfere less with normal functioning. They may or may not be associated with the above psychiatric conditions. As with the previously discussed symptoms, if this is noted to cause distress or to interfere with routine life, a more complete evaluation is indicated.

Poor Memory, Limited Attention Span,
Poor Concentration

Some symptoms which may interfere with attention or concentration have been mentioned above including the hallucinations of a psychotic process or the distractibility of attention deficit disorder (ADD). More often, these types of problems are indicators of cognitive impairment resulting from neurologic damage (dementia). The most common cause of neurologic impairment found in addiction is alcoholic dementia. It may be useful to keep in mind that many other things can lead to dementia including Alzheimer's Disease, stroke, small strokes (multi-infarct), vitamin deficiency, HIV infection, or head trauma.

A full assessment of cognitive functioning is needed to determine the usefulness of various forms of treatment (Becker, Butters, Rivoira & Miliotis, 1986). For example, a treatment which relies heavily on an educational approach in which the patient is expected to learn new material quickly would be unsuccessful for someone with impaired memory or an approach which relies on teaching problem-solving skills would have limited benefit for an individual with impaired abstract thinking. Neuropsychologic testing is a specific type of testing which can determine which of the various cognitive functions are impaired including: immediate, recent and long-term memory; ability to abstract; judgement; visual-spatial coordination; and expressive and receptive language. If specific deficits are identified in an otherwise motivated patient, treatment approaches can be developed to compensate for that deficit (Ryan & Butters, 1986; Tarter & Edwards, 1987). Consideration may be given to mental retardation in individuals who do not seem to have the intellectual capacity to process information effectively. Again, psychological testing is helpful in assessment and treatment planning.

OTHER FACTORS TO CONSIDER IN ASSESSING THE MENTALLY ILL SUBSTANCE ABUSER

The above section provides a framework by which to evaluate psychiatric symptoms as they appear in the context of substance abuse evaluation and treatment. A number of other factors may influence that assessment process including the background or attitudes of the evaluator, the context of the assessment, the treatment options available, and the availability of other assessment instruments.

Background or Attitudes of the Evaluator

Each of us bring to our clinical work personal attitudes, knowledge and feelings. These generally have a positive influence on the clinical outcome; however, sometimes personal attitudes, known as COUNTERTRANSFERENCE, may cloud the clinical picture or impede the progress of treatment. Effective professional training provides the practitioner with the valuable skill of identifying personal feelings as they develop in response to a patient. Some guidelines are offered here addressing the special countertransference issues in working with mentally ill substance abusers.

When in Doubt, Obtain a Consultation

If there are clinical symptoms or issues which do not seem to add up, if the therapeutic process seems stalemated, or if the clinician has strong negative or positive feelings toward the client, much can be gained by obtaining a second opinion. The best of clinicians have some "blind spots" or occasionally try to fit a type of treatment to a patient who is not ready or capable of benefitting. The results can be frustrating for the therapist or counselor. Another view of the situation can illuminate issues or factors which may have been overlooked or provide confirmation for the appropriateness of the current treatment. In almost any situation, a second opinion will provide information which will lead to more effective and less frustrating interactions with the client.

The Patient Is Responsible for Compliance with Treatment

Occasionally a mentally ill substance abuser will attempt to elicit a permissive attitude from the counselor by highlighting his unhappy condition of mental illness. "He's sick, he can't help himself," would be a statement representative of this attitude. An analogy may be drawn between the conditions of mental illness and that of chemical dependency. Each of these conditions can be considered a treatable disease, each involves features which temporarily render confrontation techniques ineffective (e.g., intoxication in alcoholism and psychotic symptoms in schizophrenia), each may involve denial, and in each the ultimate responsibility for obtaining and complying with treatment lies with the individual. In mental illness, as with chemical dependency, after a careful assessment has been done, effective treatment established (often done during psychiatric hospitalization), basic education about the illness and about the recommended treatment conducted, the patient can be considered to have the elements necessary to control his/her symptoms. Approaches similar to those employed in alcohol and drug counselling can be effective with the mentally ill substance abuser in helping him to move past his denial to a more responsible attitude toward his mental illness.

CASE C

One 62 year old woman had been diagnosed as having major depression which responded well to antidepressant medication. She also had a history of alcoholism for many years. During residential rehabilitation for a drinking relapse following 18 months of sobriety, she reported that she drank because she was depressed. Her counselor inquired about the sequence of events leading to relapse and found she had stopped taking her antidepressant medications two months prior to the return of symptoms of depression. She had then stopped attending AA, had become increasingly withdrawn and hopeless and had begun to drink in an effort to "kill myself with booze." On further examination of the events surrounding discontinuation of medication, the patient admitted she had begun to feel neglected by her family and thought that she could gain more of their attention if she was no longer "doing so well." Appropriate confrontation led the patient to see that she has as much responsibility to control her symptoms of depression by proper use of medication in the same way that she has responsibility to control her alcoholism through abstinence.

Situational Factors

The influence of situational factors (such as availability of various types of treatment programs, financial constraints, resource limitations within treatment programs) on clinical findings and recommendations has not been well studied. However, these influences are inevitable. How often have we thought, "What he really needs is . . . a long term residential program . . . or an opiate detox on a psychiatric unit . . . or a supportive family?" We learn to "make do" with limited resources and services without question. However, it is the dually diagnosed individuals who seldom have sufficient social and emotional reserves to apply this "make do" attitude. These are the individuals who lack the social skills needed to make themselves feel comfortable in an AA meeting, who find themselves scapegoated in residential settings ("I may be a drunk but at least I'm not crazy like him."), and in some cases, lack the intellectual capacity to make use of the usual educational and confrontational techniques used extensively in the treatment of addictions. Those of us who accept the challenge of developing treatment approaches with the dually diagnosed need to resist the "make do" attitude which has failed these complicated cases. Some questions to keep in mind when assessing dual diagnosis clients and their treatment needs may help to resist the "make do" attitude and its limiting influence on our thinking:

What would happen with no intervention? In some cases "some treatment is better than no treatment" but this is not always the case. When determining if the individual is in need of a therapeutic intervention or when assessing the effectiveness of a current treatment, this question may help to clarify the issues.

Is enough known to make a decision/diagnosis? We never seem to have enough information in the form of psychiatric or substance use history, clinical mental status examination, psychological testing, and knowledge of social and family factors to be certain that our assessment and treatment approach are accurate. The assessment process needs to be ongoing, treatment response reviewed periodically and treatment approach revised as needed.

What are the treatment goals? In order to assess the effectiveness of our treatment, we need to have a clear idea of what outcome we expect. Is abstinence a sufficient goal? Is employment? Is probation compliance? When working with clients in a residential program, we are aware of the need to assist them in the development of the skills necessary to maintain sobriety prior to discharge from a protected environment. When working with dually diagnosed patients, we may want to consider what skills or emotional factors are lacking (e.g., difficulty relating to others or poor verbal skills) and make the acquisition of these factors an initial goal of treatment.

Can existing treatments be modified to meet the special treatment needs of the patient without disruption to the treatment program or the counselor? In our zealous efforts to include mentally ill substance abusers in our treatment programs, we need to be cautious about disrupting the integrity of these programs or overextending our resources. Some elements may be relatively simple to add to existing programs such as adding a psychologist consultant to assess distracting intrapsychic symptoms, social skills, or cognitive functioning and to participate in treatment planning; or adding a psychiatrist consultant to assess patients for the usefulness of psychotropic medications and to monitor these; or adding an educational group to teach the hazards of alcohol, drug and medication combinations. Other modifications, such as maintaining supervision of acting out psychotic patients or of suicidal patients, would require significant changes in staffing patterns or specialized training for staff.

In the end we will serve our clients and society by assessing as objectively as possible the symptoms and behaviors indicating the special treatment needs of our clients and in assessing the realistic ability of the existing treatment programs to meet these needs. As we learn to see patients and their needs without the "blinders" of limited resources, we will be better equipped to garner resources to meet these needs.

CONCLUSION

This chapter provides the clinician in addictions referral and addictions treatment settings with some practical guidelines for the assessment of psychiatric and behavioral symptoms as they may influence treatment planning and treatment response. A "current symptom" focus is advocated with the belief that, in most cases, a hierarchy of treatment needs can be determined from the presenting clinical picture. Also emphasized is the need for periodic reassessment of symptoms and of treatment response to determine emerging problems or resolving issues.

REFERENCES

Balcerzak, W. S. & Hoffmann, N. G. (1985). Dual treatment rationale for psychologically disordered and chemically dependent clients. *Alcoholism Treatment Quarterly, 2,* 61-67.

Becker, J. T., Butters, N., Rivoira, P. & Miliotis, P. (1986). Asking the right questions: Problem solving in male alcoholics and male alcoholics with Korsakoff's syndrome. *Alcoholism: Clinical and Experimental Research, 10,* 641-646.

Behnke, R. H. (1976). Recognition and management of alcohol withdrawal syndrome. *Hospital Practice, NOV,* 79-84.

Cocores, J. A., Patel, M. D., Gold, M. S. & Pottash, A. C. (1987). Cocaine abuse, attention deficit disorder, and bipolar disorder. *Journal of Nervous and Mental Diseases, 175,* 431-432.

Dakis, C. A., Gold, M. S., Pottash, A.L.C. & Sweeney, D. R. (1986). Evaluating depression in alcoholics. *Psychiatry Research, 17,* 105-109.

Ewing, J. A. (1980). Editorial: Alcoholism – another biopsychosocial disease. *Psychosomatics, 21,* 371-372.

Fowler, R. C., Rich, C. L. & Young, D. (1986). San Diego suicide study: II. Substance abuse in young cases. *Archives of General Psychiatry, 43,* 962-965.

Gardner, E. R. & Hall R. C. W. (1982). Psychiatric symptoms produced by over-the-counter drugs. *Psychosomatics, 23,* 186-190.

Gawin, F. H. & Kleber, H. D. (1986). Abstinence symptomatology and psychiatric diagnosis in cocaine abusers. Clinical observations. *Archives of General Psychiatry, 43,* 107-113.

Hoffmann, H. (1971). Personality changes of hospitalized alcoholics after treatment. *Psychological Reports, 29,* 948-950.

Hoy, R. M. (1969). The personality of inpatient alcoholics in relation to group psychotherapy, as measured by the 16-P.F. *Quarterly Journal of Studies in Alcoholism, 30,* 401-407.

Kreitman, N. (1986). The critical assessment and management of the suicidal patient. In A. Roy (Ed.), *Suicide* (pp. 181-195). Baltimore, MD: Williams & Wilkins.

Leroy, J. B. (1979). Recognition and treatment of the alcohol withdrawal syndrome. *Primary Care, 6,* 529-539.

Lieberman, P. B. and Baker, F. M. (1985). The reliability of psychiatric diagnosis in the emergency room. *Hospital and Community Psychiatry, 36,* 291-293.

McLellan, A. T., Luborsky, L., Woody, G. E., O'Brien, C. P. & Druley, K. A. (1983). Predicting response to alcohol and drug abuse treatments: Role of psychiatric severity. *Archives of General Psychiatry, 40,* 620-625.

Miles, C. P. (1977). Conditions predisposing to suicide: A review. *Journal of Nervous and Mental Disease, 164,* 231-246.

Patterson, W. M., Dohn, H. H., Bird, J. & Patterson, G. A. (1983). Evaluation of suicidal patients: The SAD PERSONS scale. *Psychosomatics, 24,* 343-349.

Powell, B. J., Read, M. R., Penick, E. C., Miller, N. S. & Bingham, S. F. (1987). Primary and secondary depression in alcoholic men: An important distinction? *Journal of Clinical Psychiatry, 48,* 98-101.

Rounsaville, B. J., Dolinsky, Z. S., Babor, T. F. & Meyer, R. E.(1987). Psychopathology as a predictor of treatment outcome in alcoholics. *Archives of General Psychiatry, 44,* 505-513.

Ryan, C. & Butters, N. (1986). The neuropsychology of alcoholism. In D. Wedding, A. M. Horton & J. Webster (Eds.). *The Neuropsychology Handbook: Behavioral and Clinical Perspectives* (pp. 376-409). New York: Springer.

Slovenko, R. (1985). Law and psychiatry. In H. I. Kaplan & B. J. Sadock (Eds.). *Modern Synopsis of Comprehensive Textbook of Psychiatry/IV* (pp. 1960-1990). Baltimore: Williams & Wilkins.

Tancredi, L. R., Lieb, J. & Slaby, A. E. (Eds.). (1975). *Legal Issues in Psychiatric Care*. Hagerstown, MD: Medical Dept., Harper & Row.

Tarter, R. E. & Edwards, M. L. (1987). Brief & comprehensive neurological assessment of alcohol and substance abuse. In L. C. Hartlage, M. J. Asken & J. L. Hornsby (Eds.). *Essentials of Neuropsychological Assessment* (pp. 138-162).New York: Springer.

Wallen, M. & Weiner, H. (1988). Guidelines for individual counseling with dually diagnosed patients. Presented at *The Mentally Ill Substance Abusing Person: Yours, Mine, or Ours?* The Medical College of Pennsylvania, May 19 & 20, Philadelphia, PA.

Zarcone, V. P., Jr. (1978). Residential treatment for drug dependence. In R. J. Craig & S. L. Baker (Eds.), *Drug Dependent Patients: Treatment and Research* (pp. 67-89). Springfield, IL: Charles C. Thomas.

Four Perspectives on Dual Diagnosis: An Overview of Treatment Issues

Linda Rubinstein, MSW
Frances Campbell, MSN
Dennis Daley, MSW

INTRODUCTION AND REVIEW OF RESEARCH

Working with the dual diagnosed patient presents complex and challenging situations. Traditional treatment approaches do not always work, and new approaches based on the understanding of both the problems and abilities of the individual are called for.

One approach to understanding dual diagnosis is to examine it from four perspectives which define the scope and the complexities of the problem. These perspectives are: (1) the *patient*, who must deal with the realities of two or more disorders; (2) the *family* whose support and involvement may be needed to help the patient, and who may have special treatment needs of their own; (3) the *counselor/therapist*, who must expand the knowledge base and skill level used to work with these patients; and (4) the many other *systems* needed to help this multi-problem group. This paper will focus primarily on the first two perspectives since these are the areas in which literature is available.

Studies profiling the person with chemical dependency have increased in recent years. What has been discovered in the emergent research is that many chemically dependent persons also have additional psychiatric diagnoses which complicate recovery and lead to poorer outcomes (Rounsaville, Iolinski, Babor and Meyer, 1987).

Linda Rubinstein, Frances Campbell, and Dennis Daley are affiliated with the Comprehensive Alcohol and Drug Abuse Program, Western Psychiatric Institute and Clinic, Department of Psychiatry, University of Pittsburgh School of Medicine, Pittsburgh, PA 15213.

There are many more individuals with dual diagnoses than were once believed. For example, Hesselbrock, Meyer and Keener, (1985) in a study of hospitalized alcoholics found that 77% of these individuals met criteria for another DSM-III diagnosis at some time in their life including drug abuse and dependence. Analysis of data from the Epidemiologic Catchment Area survey examining comorbidity between alcohol use disorders and nonsubstance psychiatric disorders reveals that every one of the psychiatric disorders examined was more likely to occur in alcoholics than nonalcoholics (Helzer and Pryzbeck, 1988). Several studies have shown an association between depression and opioid dependence (Maddux, Desmond and Costello, 1987; Rounsaville, Kosten, Weissman and Kleber, 1985). Numerous other studies and reports also document significant rates of comorbidity among patients with alcohol or drug use disorders (Mirin, Weiss and Michael, 1988; Schuckit, 1986; Bedi and Halikas, 1985; Merikangas, Weissman, Prosoff, Pauls and Leckman, 1985; Carroll and Sobel, 1986). It is generally accepted that there are "other problems" for the chemically dependent (Wallace 1987).

Treatment outcomes are generally poorer among patients with a coexistent psychiatric disorder (Rounsaville et al., 1987). Studies by McLellan and colleagues (1983) evidence that patients with high psychiatric severity as measured by the Addiction Severity Index show virtually no improvement in any treatment. High dropout rates from outpatient care for dual disordered patients have also been reported (Kofoed, Konia, Walsh and Atkinson, 1986).

When interpreting these findings, several facts should be kept in mind. First, studies of the dual diagnosed have been conducted most frequently on patients in inpatient treatment facilities. This population represents a more problematic group than those who do not require inpatient treatment. Second, some studies report "lifetime rates" of psychiatric illness, which implies that the psychiatric disorder occurred during the persons lifetime but may not be present now. Some individuals experience single episodes of psychiatric illness, while others experience recurrent episodes. Chronic disorders such as schizophrenia, refractory depression and bipolar disorder typically require long-term or even lifelong care.

Another factor which complicates these reports is the time frame in which the psychiatric diagnosis is made. It is often necessary for patients to be abstinent for several weeks or longer before an accurate psychiatric diagnosis can be made. Some cases even require longer periods of abstinence. During early withdrawal and recovery, many symptoms may appear which mimic psychiatric illness. This is true especially for depressive symptoms which are very common in patients in early recovery, but which do not indicate a major depression. Even psychotic symptoms may occur during detoxification and withdrawal which might be interpreted as schizophrenia, but given time will resolve without treatment.

Clinicians are advised to increase their observation skills and to view the client and his symptoms in an objective manner so that additional conditions that must be addressed in treatment are neither overlooked or misdiagnosed. The clinical use of diagnoses must be understood as a tool to guide treatment and not a method for labelling patients in a negative manner. Strengths and health must always be assessed in the client (Daley, Moss and Campbell, 1987).

Another caution for the therapist is to attend to the differences between those patients who show behavioral traits but do not present with full criteria for a diagnosis. For example, many addicted persons show antisocial behavior while in the active phase of addiction. However, these traits may not constitute the DSM-III-R diagnosis of Antisocial Personality and thus patients should not be labeled with this disorder. Labels in such cases may serve to limit patients rather than to help. For example, labeling may occur in instances where symptoms of depression are seen in a newly recovering person, and often the diagnosis of major depression is given. This condition may be a secondary depression (one which may be induced by the chronic and abusive use of alcohol or drugs); these depressions are often misdiagnosed as a major depression and treated with antidepressants. Secondary depressions however, usually remit within a week or so after substance use is stopped. Clinicians must be cautioned to avoid making premature or incorrect interpretation of symptoms so that patients can be treated in the most beneficial manner.

PERSPECTIVE 1: THE PATIENT

Dual disordered patients are reported to be difficult, noncompliant, and resistant to treatment. They tend to become crisis users of the emergency room and of in-patient psychiatric and medical detoxification services (Hellerstein and Meehan, 1987).

The literature has at times suggested a cause-effect relationship between chemical dependency and mental illness, however, we are not aware of reliable or valid research to corroborate this. Still, chemical dependency and mental illness interface in a multiplicity of complex ways. Khantzian and Treece (1985) have observed that the effects of a drug used and the emotional and defense states of the users become inextricably intertwined, each effecting the other in turn. In one study, young (age 19-39) adult chronic patients with psychiatric and chemical dependency disorders were reported to have had an annual rate of psychiatric hospitalization that was over 2 1/2 times than that of each of the comparison groups. In most patients the chemical dependency was interactive, exacerbating the patients psychotic pattern and/or paranoid outlook (Safer, 1986). Other literature supports findings implying that the compounding of alcohol and drug abuse with other psychiatric problems will result in poorer treatment progress and outcome (Alterman, Erdlen and Murphy, 1981; Cohen and Klein, 1970). We have seen schizophrenic patients who left the hospital stabilized on neuroleptics decompensate when they began to abuse alcohol again.

Psychiatric symptoms can trigger the urge to drink or use drugs in an attempt to self-medicate. For example, a patient diagnosed as Borderline Personality Disorder used drugs whenever she experienced difficult emotions. However, when she was high her impulse control was poor, and she was most at risk to perform physically self-damaging acts such as cutting her arms with pieces of glass. Through counseling which addressed both the mental health issues and the chemical addiction issues the patient eventually joined AA, and began to identify self as an addict. Through counseling and sponsorship in the 12 step program, the client increased her ability to cope with feelings in healthier ways resulting in fewer hospitalizations. Freed (1975) reports that schizophrenic alcoholics use alcohol to produce "social" amelioration of schizophrenic symptoms. Others have conceptualized alcohol as a tool to re-establish emotional homeostasis. Depressed individuals may use mood altering chemicals to feel better or to perform activities of daily living. Agoraphobics may use alcohol to relieve anxiety and fear when experiencing a panic attack. As evidenced by these examples there are many symptoms that patients attempt to control through self-medication.

Few studies have looked at how drug and alcohol use effect the metabolism and utility of neuroleptics. However, Knudsen and Vilmar, (1984) have suggested a hypothesis of possible antagonistic interaction between cannabis and neuroleptics. The authors conclude that cannabis use is a risk for schizophrenic patients, even when they are taking adequate neuroleptics.

In another study, Mellaril was shown to leave the blood more rapidly, decreasing the neuroleptic level in the blood, in the schizophrenic drinking large amounts of alcohol. However, if the dose of Mellaril was taken with smaller amounts of alcohol (two shots), the alcohol actually helped aid in increasing the level of Mellaril in the blood. Therefore, schizophrenics who are attempting to self-medicate may find alcohol at times to be of help (Bradwejn, Jones, Annable, Greese and Chouldnard, 1983), and clinicians must be sensitive to this possibility. Several other reports indicate decreased effectiveness of anti-depressants in alcoholics who continue to drink (Ciraulo, Barnhill and Jaffe, 1988).

TREATMENT ISSUES

Although the literature suggests that treating dual diagnosed patients is difficult, there is a paucity of information regarding what treatment strategies might be useful. Dual diagnosed patients are difficult to treat because they have two or more disorders that are distressing, often denied, chronic, and prone to relapse.

Denial

Much has been written about the denial associated with chemical dependency. Denial, which takes the form of resistance, minimization, rationalization, anger and blaming, is also common among patients who have other psychiatric disorders. Dual diagnosed patients often deny one or both of their disorders. Yet, it is the understanding and acceptance of their disorders that is at the heart of recovery. Education combined with other interventions facilitates patients' understanding that they have not one but two disorders that are interrelated and must both be treated.

Clinically, we have come across a wide range of reactions from patients with dual disorders. Many have been confused by their symptoms and have wondered what was wrong. Others have voiced feelings such as "Why be sober and miserable?" Still others have talked about feeling angry that they have not one but two or more disorders to contend with and felt this was unfair, proclaiming, "Why me?" We have also seen patients avoid dealing with both disorders by focusing on one disorder, and attributing all their problems to it. Many patients and families tend to look for a cause effect relationship between mental illness and chemical dependency. Some patients use their mental illness as an excuse to use drugs and alcohol, or avoid dealing with the chemical dependency by focusing only on the mental illness. Thus it seems most important that professionals assess their patients perceptions, thoughts and feelings regarding their dual problems. This requires empathy on the part of the professional and the belief that denial and misinformation will continue to result in poor treatment outcomes for patients.

Patient Education

Educating patients about their illnesses, causes or factors that contribute to the illness, and the symptoms associated with their problems is important if patients are going to manage their symptoms. For an example, by daily monitoring of symptoms schizophrenics may be in a position to identify warning signs of relapse and can then seek professional help in dealing with symptoms (UCLA Dept. of Psychiatry, 1988). The same can be said for the use of relapse prevention with chemically dependent patients. Educating chemically dependent patients about early warning signs is helpful in preventing relapse (Daley, 1986).

Skill Development

Many dual diagnosed patients identify emotions such as anger, guilt and shame as particularly difficult to cope with. In retrospect, patients often recognize how their feelings build up and eventually result in psychiatric relapse or a strong desire to drink or use drugs to escape or numb how they feel. Therefore, identifying and appropriately managing feelings are an important part of recovery for many patients. For many, learning to identify and express feelings requires developing new skills. Skills training programs can be a useful treatment intervention for the patients.

Cognitive therapy techniques can be particularly useful to decrease depressive feelings and change faulty thinking that many chemically dependent patients suffer from, and which may contribute to relapse. Cognitive therapy is a treatment approach that aims to help patients modify maladaptive thoughts, assumptions, or beliefs and teaches specific problem solving or adaptive cognitive skills (Beck, 1976).

Identifying and handling urges or cravings to use alcohol or drugs is another common treatment issue. It is common at times to experience urges or cravings to use drugs and alcohol in recovery. Thus, it is important to be aware of stimuli which may trigger an urge, physical and psychological signs, and coping strategies. Such strategies as talking with others, redirecting activities, changing thoughts and avoiding threatening situations can be taught to patients (Daley, 1986).

Leisure time activity is another area that can be addressed with dual diagnosed patients to help prevent relapse and add structure to their lives. Many patients gave up friends and leisure time activities due to their psychiatric difficulties, chemical dependency and addictive lifestyle. They are concerned about having fun in recovery and structuring their days in a productive way. Boredom and lack of constructive activities can be dangerous to the dual diagnosed patient. Compounding this problem are patients who grew up in a rigid, restrictive and unpredictable environment such as an alcoholic home where spontaneity and learning to play is a new and sometimes awkward undertaking.

Linking patients with recreational/social activities and resources in the community can be helpful. For instance, twelve step self-help fellowships offer leisure time activities. AA and NA sponsor dances and picnics for fun and socialization. Also, in many communities recovery clubs exist that hold meetings along with recreational activities. Mental health programs in communities also offer patients structured programs. For example, partial hospitalization programs provide leisure activity through recreational programming along with therapy groups.

Treatment Compliance

Medication compliance and its usefulness in managing psychiatric symptoms is a common issue with many patients. Patients need to understand the differences between psychoactive and psychotropic drugs. Educating patients about their mental illness and need for medications is crucial to preventing psychiatric relapse and a return to mood altering chemicals. Laboratory studies to determine medication compliance is useful in assessing medication compliance.

Complying with outpatient care is also a common treatment issue. An early warning sign that patients are heading toward trouble is when they begin to cancel or fail to show for appointments. Stressing the importance of follow-up and the patients responsibility in maintaining and utilizing therapy appointments is an issue that can be spelled out in a treatment contract. Utilizing AA and NA, and other services and resources in the community such as partial hospitalization programs and mental health support groups should be part of a patient's treatment when appropriate. Collaborating with other treatment sources and services such as supervised living arrangements can help assure treatment compliance for dual diagnosed patients. Likewise, through collaboration a patient's response to treatment can be monitored.

Use of Twelve Step Programs

The use of twelve step self-help groups is a well accepted and regularly utilized adjunct to treatment for chemically dependent patients. However, for some dual diagnosed patients new questions emerge regarding the role of A.A. and N.A.

As mentioned previously, for dual diagnosed patients the use of psychotropic medications is sometimes necessary to relieve a patient of psychiatric symptoms that interfere with functioning. Yet, there has been controversy within some twelve step programs regarding psychotropic medications. Using prescribed and needed psychotropics does not mean a person has had a slip and is not "clean" or "sober." Fortunately, A.A. has, in fact, addressed this very issue. An A.A. pamphlet entitled *The A.A. Member—Medications and Other Drugs*, a report from a group of physicians in A.A., is available to patients and professionals.

Support groups have been of great benefit to chemically dependent patients. Identifying with others and recognizing they are not
alone have great therapeutic benefit. For many patients they have
felt different long enough. However, for some dual diagnosed patients revealing at an A.A. or N.A. meeting that they have both an
addiction and mental illness may cause them to feel more different.
Clinicians must be particularly sensitive to this issue and counsel
patients regarding the pros and cons of sharing with others their
dual problem. We have found sensitive members of A.A. and N.A.
who have accepted our patients dual problem, were supportive and
did not attempt to interfere with the patients' treatment. However,
in fewer cases we have been told about A.A./N.A. members' discomfort and less than supportive response to patients' admissions of
psychiatric problems and use of psychotropics.

A patient who is dual diagnosed can benefit from sponsorship if a
sponsor is chosen who is sensitive and accepting of his/her dual
problems. However, in certain cases a patient may find putting
one's trust in a sponsor is too difficult. For example, a schizophrenic who is paranoid may not feel comfortable utilizing a sponsor.
This patient can be encouraged to attend "speaker" meetings that
are less threatening than discussion meetings. Clinicians can also
help connect patients with members of A.A. and N.A. who can
escort them to their first meetings. Thus, for many dual diagnosed
patients A.A. and N.A. can be of great benefit, but a clinician must
remain sensitive to potential problems and the particular needs of
their patients. Some patients may find involvement in A.A./N.A. in
addition to another twelve step program such as Emotions Anonymous or newly forming Double Trouble groups is ideal so that both
problems can be addressed. For others A.A. and/or N.A. along
with out-patient treatment is sufficient in obtaining the help and
support they need.

Peer support is primary in twelve step self-help groups. It is our
belief that not only the support but the twelve steps and principles of
A.A. and N.A. can also be of benefit to many dual diagnosed patients. For instance, the twelve steps provide concrete guidelines for
recovery and advice on daily living. Steps focusing on "defects of
character" suggest making personality changes, a therapeutic guide
for patients with personality disorders. Making amends, admitting

wrong doing and practicing honesty also involve taking responsibility for ones behavior and making efforts to change.

Many people also find great strength and meaning utilizing the spiritual aspect of A.A. and N.A. This spiritual belief in a power greater than oneself has aided many patients. The literature suggests that spirituality can be an effective stress reliever. Spirituality can also add a richness, dimension and depth to living that celebrates the entire being. Likewise, spirituality can be seen as a way through and a way out of suffering (Whitfield, 1984; Wallace, 1985; Berenson, 1987).

Taking things "one day at a time" can also be a useful recovery tool for coping with both an addiction and mental illness. Another useful idea involves "time out," a common behavioral technique. Just as the craving to get high eventually dissipates if the addict does not give in to it, an addicted borderline might also find that the urge to hurt him/herself would dissipate too if given the chance. Techniques that are used in addictions counseling such as prayer, meditation, calling someone to talk to about how they are feeling or utilizing a host of redirecting activities could be taught and used. Thus, the "tools" of recovery for dependent individuals can be useful to the dual diagnosed patient.

Building a new peer group with positive role models who share similar experiences helps to increase identification as an addict. Developing an identity as an addict is needed for ongoing recovery from substance dependence. This developing identity may be particularly helpful to a borderline who, as part of his/her disorder, suffers from identity disturbance. Also, becoming a responsible group member who has something to offer others meets altruistic needs that many individuals have.

As professionals, we have been struck by members unconditional acceptance and caring for individuals in the fellowships. Although relapse is possible members are always welcome back into the programs. Much can also be said for the on call availability of group members for each other. Considering the crisis oriented nature of some dual diagnosed patients it is a comfort to many professionals that their patients have a support network that is available to them.

Support Groups for Psychiatric Illnesses

Support groups also exist for psychiatric patients. Many community mental health centers have organized or supported groups comprised of patients with particular psychiatric disorders. Depression and schizophrenia support groups, among others, provide needed support and identification. Some support groups are facilitated by a professional while others are patient facilitated. As with support groups for the chemically dependent, these groups help to lessen patients' isolation and the feeling of being alone, different, and misunderstood.

PERSPECTIVE 2: THE FAMILY

Issues to consider from the family perspective include: (1) evaluating the impact of the dual diagnosed patient on the family system and individual members; (2) evaluating the impact of the family on the patient; (3) engaging the family in the treatment process when appropriate; and (4) delineating family treatment goals.

Effects on the Family

In recent years there has been a proliferation of literature addressing the problems and treatment of chemical dependency in the family. This literature has focused on the family system (Kaufman, 1986; Steinglass, 1986), and children (El-Guebaly and Offord, 1977; Woodside, 1982, and 1983; Ackerman, 1987). There also is increasing literature addressing the problems and needs of families in which a psychiatric disorder exists (Hatfield and Lefley, 1987; McElroy, 1987). Considerable information is available as well on families and/or offspring of patients with specific disorders such as schizophrenia (Torrey, 1988; Hogarty, Anderson, Reiss, Kornblith, Greenwald, Javna and Madonia, 1986), depression (Jacob, Frank, and Carpenter, 1987; Merikansas, Weissman, Prosoff, Pauls and Leckman, 1985), and anxiety disorders (Turner, Beidel and Costello, 1987).

Since the chemical dependency and mental health fields have yet to converge, there is a paucity of information available concerning the families of dual diagnosed patients. Although comorbidity may complicate assessment and treatment, the concerns and problems of families appear to be similar to those identified by families of the chemically dependent, and families of patients with specific psychiatric illness. Differences are more related to the degree and extent to which specific problems exist.

Families affect, and are affected by, the dual disordered member, sometimes in profound ways. Yet not all families, nor every member within the same family, experience similar effects. The specific impact in a given case will be mediated by many variables. The clinician should keep these in mind when assessing families. These variables include:

1. *Severity of problem*: Families exposed to more serious types of psychopathology such as psychotic episodes, suicide attempts, or grossly disturbed behavior face more stress and problems than those exposed to less severe problems. In some instances, measures must be taken to protect the dual disordered member and the family through such means as involuntary commitment. Similarly, multiple relapses to substance use following periods of recovery can frustrate and drain the family.

2. *Length of problem*: Long-term exposure to a chronic psychiatric condition often drains families of energy and resources, particularly when multiple hospitalizations are involved as a result of exacerbations of symptomatology. Acute, single episodes typically do not cause the same type of ongoing stresses as chronic conditions such as schizophrenia or refractory depression.

3. *Behavior of the family member with the dual disorders*: Unpredictable, self-destructive, aggressive, violent and manipulative behaviors tend to generate strong reactions. These behaviors may contribute to fears (e.g., of personal safety; of person hurting him/herself), or other kinds of problems (financial, social, etc.). In some cases, considerable time, attention and energy is directed towards the impaired member. Consequently, others may feel their needs are ignored. A brother of one patient stated that "my parents spend all their time and energy on my sister who's always having trouble. Seems like me and my other sister don't get much attention at all. When we do well in school, it isn't noticed very much. Everything gets focused on my sister's problems."

4. *The unique relationship between the dual disordered person and the family members*: In one family seen by the authors, the

parents of a patient were constantly at odds with each other over their son. The mother was extremely supportive and nurturing, accepting her son regardless of what he did. She was quick to overlook his irresponsible behaviors and "help" him any time he was in a bind. The father was just the opposite. Quick to anger whenever his son got drunk or acted inappropriately, his position was one of being "tough" and firm. He believed that his son should not be nurtured and taken care of and should assume responsibility for his life. Each parent had a unique relationship with their son that was different and that dictated how they felt. These different responses, however, contributed to marital discord.

5. *The family member's unique perception*: How the dual disordered member and his/her problems are viewed is often based on one's understanding of chemical dependency and psychiatric problems, and the effects of these on the family and oneself. In the case cited above, the mother believed that her son was ill and needed acceptance and understanding. The father believed his son was lazy and irresponsible, and that his problems stemmed mainly from drinking too much. Each parent's unique perception impacted on how they dealt with their son and with each other.

6. *Offsetting factors*: Relationships with others who are supportive, have knowledge of the illnesses, and skill in dealing with crises may help to counteract potential adverse effects. The wife of an alcoholic with a bipolar disorder relied heavily on her sister and Al-Anon support group during her husband's periodic relapses. The emotional support she received helped to sustain her through difficult crises. Also, her awareness of signs that he was deteriorating allowed her to take quick action when manic symptoms returned. As a result, she felt a greater sense of control over what could be done.

7. *For children, how the parents function*: When one or both parents have mental health and/or alcohol or drug related problems, the ability to fulfill parental responsibilities then suffer. In more severe cases, the dual disordered person is limited in the guidance and nurturance provided to his/her children. Sometimes, the other parent can help offset the adverse consequences of this, particularly when they are competent, nurturing and responsive to the needs of their children. When both parents have mental health and/or chemi-

cal dependency problems, the potential adverse impact on the children is even greater.

When the family is accessible and it is appropriate to engage them in the treatment process, the clinician can begin to assess how the family system has been affected. Areas to evaluate include: family history of illness, atmosphere or mood, communication and interaction within the family, roles assumed, rules governing family behavior, relationships to the outside world, family self-esteem, level of denial, enabling, financial condition, and strengths. In some instances, the clinician may also assess individual family members' physical and mental health, interpersonal relationships, social, occupational (or school), and spiritual areas of functioning. The clinician should not underestimate the burden families experience, particularly with the more chronic and severely disabling illnesses.

The Family's Impact on the Dual Disordered Member

Numerous investigators have established alcoholism and other psychiatric disorders as familial illnesses. There appears to be an inherited vulnerability or predisposition to develop certain disorders (Schukit, 1986).

Environmental factors play a role as well. It is well documented for example, that children of alcoholics are more susceptible than those of non-alcoholics to experience a variety of health and psychosocial problems. Many dual disordered patients are also sons or daughters of parents who have chemical dependency and/or psychiatric disorders. Thus, there may be important family of origin related issues that the patient will need to face if recovery is to progress. The proliferation of programs for adult children of alcoholics is evidence that many people have experienced adverse effects of a parent's addiction and felt some type of help was needed.

The family may also affect the course of the illness of the dual diagnosed member. For example, if the family passively tolerates intoxication or inappropriate behaviors, the impaired member receives less feedback about his or her behavior. As a result, change is less likely to occur. The family can "enable" the illness to continue, albeit unintentionally, through over-functioning behaviors and tolerating difficult behaviors. The result is that the dual disordered member is less likely to see a need for help and less likely to become engaged in treatment. Conversely, the family can have a positive impact by taking a proactive approach in identifying problems early and intervening so that the impaired member gets help. Families can continue to play a major and positive role during the ongoing recovery from the dual problems. However, clinicians should be cognizant that although families often have good intentions they may become overwhelmed with serious pathological behaviors they face with the ill member. They may find it necessary to detach for their own survival.

Engaging the Family in Treatment

Once it has been established that family involvement is needed and feasible in a given case, the goal is to engage the family in the treatment process. In general, the earlier in the patient's illness the family is contacted, particularly during crises, the easier it is to involve them in treatment. Families are more likely to cooperate if approached in a supportive manner by clinicians. Outreach efforts are often needed to engage families.

It is of utmost importance to "connect" with the family so that they view the clinician as someone who understands their experience whom they can trust and work with collaboratively. It is also important that the clinician not place blame upon them for the patients' illnesses. Initially, the family can be engaged to "help" the clinician help the dual disordered member. As the assessment and treatment proceeds goals may shift from the individual patient to the family system.

Working with families sometimes requires the clinician to deal with personal attitudes and perceptions of families. Negative or judgmental attitudes towards families, unrealistic expectations concerning progress, failure to understand family systems and the reciprocal relationship between the patient and the family, failure to communicate sufficiently with the family concerning the illness and course of treatment, and failure to work collaboratively to help the family are several of the many potential obstacles with which the clinician should be familiar. Clinicians with inadequate training or lack of experience with mental illness in their own family may have difficulty validating the pain of the patient's family (Group for the

Advancement of Psychiatry, 1986). Only by understanding the "experience" of families living with a dual disordered member can the clinician be sensitive to their needs.

What Families Need: Family Treatment Goals

Family treatment goals generally involve acquiring knowledge, increasing self-awareness, making changes in the family system, individual members making changes, and maintaining involvement in ongoing recovery (professional and/or self-help support groups). Ongoing treatment can be especially helpful in addressing the specific needs of parents, children or spouses of the dual diagnosed.

Numerous reports have discussed the usefulness of professional and self-help interventions for families of patients with psychiatric disorders (Hogarty et al., 1986; Hatfield and Lefley, 1988; McElroy, 1988; Jacob et al., 1987; and Torrey, 1988). Such interventions often help to decrease the family burden by providing families with information and skills to better cope with the impaired member on a day to day basis. For example, the family of the alcoholic schizophrenic who helps him/her comply with medications and avoids intense emotional interactions will facilitate recovery.

Families want to be listened to with empathy, engaged as allies in treatment, provided with emotional support and practical advice on how to deal with the impaired member. They need information on the causes, effects, onset and course of the illnesses, the treatment process, treatment resources, cost of professional care, and what their role will be. Families need help in developing skills to deal with the dual disordered member. Self-destructive, violent, psychotic and bizarre behaviors can be frightening to families and create considerable turmoil. The support and help provided by clinicians can be invaluable in helping families discover which areas they have control over and which they do not. Learning, for example, when hospitalization is indicated, or which types of disorders require medications can be extremely helpful to the family.

Some families also need help with economic and social services to insure that the impaired family member's basic needs are met. The clinician can play a major role by helping the family deal with treatment facilities or legal systems since dual disordered patients frequently use these systems.

Other areas in which the clinician can help the family are with their emotional reactions, attitudes and expectations, and behavioral reactions. Affectively charged issues that family members may have to deal with include guilt, shame, embarrassment, anger, resentment, hatred, grief, fear, depression, and isolation. Families of patients more severely disabled with dual disorders may have to adjust their expectations. This can be particularly difficult as in the case of a parent giving up or significantly modifying dreams and hopes for an ill child who once showed great potential. Families may need help modifying their behaviors and lifestyle as well.

PERSPECTIVE 3: THE PROFESSIONAL CAREGIVER

Working with dual diagnosed patients is challenging for professional caregivers. Many are unfamiliar with psychiatric diagnosis and the effects of substance abuse on these disorders. These factors lead to confusion and stress for professionals. Caregivers must expand their knowledge of dual diagnosis and increase their ability to interact therapeutically with the patients. Accepting that this group of individuals is sometimes difficult to work with is important for caregivers. Acceptance leads professionals to adjust their expectations and approaches to accommodate these patients who present with divergent behaviors.

There are basic elements of treatment which are the same for dual diagnosed patients as for any other person who seeks services. Establishing a therapeutic relationship is still the most important factor in treating the dual diagnosed patient. However, the process of building this relationship may differ dramatically with the dual diagnosed client. In some cases patients never achieve an active therapeutic alliance; in others the progress may be slow. Caregivers must not give up hope when progress is slow. It is helpful for professionals to set realistic goals for individuals based on an understanding of the patient's strengths.

The attitudes, perceptions and expectations of the caregiver also affect the dual diagnosed patient. These attitudes, whether positive or negative, are transferred in subtle ways. Professionals must examine their attitudes toward patients and recognize that they are potent factors in the helping relationship. Patients with a dual diagnosis will be affected by rejecting and hopeless attitudes in the same way that any patient is affected by the negative attitudes of therapists. Professionals who have negative attitudes and unrealistic expectations can create problems for the patients. Realistic assessment of the abilities of the patient is an extremely important skill for the professional caregiver to develop. The key to understanding what patients can do is based on the professional's understanding of the disorder, and knowledge of the individual. Some dual diagnosed patients whose progress is slow may be further hindered by unrealistic or rejecting attitudes of the caregiver.

Professionals who identify problematic attitudes in themselves must address these issues out of a sense of fairness to themselves and their patients. Because attitudes are affected by one's own personal experiences and beliefs, family of origin issues with psychiatric illness or substance abuse should be addressed. It is painful for therapists to work with patients when these personal issues remain active and unresolved. Patients feel the tension and negative transference of the counselor in such pain.

For professionals who choose to work with dual diagnosed patients, supervision is a valuable tool which helps to develop professional skills as well as identify personal issues that may be present. Supervision is especially important for the professionals who work with dual diagnosed patients because they precipitate stressful situations which can lead to frustration and burnout. Professionals are also encouraged to develop an active network of colleagues who will provide additional information and support.

Understanding the differences seen in the dual diagnosed can spur professionals to make adjustments in their approaches to these patients. Making adjustments requires professionals to actively seek continued education and training. The investment of time and energy in these pursuits can make a difference to those who deal with the dual disordered patient.

PERSPECTIVE 4: SYSTEMS

Dual diagnosed patients are frequently multi-problemed individuals who may be involved with several service systems at once. In addition to the substance abuse treatment system and the psychiatric treatment system, these individuals may be in the legal system, the medical treatment system, financial and vocational help systems, homeless programs and a host of other social and community agencies.

Many of these "other" systems report poor success rates in their work with the dual diagnosed. These patients are viewed as difficult and non-compliant. However, some of the problems that occur may be due to a lack of understanding on the part of other professionals about the degree of impairment these patients experience. Expectations of what an individual can do may be unrealistic and workers may misinterpret slow progress as total resistance.

These other systems can be helped by receiving more information from the primary therapists about patients' current level of functioning. It is also important that primary treatment professionals not involve other systems too early in recovery (i.e., vocational training, etc.).

Services such as housing and financial aid may be needed immediately. Some patients require many reminders from caseworkers to comply with requirements needed to gain benefits. Caseworkers can reinforce the need for patients to work closely with other systems' workers who can help them.

With more understanding of the varying needs and limits of patients, the chaos, stress and frustration experienced by both the client and the system can be reduced. It is the responsibility of the primary therapist to coordinate the client's involvement in most other systems. This function as coordinator and patient advocate is a real help to all parties concerned, as the individual progresses in his recovery, health and well-being.

CONCLUSION

In summary, recent literature suggests that a significant number of chemically dependent people are also experiencing psychiatric disorders. Recognizing and appropriately treating the dual diagnosed patient should result in improved outcomes. The patient, the patient's family, the professional caregiver and other systems involved with the patient or family are all impacted by the chemical dependency and psychiatric disorders. Likewise each perspective has the potential to impact on other perspectives. Looking at the dual diagnosed patient through the lenses of the four perspectives reveals that these patients present with complicated problems which offer new challenges to clinicians. Approaches to treatment must be specialized, incorporating knowledge from both the addiction and psychiatric fields. The use of collaboration, consultation and supervision can improve treatment and offers much needed support to professionals working with the complicated problems of the dual diagnosed patient

REFERENCES

Alterman A, Erdlen F and Murphy E (1981): Alcohol abuse in the psychiatric hospital population. *Addictive Behaviors*, 6:69-73.

Beck A (1976): *Cognitive Therapy and the Emotional Disorders*. International Universities Press, New York.

Bedi A and Halikas JI (1985): Alcoholism and Affective Disorder. *Alcoholism: Clinical and Experimental Research*, Vol. 9(2):133-134.

Berenson, D (1987): Alcoholics anonymous from surrender to transformation. *Networker*, 25-31, July-Aug.

Bradwejn J, Jones BD, Annable L, Greese I and Choulnard A (1983): Neuroleptic blood levels. Proceedings of the annual meeting, Society of Biological Psychiatry, pg. 103.

Carrol J and Sobel B (1986): Integrating Mental Health Personnel and Practices into a Therapeutic Community. Therapeutic Communities for Addictions: Readings in Theory, Research and Practice. G. DeLeon and J. Zeingerfugy Jr., (Eds), Chicago: Charles C. Thomas.

Ciraulo, Barnhill and Jaffe (1988): Clinical Pharmacokinetics of Imipramine and Desipramine in Alcoholics and Normal Volunteers. *Clinical Pahrmacol Ther*, 509-518.

Clinical Research Center for Schizophrenia and Psychiatric Rehabilitation, "Symptom Management: A rehabilitation program for training in community adaptation skills" (1988) UCLA Department of Psychiatry, Brentwood Division W. LA VA Medical Center and Camarillo State Hospital. Unpublished Manuscript.

Cohen M and Klein D (1970): Drug abuse in a young psychiatric population. *American Journal of Orthopsychiatry*, 40(3):448-455.

Daley D (1986): *Relapse Prevention Workbook for Alcoholics Drug Dependent Persons*. Learning Publications, Inc.

Daley, D, Moss, H and Campbell, F. (1987) *Dual Disorders: Counseling Clients with Chemical Dependency and Mental Illness*. Center City, MN: Hazelden.

El-Guebaly, N and Offord, D (1977): The Offspring of Alcoholics: A Critical Review, *The American Journal of Psychiatry*, 134(4):357-365.

Freed E: Alcoholism and Schizophrenia (1975): The search for perspectives. *Journal of Studies of Alcohol*, 36(7):853-881.

Group for the Advancement of Psychiatry (1986): *A Family Affair: Helping Families Cope with Mental Illness.* New York: Brunner Mazel.

Hatfield, A and Lefley, H (eds) (1987): *Families of the Mentally Ill: Coping and Adaptation.* New York: Guilford Press.

Hellerstein D and Meehan B (1987): "Out-patient Group therapy for schizophrenic substance abusers." *American Journal of Psychiatry* 144:1337-1339.

Helzer J and Pryzbeck T (1988): The Occurrance of Alcoholism with Other Psychiatric Disorders in the General Population and its Impact on Treatment. *Journal of Studies on Alcohol*, Vol. 49(3):219-224.

Hesselbrock M, Meyer R, Keener J (1985): Psychopathology in Hospitalized Alcoholics. *Archives of General Psychiatry*, Vol. 42:1050-1055.

Hogarty, G, Anderson, C, Reiss, D, Kornblith, S, Greenwald, D, Javna, C and Madonia, M (1986): Family Psychoeducation, Social Skills Training, and Maintenance Chemotherapy in the Aftercare Treatment of Schizophrenia. *Archives of General Psychiatry*, Vol. 43, 633-642.

Jacob, M, Frank, E, Kupfer, D and Carpenter, L (1987): Recurrent Depression: An Assessment of Family Burden and Family Attitudes. *Journal of Clinical Psychiatry*. Vol. 48(10), 395-400.

Kaufman, E (1986): A Contemporary Approach to the Family Treatment of Substance Abuse Disorders. *American Journal of Drug and Alcohol Abuse.* Vol. 12(3), 199-211.

Khantzian E and Treece C (1985): DSM III Psychiatric Diagnosis of Narcotic Addicts: Recent findings. *Archives of General Psychiatry*, 42:Nov.

Knudsen P and Vilmar T (1984): Cannabis and neuroleptic agents in schizophrenia. *Acta Psychiat. Scand.*, 69:162-174.

Konia J, Alkenson R and Kofoed L (1986): Outpatient Treatment of Patients with Substance Abuse and Coexisting Psychiatric Disorders. *American Journal of Psychiatry*, Vol. 143(7):867-872.

Maddux J, Desmond D, Costello R (1987): Depression in Opioid Users Varies with Substance Use Status. *American Journal of Drug and Alcohol Abuse*, Vol. 13(4):375-385.

McLellan AT, Luborsky L, Woody GE, O'Brien CP, Druley K (1983): Predicting Response to Alcohol and Drug Abuse Treatments. *Archives of General Psychiatry*, Vol. 40:620-625.

McElroy E (1987): *Children and Adolescents with Mental Illness: A Parents Guide*. Kensington, MD: Woodbine House.

Merikankgas K, Weissman M, Prusoff B, Pauls D and Leckman (1985); Depressives with Secondary Alcoholism: Psychiatric Disorders in Offspring. *Journal of Studies on Alcohol*, Vol. 46(3):199-204.

Mirin S and Weiss R (1988): Psychopathology in Substance Abusers: Diagnosis and Treatment. *American Journal of Drug and Alcohol Abuse*, Vol. 14(2).

O'Sullivan K, Whillans P, Daly M, Carroll B, Clare A and Cooney J (1983): A

Comparison of Alcoholics With and Without Co-existing Affective Disorder. *British Journal of Psychiatry*, Vol. 143:133-138.

Rounsaville B, Iolinsky Z, Babor T, Meyer R (1987): Psychopathology as a Predictor of Treatment Outcomes in Alcoholics. *Archives of General Psychiatry*, Vol. 44:505-513.

Rounsaville B, Kosten T, Weissman M, Kleber H (1985): Evaluating and Treating Depressive Disorders in Opiate Addicts. *Treatment Research Monograph Series*. U.S. Department of Health and Human Services.

Safer D (1986): The young adult chronic patient and substance abuse. Department of Psychiatry, Johns Hopkins University School of Medicine, Unpublished Manuscript.

Schuckit M (1986): Genetic and Clinical Implications of Alcoholism and Affective Disorder. *American Journal of Psychiatry*, Vol. 143(2):140-147.

Steinglass, P (1985): Family Systems Approaches to Alcoholism. *Journal of Substance Abuse Treatment.* Vol 2, 161-167.

The A.A. Member-Medications and Other Drugs (1984), A report from a group of physicians in A.A. Alcoholics Anonymous World Services, Inc.

Torrey, E. (1988): *Surviving Schizophrenia: A Family Manual*, 2nd. ed., New York: Harper and Row.

Turner, S, Beider, D and Costello, A (1987): Psychopathology in the Offspring of Anxiety Disorders Patients. *Journal of Consulting and Clinical Psychology*, Vol. 55(2), 229-235.

Wallace, J (1985): *Alcoholism: New light as the disease*, Edgehill Publications.

Wallace J (1987): The Other Problems of Alcoholics. *Journal of Substance Abuse Treatment.* Vol. 3:163-171.

Whitfeld C (1984): "Principles of spirituality during recovery," *Focus on Family*, 14-17, March/April.

Woodside, M (1982): *Children of Alcohlics*. New York: NY State Division of Alcoholism and Alcohol Abuse.

Woodside, M. (1983): Children of Alcoholic Parents: Inherited and Psycho-social Influences. *Journal of Psychiatric Treatment and Evaluation*, Vol. 5, 531-537.

Woody G, Luborsky L, McLellan AT, Obrien C, Beck A, Blaine J, Heman I, Hole A (1983): Psychotherapy for Opiate Addicts. *Archives of General Psychiatry*, Vol. 40:639-645.

Anxiety Disorders and Substance Abuse

Charles J. Hudson, MD

INTRODUCTION

The purpose of this article is to review the anxiety disorders as presented in the DSM III R and the known relationships of these disorders to substance abuse. It is exceedingly important for clinicians to realize that these disorders, in the majority of cases, existed before the substance abuse began. These afflicted individuals have begun to medicate themselves, literally, because they have been, at times, stricken with the fear of death.

Many people in the population are not knowledgeable enough to recognize the onset of alien feelings as symptoms of an emotional disorder, or are ashamed to seek help. Delays in seeking help are one of the reasons that afflicted individuals may turn to the most readily available agent that might give relief, such as alcohol, cannabis or someone else's tranquilizer. These agents will be taken as long as they are available. Unfortunately the agent of abuse may in turn produce euphoria, thereby increasing dependence on it. Recreational drug use, on the other hand, is the conscious attempt to produce euphoria or similar mood states, commonly with illegal substances, and often with an element of thrill seeking or antisocial motivation.

There are other psychiatric disorders which may occur during the period that an individual engages in substance abuse, but we will not discuss intercurrent or subsequent psychiatric disorders. Although temporal relationships of psychiatric disorder to substance abuse are important, we feel that a focus on disorders that predate

Charles J. Hudson is Medical Director, Schoharie County Mental Health Center and Assistant Clinical Professor of Psychiatry, Albany Medical College.

substance abuse is of particular importance and practical value. Through attention to conditions which are likely to lead to substance abuse, the treatment of them and the education of the public on the nature and symptoms of panic and other anxiety disorders, the current epidemic of substance abuse may be reduced. We feel this is a vital, much needed public health function because, as the ECA[1] study has indicated, substance abuse, excluding tobacco addiction, currently afflicts ten percent of the population.

To emphasize the close relationship between psychiatric disorder and substance abuse, one recent study (Ross, 1988) reviewed 501 patients who entered an addiction center for treatment: 61.9% had lifetime diagnoses of anxiety disorders in addition to alcohol and other drug abuse problems.

On a clinical level, the worker in the field of substance abuse needs to be constantly aware of the diversity of the U.S. population. Socioeconomic differences, geography and ethnicity all have a bearing on substance abuse. It is all too easy to stereotype the ghetto or inner city abuser, "junkie," "polyabuser" or "pothead" and write them off as lost causes or failures. Some of the most "hardened" or recalcitrant patients may, underneath, have a treatable anxiety disorder, which should be aggressively treated. Individuals who come from socially disorganized settings have higher rates of psychiatric disorder than middle class Americans, but less access to quality medical care and mental health care. Poor people, especially those who differ ethnically from the main population, may have several barriers between them and effective intervention. There may be a language barrier, they have more employment problems and they are seen as "being different." They may also be distrustful of official agency treatment programs.

What kind of treatment is a less articulate or minority group person apt to receive when the symptoms of an anxiety disorder occur? The chances are higher that a street drug or some form of alcohol will be used, or there may be multiple agents. The social milieu is more likely to determine treatment than the local mental health clinic. Thus, one segment of the population may receive prompt attention and treatment with psychotherapy and imipramine, while another individual from a slum, with the same disorder, is ushered into a substance abuse career, a correctional facility and even

AIDS. Serious social inequities still exist in our society, and the health and mental health systems care delivery systems are deficient. Large segments of the population, for example the working poor, have little or no health care coverage. These are only some of the issues that the worker in addictionology needs to keep in mind.

PANIC DISORDER

The three panic disorders, social phobia, panic disorder and agoraphobia with panic attacks, have as their major, central symptom, the panic attack. These disorders were defined with diagnostic criteria in the DSM III, first published in 1981 and later revised in the DSM III R.

A panic attack is the sudden onset of an intense fear—some patients even call it terror—accompanied by an increased heart rate, sweating, palpitations, agitation, increased respirations, shortness of breath, difficulty swallowing, cold sweaty palms, tremor, catastrophic thinking, nausea, numbness, tingling, depersonalization or derealization and weakness and faintness. Catastrophic thinking is characterized by sudden thoughts of dying, losing control, going insane or committing some kind of violence. The best understanding of a panic attack comes from seeing one and talking to the individual experiencing it, or, better yet, experiencing one. Thus far elective panic attacks for training purposes are not feasible.

In panic disorder without agoraphobia, the attacks can occur at any time or place, usually causing the afflicted person to get up, pace, or leave the situation, especially if it is a social event, restaurant, etc. In expectation of a panic attack panic-prone individuals may sit near an open door to leave more easily. Some situations may be avoided because of lack of a ready exit.

Westphal (1871) originated the term "agoraphobia" to describe a complication that he observed. This Greek term means fear of the market place or fear of public places, which he thought his patients had. It now appears that agoraphobia is a complication of panic disorder. With panic disorder some patients become too frightened to leave the security of the home even though they continue to have panic attacks at home, which simply feels safer. Going out may necessitate having a companion, enduring severe anxiety, and having to avoid many public situations. This is a stressful enough endeavor that alcohol may be used routinely to go outside the home. The great majority of the population cannot imagine or accept that such an experience exists and that it is not under the control of the will. This is part of the burden of the panic stricken; they are subjected to repeated attacks which defy description and which they are often ashamed to admit. Many friends and family members don't understand why the afflicted "just can't pull themselves out of it." Strongly implied is the notion that the anxious person doesn't want to get well and is somehow responsible for continuing their disorder.

Panic disorder exists as two sub-types, panic disorder with agoraphobia and panic disorder without agoraphobia. The panic attacks may be relatively infrequent and benign or occur multiple times each day with an intensity which wilts the brave and humbles the bold. The panic attacks may be totally random in their occurrence, or they may cluster in certain situations.

Social phobia is an example of their appearing when the individual is in a social situation, in crowds, giving a public performance of any kind, or simply being looked upon by another person. It is less common than panic disorder and is differentiated from paranoid disorders by the lack of delusional thinking.

Isaac Marks (1969) made a significant contribution to the understanding of these disorders with the publication of his book, *Fears and Phobias*. Marks noted briefly that "some individuals afflicted with severe anxiety had learned to treat themselves with alcohol and sedatives, but they are able to give these up with treatment." This was an early observation that some substance abusers are treatable, but first it is necessary to recognize that another serious disorder, i.e., panic disorder, is involved and must be dealt with. Marks' book was important also in calling attention to the disability and varied symptomatology that is possible with this group of anxiety disorders.

Klein (1964) published an important study showing that panic attacks could be reduced or eliminated with imipramine. In one of the few double blind studies published in the early literature in this field, he compared three groups of patients, one treated with placebo, one treated with imipramine and one with chlorpromazine.

The improvement in the imipramine group was significantly superior to the placebo and the chlorpromazine treated groups. Another study by Klein's group (Quitkin, 1972) described treatment of a group of "addicts," individuals who had learned to treat their anxiety with alcohol, sedatives and barbiturates. These investigators went on to expand our knowledge of anxiety disorders by observing that those individuals who indulged in self-medication were treating anticipatory anxiety, and that alcohol and other drugs had little effect on the panic attack itself. Thus was established the fact that individuals stricken with panic disorder in time develop a second, anticipatory anxiety which is different from the panic attacks, and which may become as disabling as the panic attacks. Comparing their data with that of Marks, the Klein group concluded that 5-10% of "phobic anxious" people become serious drug abusers. One of their comments is worth noting because it contains one of the most important bits of wisdom in the field of addictionology: "If a careful history of the period prior to the onset of drug abuse is not taken, the true clinical picture will be obscured by the more obvious drug abuse." All workers in the field of substance abuse must take this statement as one of the cornerstones of their work, not just for the anxiety disorders but for all psychiatric disorders. The converse is also true, that psychiatric patients must be carefully questioned about their self-medicating, whether with alcohol, over the counter nostrums, street drugs or benzodiazepines obtained over the back fence from a neighbor. When any doubt exists, urine screens or liver enzyme studies may be ordered.

Reinforcing the points just made, Mullaney and Trippitt (1979) reported on the screening of 101 patients at an English regional alcohol treatment center. Careful studies of the patient population with interview and questionnaires arrived at the conclusion that at least 40% of those patients also suffered from serious anxiety disorders which predated the alcohol abuse. Mullaney and Trippitt also emphasized the importance of screening for phobic anxiety disorders, although they presented no data to illustrate the importance and logical consequence of their findings for treatment. It seems clear from the work reviewed that there is firm, convincing data with the panic disorders to stress the critical importance of history taking and the DSM III diagnostic approach. The picture of this process is still emerging with the other anxiety disorders, which are less well understood and where successful treatment is lagging behind the panic disorders.

The following individual was seen by the author in an upstate New York clinic, and is an illustration of what is possible with appropriate diagnosis and treatment.

Case Report

A 47-year-old married woman, who lived several blocks from a rural New York state clinic, had had symptoms of anxiety for five years, with occasional but ineffective visits to the local clinic. She became so anxious that she was unable to continue her job in the village, and simply stayed home, with worsening anxiety. She began to drink daily to control her anxiety, especially if for some reason she had to leave home. For nearly two years she drank daily, usually vodka spaced during the day and increased at times of anticipated stress. Feeling that no progress was being made, her husband contacted the author and asked that a home visit be made. The visit revealed a reasonably well kept middle class home and a white female appropriately dressed and groomed, but with slurred speech, unsteady gate. She gave a clear history of panic attacks and anxiety of a non-panic, anticipatory nature. There was no indication that she had any other psychiatric disorder, and she readily admitted to her alcohol intake as a means of attempting to cope with her anxiety. She was begun on imipramine, urged not to drink, and in a matter of weeks indicated that her panic was under control. In three months she was free of panic and beginning to resume many of her previous activities. She remained remarkably symptom free for three years, when an attempt was made to taper her medication. When the panic began to return, the dose was raised back to therapeutic level.

Diagnostic Impression
Axis 1 Agoraphobia with Panic Attacks
    Alcohol Abuse.

OBSESSIVE-COMPULSIVE DISORDER

The DSM III R (1985) has presented criteria for the diagnosis of obsessive compulsive disorder (OCD). In the DSM III diagnostic system OCD is diagnosed on axis 1 and is not to be confused with obsessive-compulsive personality disorder, which is not an anxiety disorder and which will not be dealt with here.

Obsessions are recurrent, persistent, involuntary thoughts, ideas, images or impulses. They are intrusive, senseless or repugnant. They may be benign, such as the persisting thought of a tune, but they may also be recurring violent thoughts involving doing harm to one's self or others. Compulsions, however, are repetitive behaviors, seemingly purposeful actions, performed in a stereotyped fashion. The behavior seems designed to prevent a future event or to undo a past, troubling situation. It is performed commonly with a subjective sense of repugnance and a desire to resist the compulsion. The individual recognizes the senselessness of the behavior and derives no pleasure from the act but may experience some temporary relief.

Obsessive or compulsive traits may exist in normal people or may occur as part of another psychiatric syndrome, such as schizophrenia, and indeed, in more bizarre or unusual cases, the two disorders may be mistaken for each other. Clinically this disorder was thought to be rare, but the ECA study (Robins, 1981) gave a prevalence rate of 2% in the general population, which is higher than that of schizophrenia. The reasons why this discrepancy exists between clinical and epidemiological experience is not yet known, and can only be conjectured. Part of the discrepancy might result from some individuals with OCD being missed altogether if they are being seen in substance abuse programs, where their symptoms are not being noted. Patients may also hide their symptoms. For example the author heard of one patient who was seeing a dermatologist for a persistent skin rash on both hands; the fact that she was washing her hands numerous times daily because she suffered from OCD was not discovered until the dermatologist decided to ask for a psychiatric consultation.

Individuals with this disorder are "challenging" to treat; they are repetitive and ritualistic. They may come hours early for their appointment, overstay their appointment, then return to knock on the door to request clarification of a matter just explained to them. They may bring lists of questions, some from the Physicians Desk Reference. They then may phone later, apologetically, to ask the same questions or variations of them. Their focus of worry or concern may be some event in the past which comes back to haunt them. The disturbing thoughts continually return with other possible tragic outcomes, for which no reassurances are possible or accepted. The afflicted individual now is left with repetitive acts to try to undo distressing thoughts.

Along with their symptoms may be substantial generalized anxiety and ultimately also depression. Many therapies of all kinds have been tried through the years, including lobotomy, psychoanalysis, behavior therapies, many medications, many varieties of psychotherapies, alone and in combinations. No group studies pointing to any definitive approach have occurred until recently.

Because of the variable nature of the disorder, frequently some tranquilizing or antidepressant medication will give some relief. The disorder is uncommon in clinical practice making it difficult to gather enough numbers for comparative treatment studies. Presently there is considerable interest in clomipromine, (Ananth, 1986) a tricyclic antidepressant drug widely used in Canada, which appears to have some specificity for OCD. It is not yet licensed in the United States.

Little is known about the cause of OCD, but more recent focus has been on biological causation; some cases have been known to occur after head injury (McKeon, 1983) and other recent work has focused on changes found on brain imaging in individuals with the disorder, (Swedo, 1988), strongly suggesting that OCD is an organic brain disease.

The relationship of OCD to substance abuse is poorly understood and relatively unexplored. In a study of 500 alcoholic males, Powell, (1982) using Feighner's diagnostic criteria (1972), found that 12% of the alcoholic population he surveyed had OCD. He further noted that the alcohol abuse seemed to come on at the same time as the obsessive compulsive symptoms, rather than to predate them.

Another study of 49 patients at a V.A. facility (Lydiard, 1988) revealed that 2% had OCD. Life time prevalence in a Canadian study of 501 alcohol and drug abuse patients was 10.3% (Ross, 1988). Thus, the three studies cited here report 2%, 10% and 12% of OCD patients in their clinical study populations. It is possible that the reason so few cases of OCD are being seen in general psychiatric clinics is because some are in chemical dependency populations or even in other medical clinics. A more systematic means to scan for OCD is useful; the authors of the Canadian study used the DIS, the Diagnostic Interview Schedule of the DSM III R. Also available in the DSM III R is a symptom check list for OCD. It seems that these or similar items would be very useful in searching for the "hidden obsessive-compulsive patients" who are, as suggested by the studies just reviewed, more common than anticipated in populations attending substance abuse clinics and addiction centers. If clomipramine is as helpful as Canadian writers indicate, the future may be quite a bit brighter for this disorder. Nevertheless, at this point in time, it must be said that far too little is known about OCD, its recognition, treatment, and relationship to substance abuse issues. Workers in the field of addictions should ask about repetitive thinking, observe for ritualistic behavior and consider using one of the diagnostic aids just mentioned.

A Case of Obsessive-Compulsive Disorder

A 30-year-old white female was referred to a rural New York clinic by her live-in boy friend of eight years. When she presented to the clinic she was a well dressed, well groomed, intelligent individual who seemed initially reluctant to discuss why she came to clinic. After some hesitation, she said that over the past six months she became increasingly distressed about her thinking, which involved worsening preoccupation with an incident that had occurred during a chemistry course she had taken as a college undergraduate. During an experiment one day she spilled on the counter top a container of a toxic chemical, which ran onto the floor. Special personnel were called in to clean up the spillage. The incident not only ruined the experiment, but angered the instructor, and exposed other members of the class to the chemical. At the time of the original episode, she had become depressed and had constant thoughts about the chemical, how well it had been disposed of, and whether the other students and lab workers would suffer some irreparable harm in years and generations to come. She dropped out of college the rest of the semester and saw a psychiatrist for nearly six months. He had placed her on medication, however she remembered very little about the sessions or the name of the medication.

Her lover reported that she had also begun clandestine alcohol usage, and although never frankly intoxicated, her alcohol use was becoming increasingly apparent to other members of the rural community and caused her to be increasingly impaired at her job on the local arts council. Her obsessional thinking centered on the chemical spillage, whether the cleanup had been adequate, and should she recontact the school to obtain the class list, to determine whether any symptoms of toxicity had occurred in the class members. These thoughts were related with distress and an increasingly bizarre quality as the sessions progressed. Psychotherapy seemed to make no change in her clinical state, and several psychotropic medications, both tricyclic antidepressants and neuroleptics were tried without success. Finally after nearly six months of treatment she reported that her mother remembered the name of the psychiatrist who first treated her. He was contacted, and his case notes received. His diagnostic impression of obsessive compulsive disorder was in agreement, and he had used for treatment a monoamine oxidase inhibiting antidepressant, phenelzine. This medication was begun, with definite improvement over the following month. Her use of alcohol stopped, of necessity on this medication. Obsessional thinking greatly decreased, and depression and anxiety were less severe. Unfortunately soon after going into remission her boyfriend was killed in an automobile accident. Although grief-stricken, she suffered no worsening of her original symptoms. Attempts to lower the medication were followed by a return of the disturbing thoughts of the chemical spill.

Diagnostic Impression
Axis I Obsessive-Complsive Disorder
Alcohol Abuse

GENERALIZED ANXIETY DISORDER

Generalized anxiety disorder, or GAD, is defined by the DSM III R as a generalized, persistent anxiety, manifested by symptoms from at least three of the following groups: motor tension, autonomic hyperactivity, apprehensive expectation, vigilance and scanning, and with anxious mood present for at least one month. The clinical recognition of GAD in addictionology is crucial; a recent Canadian study of 501 patients seen at a treatment center (Ross, 1988), revealed that 41.1% had a lifetime prevalence of GAD. Unlike the panic disorders, GAD is unfocused and continual. Both disorders may be similar in severity, but extensive interviewing of the GAD patient fails to elicit the typical pattern of panic attacks.

Continuous anxiety of some degree may accompany other psychiatric syndromes, such as schizophrenia or the depressions, but the symptomatology of those disorders is more prominent and GAD is seldom diagnosed separately.

Paradoxically, the major characteristic of GAD is its lack of distinctiveness. The intensity of the anxiety may vary considerably from one individual to another and even in the same individual over time. A major stress or precipitating event may have occurred in a significant number of cases. In its most severe form, the patient is demoralized, dysfunctional, anguished, and ultimately depressed. For those afflicted with this disorder the only relief comes either with sleep or from the sedation induced by tranquilizing medications, which must be used in heavy doses at times.

The cause of GAD is unknown, but is presumably biological in nature. Weissmann (1985) has presented preliminary data in the ECA (Robins, 1984) study indicating genetic linkages with major depressive disorder and panic disorder, although more study is needed to confirm this observation. Weissmann (1985) also noted an increased risk of alcoholism with GAD.

A clinician requires an elevated index of suspicion for the diagnosis of GAD in a tremulous, hyperalert individual with increased autonomic activity and who is undergoing detoxification from alcohol. It is likely that some cases of GAD are missed and attributed to withdrawal syndromes, but this is an area that needs further study.

One confirms the diagnosis in this situation by obtaining a history of continuous anxiety existing well before the alcoholism. There may be a history of tranquilizer abuse as well. If GAD occurs with a withdrawal syndrome, the patient at times begs for relief from the anxiety and for continuation of whatever agent is used during withdrawal. Some patients will simply sign out of the hospital if their symptoms become intolerable.

For uncomplicated GAD, a number of treatment approaches have been tried, including the gamut of psychological and verbal therapies, and many medications or combinations of medications and other therapies. Not uncommonly tranquilizer abuse may result. Is the answer to give these patients enough benzodiazepine dosage so it is unnecessary for them to raise their dose themselves? There are no easy answers, but one outcome of treatment is long term benzodiazipine use. If this is the case, the issues should be faced with the patient and family, and the medications closely monitored.

Feighner (1987) has reported on a multicenter study involving five hundred GAD patients who were treated with buspirone, a recently marketed medication said to lack some of the problems of the benzodiazepines and to have very low abuse potential. This study reported favorable results, as have others, but the Feighner study had a dropout rate of 66% by six months, and the dropout rate was not commented on. Certainly this agent may be given a trial and continued in those cases where it is successful. It is wise to combine biological with other forms of social or psychological therapies as seems appropriate to each individual.

In a number of cases seen by the author in recent years, multiple treatments had been tried, with minor improvement, as the patient became increasingly dependent on the care givers, the support system wore down and ultimately the patients wanted to relate directly to the physician on the treatment team, for medication. This situation sets the stage for possible conflict between the physician and the non-physicians on the treatment team: polypharmacy becomes tempting, the patient may doctor shop, and of course medication abuse may occur.

One of the other unfortunate aspects of this disorder is that the patient has little or no control over it, complains that nothing works, then is blamed for the disorder and for not trying hard enough to get better. How much to medicalize treatment becomes an ethical dilemma for the physician on the treatment team.

There are many unknowns with GAD, indeed, whether it is even one disorder or a collection of disorders. The fundamental issues of its nature and effective treatment must await further, extensive research.

Case Report

A 47-year-old divorced woman was referred to a rural New York substance abuse program by a county court after having been arrested on a harrassment charge while under the influence of alcohol and valium. She was living with her mother, was unemployed and on public assistance. Her chief complaint was that she "was a wreck without alcohol and Valium." She had attended outpatient counseling for over a year, and during this time she was under the care of a local physician who agreed to treat her with tranquilizing medication. As treatment progressed she stopped using alcohol, was employed, while continuing to be treated with medication. Her job, caring for an elderly person became more stressful, her medication usage increased. She was urged to enter psychiatric treatment on the acute inpatient unit of a nearby general hospital. Upon entering the hospital her chief complaints were that she was feeling "down and anxious" and reported that her medication, alprazolam, no longer helped her. She had trials of several different medications without improvement, finally being switched back to maximum dosage of alprazolam to control her anxiety. She was said to be a difficult patient because of her constant complaints of not feeling better. After discharge she returned to substance abuse counseling, with many of the same issues, i.e., poor relationship with mother, unemployment, lack of support from other family members, unresolved grief from her father's death, and a general lack of positive supports. After two months she decided to terminate therapy. Her diagnoses were: generalized anxiety disorder, alcohol dependence in remission and benzodiazopine abuse.

She was still seen intermittently in treatment and noted to be abusing her prescription medication, alprazolam, which she was getting from several sources. The consulting psychiatrist and the substance abuse staff referred her to a special hospital unit for detoxification, and all medication was uneventfully discontinued. She was discharged to return to outpatient substance abuse counseling. She was not consistent in attendance, so her case was closed, but she did maintain phone contact and was continued on a monoamine oxidase inhibitor, phenelzine, by the psychiatrist, who thought that she had generalized anxiety disorder. Improving on this medication, she moved away from her mother's home to a rented room, and was doing more than she had in months. Her improvement was also marked by the fact that she came to clinic much less frequently. On a phone call to the clinic she was thought to sound paranoid. Because side effects were feared, the medication was discontinued. A month later she was brought to the clinic by her landlord who noted that in a month she had deteriorated, ate poorly, and at times did not make sense when she spoke. Because she clearly could no longer care for herself, she was certified to a public mental hospital. Subsequent medical evaluation revealed marked blood electrolyte imbalance, the cause of which was traced to a cancer of the colon. The tumor was removed surgically and the patient received radiation, with marked improvement in her overall condition and mental state. She was discharged home, much improved. She still had a lower level of continuous anxiety every day, for which she took no medication. She preferred to stay confined to her apartment.

She had had anxiety disorder for many years, with numerous hospitalizations, and like many people with anxiety disorders was a heavy smoker. The rather rapid appearance of a lung cancer, which her internists thought caused the disturbance in her blood electrolytes, was a complete surprise. Her anxiety was clearly improved after the cancer was treated, but did not disappear. Her treatment team did not know of a direct connection between the tumor and anxiety. Her heavy smoking was thought to be related to her anxiety, however, and is a reminder of just one of the medical consequences of anxiety disorders.

POST TRAUMATIC-STRESS DISORDER

Stress or traumatic disorders have been known since the ancient Greeks, a case having been described by the Greek historian Herodotus (480 B.C.). It was not until 1981, however, that the DSM III clearly defined criteria for post traumatic-stress disorder. This entity has undoubtedly been present in large numbers with the advent of modern warfare, with its increasing emphasis on technology dedicated to the more efficient destruction and mutilation of humans. The disorder had not received as much attention as it has since the Viet Nam conflict, but it also is not appreciated by the general public and many professionals that PTSD occurs sporadically in the civilian population as a result of natural disasters, automobile accidents, criminal assaults, and industrial accidents. Not mentioned in the ECA study, PTSD is uncommon in clinical practice.

An important part of the understanding of PTSD is its definition as a disorder which will occur in most individuals who are exposed to an extraordinarily stressful event. The DSM III R lists two subtypes of PTSD, immediate and delayed, the latter appearing more than six months after the stress, and said to be the more severe. The symptomatology consists of flashbacks of the stressful event, disturbing nightmares, problems with mental concentration, loss of feelings of closeness to others, heightened alertness, and significant anxiety and/or depression. In its most severe forms it is incapacitating, disrupting personal, social and occupational spheres of functioning, and complicated by chemical abuse and dependency.

The cause of PTSD is unknown, and despite the hundreds of thousands of cases estimated to have resulted from the Viet Nam conflict alone, no large organized, sophisticated group studies have been done to assess treatment efficacy. The proliferation of treatment approaches in the professional literature reflects the confusion over treatment, with antidepressants, tranquilizers or other medication approaches mentioned. Peer group therapy is a common approach, relying on the group to unite and give each member the support he had not received elsewhere. Members share the unspeakable, numbing effects of senseless tragedies they experienced.

Kolb (1982), working at the Albany, New York, V.A. facility, has reported on his work, including a large, open study with approximately ninety patients. He indicates promising results with modified techniques used by the British in World War II, called narcosynthesis. This approach, through the use of hypnosis or medication, attempts to produce an abreaction, an actual emotional reliving of the traumatic event, (Sargent, 1957). Kolb uses recordings of battle sounds to simulate combat, as well as medication to facilitate the expression of affect laden, unconscious material. Narcosynthesis was used in both world wars to treat traumatic neuroses of combat, and may still be a widely applicable form of therapy for PTSD. No controlled group study has been done to see how it compares with an untreated group of individuals also suffering from PTSD.

In a double blind study (Frank, 1988), comparing the drugs imipramine and phenelzine, both drugs were found to significantly reduce the symptoms of PTSD, but without producing complete remission of symptoms.

During the course of the Viet Nam conflict more and more fighting men were found to have abuse and dependency problems when they returned home. Some were able to discontinue their drug habits on their own, but PTSD became increasingly linked to long term drug abuse and dependency problems. There is now a profusion of professional writings on many aspects of PTSD, too many to attempt to review here. Hard data are still scarce, and one must retreat to such statements as "PTSD is a common disorder among veterans of the Viet Nam era, and it is commonly accompanied by drug abuse and dependency problems, again for self treatment. Most Veterans Administration facilities are geared to recognize and treat this combined problem, with a mix of individual or group psychotherapy and the physicians choice of a pharmacological agent."

SIMPLE PHOBIA

Simple phobias are uncomplicated and benign disorders related to specific objects or situations, such as animals, insects, thunderstorms, dirt, etc. Nearly three hundred such phobias are now listed. They are the commonest of psychiatric disorders, occurring in 19% to 40% of the population, and cause little in the way of serious symptomatology compared to the other anxiety disorders. It is very uncommon for them to require treatment. Most people simply avoid the feared object or situation. There are at least two instances, however, where they are more likely to cause problems; those phobias involving medical procedures, and those involved with flying.

Mental health professionals working in medical settings are apt to receive referrals from medical colleagues because an individual is fearful of a certain medical procedure, such as venipuncture, minor surgery or general anesthesia. Some medically phobic people have postponed procedures for years. Generally a careful discussion with the patient, working with the appropriate physician and alerting the other personnel to be supportive and comforting is all that is needed.

Flying is said to be the commonest simple phobia, and is not a problem as long as the individual avoids this type of transportation. In our highly mobile world, many more people fly for business or personal reasons than ever before, and when one reaches a certain economic level in our society, avoiding flying may become very limiting and awkward. With alcohol so easily available in airports and on board aircraft, one would predict that a certain percentage of those people with simple flying phobia would fall victim to some degree of alcohol abuse. The author could find no literature linking this particular phobia to alcoholism, yet it must be mentioned as a possibility. A well known baseball player of the 1950s was said to suffer from a flying phobia and alcoholism.

A Canadian study cited earlier (Ross 1988) listed simple phobia as being present in 18.2% of their treatment population of 501 individuals. It is difficult to know whether the phobia played any role in the drug or alcohol problem in this large study, since the prevalence of simple phobia in the general population is similar to that quoted in this Canadian study.

Behavioral treatments are said to be most helpful, while medication is not seen to be of benefit in the treatment of simple phobia. Certainly it is wise to inquire about simple phobias or to use a questionnaire when doing a clinical assessment.

AGORAPHOBIA WITHOUT PANIC ATTACKS

Agoraphobia without panic attacks is described in the DSM III R, but this is an elusive disorder on which to obtain data. There is confusion as to whether it is a distinct entity or simply a variant of GAD which has an agoraphobic component as a complication. Without adequate data on its epidemiology and relationship to substance abuse, it will not be discussed here.

CONCLUSION

Progress in the basic and clinical research of the anxiety disorders has been remarkable in the last decade, but there is a great disparity among the anxiety disorders. Most progress seems to have been made in the treatment of the panic disorders, with hope for the treatment of OCD, but the therapeutic research for GAD and PTSD is less positive at the present time. The point to be stressed for all of these disorders, however, is a pluralistic treatment approach, with competent screening for medical disorders, then verbal and psychological therapies followed by psychiatric medications when necessary. A multidisciplinary team is necessary, and the substance abuse counselor or alcohol counselor must be part of the team. Abuse and dependence issues must be faced squarely, as well as the treatment of the primary anxiety disorder.

The use of medications to treat these disorders will always be a double edged sword and runs the risk of replacing one dependency with another. There is also the risk that the agent of abuse will be taken in addition to the prescribed medication. There is still, however, the benefit of the physician's proscription of all other agents while the medication is used, and hoping it will be followed. In the case of alcohol, the question arises whether controlled or social drinking can be an option for the person whose disorder is in remission and who is not on medication. The author recommends against this option, realizing that many patients will not follow this advice.

NOTE

1. The ECA study was an important source of information for this article. The Epidemiological Catchment Area Study (Robins 1984) is the most comprehensive study published on the mental health of the American people and involved cooperation between the federal government and three university departments of psychiatry in Boston, Baltimore and Saint Louis. Thousands of people from urban, suburban and rural areas were interviewed in depth to obtain community prevalence rates for most psychiatric disorders. The prevalence of substance abuse was determined to be 10% of the general population, thus presenting as one of the most serious public health problems of the United States.

REFERENCES

Ananth, A. (1988). Clomipramine: An antiobsessive drug. Canadian Journal of Psychiatry, 31, 253-257.

Diagnostic and Statistical Manual III R (1985). Washington, D.C. American Psychiatric Association Press.

Feighner, J., Robin, E., Guze, S., Woodruff, R., & Munoz, R. (1972). Diagnostic criteria for use in psychiatric research. Archives of General Psychiatry, 26, 57-63.

Feighner, J. (1987). The Impact of anxiety therapy on patients' quality of life. American Journal of Medicine, 82, 14-19.

Frank, J.B., Kosten, T.R., Giller, E.L. & Dan, E. (1988). A randomized trial of phenelzine and imipramine for post-traumatic stress disorder, American Journal of Psychiatry, 145 (10), 1289-1291.

Herodotus. (1983). The Histories. Middlesex, England. Penguin Classics, 430.

Hudson, C.J., & Perkins, D. (1984). Panic disorder and alcohol misuse. Journal of Studies on Alcohol, 45, 462-464.

Jelinek, J.M. & Williams, T. (1985). Post-traumatic disorder and substance abuse in Viet Nam combat veterams: Treatment, problems, strategies and recommendations, Journal of Substance Abuse and Treatment, 1 (2), 87-97.

Kein, D. (1964). Delineation of two drug responsive syndromes. Psychopharmacologia, 5 (6), 397-408.

Klein, D. (1967). Importance of psychiatric diagnosis in prediction of drug effect. Archives of General Psychiatry, 16, 119-125.

Kolb, L.C. & Mutalipassi, L. (1982). The conditioned emotional response: A sub-class of the chronic and delayed post-traumatic-stress disorder. Psychiatric Annals, 12 (11) 979-987.

Luxenberg, J.A., Swedo, S.E., Flament, M.F., Friedland, R.P., Rapoport, J. & Rapoport, S.I. (1988). Neuroanatomical abnormalities in obsessive-compulsive disorder detected with quantative x-ray computed tomography. American Journal of Psychiatry, 145, 1089-1093.

Lydiard, R., Howell, E.F., Malcolm, R. & Ballenger, J.C. (1988). Prevalence of anxiety disorders among alcoholics. Poster Display, American Psychiatric Association Annual Meeting, Montreal.

Marks, I. (1969). Fears and Phobias, New York, Academic Press.

McKeon, J., McGuffin, P. & Robinson, P. (1983). Obsessive-compulsive neurosis following closed head injury: A report of five cases. British Journal of Psychiatry, 190-192.

Modlin, H. (1983). Traumatic Neurosis and other injuries. Psychiatric Clinics of North America, 661-681.

Mullaney, J.A. & Trippitt, C.J. (1979). Alcohol dependence and phobias. British Journal of Psychiatry, 135, 565-573.

Powell, B.J., Penick, E.C., Othmer, E., Bingham, S.F. & Rice, A.S. (1982). Prevalence of additional syndromes amongst male alcoholics. Journal of Clinical Psychiatry, 43 (10), 404-407.

Quitkin, F., Rifkin, A., Kaplan, K. & Klein, D. (1972). Phobic anxiety syndromes complicated by drug dependence addictions. Archives of General Psychiatry, 27, 159-162.

Robins, L., Helzer, J.E., Weissman, M.M., Orvaschal, H., Gruenberg, E., Burke, J.D. & Regier, D.A. (1984). Lifetime prevalence of specific psychiatric disorders in three sites. Archives of General Psychiatry, 41, 949-958.

Ross, H.E., Glasser, F.B. & Germanson, T. (1988). The prevalance of psychiatric disorders in patients with alcohol and other drug problems. Archives of General Psychiatry, 45, 1023-1031.

Roy-Byrne, P. & Katon, W. (1987). An update on the treatment of anxiety disorders. Hospital and Community Psychiatry, 38 (8), 835-843.

Solursh, L. (1988). Combat Addiction and Post-traumatic stress reexplored. Psychiatric Journal of the University of Ottawa, 13 (1), 17-20.

Weissmann, M.M. (1985). The epidemiology of anxiety disorders: Rates, risks and familial patterns. In Tuma, A. H. & Maser, J.E. (Eds) Anxiety and the Anxiety Disorders, New Jersey, Lea.

Westphal, C. (1871). Die agoraphobie: eine neurpathische und eischeingung. Archiv fur Psychiatrie und Nervenkrankheiten, 3, 138-171, 219-221.

Winokur, G. & Coryell, V. (1988). (Eds.) Biological Systems: Their relationships to anxiety. Psychiatric Clinics of North America. 11 (2).

Affective Disorders
and Affective Symptoms in Alcoholism

Richard L. Weddige, MD
Mary Beth Ostrom, MD

The relationship between alcoholism and affective disorders has generated much interest among clinicians and researchers. The incidence, coexistence, and lifetime prevalence of each disorder has been studied. The suggestion or assumption that people drink because they are depressed has been challenged. Mayfield and Coleman in 1982 examined the changes in drinking pattern associated with three mood states, mania, depression and cyclothymia in 59 patients with a documented cyclic affective disorder. They also looked at the relationship between drinking and depressive disorder in 21 patients with a history of excessive drinking and depressive disorder. They found that 20% of patients with a cyclic mood disorder had excessive drinking and 50% of those who drank had a change in drinking during an episode of affective disorder. Within the depressive group 33% exhibited some relationship between excessive drinking and a depressive episode. Also the drinking behavior was positively and consistently related to elation but negatively and inconsistently related to depression in those with cyclic mood disorders. Loskow, Mayfield, Thiele in 1982 in a discussion of a case involving an individual with a diagnosis of bipolar disorder and substance abuse emphasized the need to consider and evaluate

Richard L. Weddige is Professor and Director of Residency Training; Mary Beth Ostrom is Chief Resident, Texas Tech University, Health Sciences Center, Department of Psychiatry, Lubbock, TX 79430.

The authors wish to thank Mrs. Cindy Rosenblatt for her assistance in typing and proofreading.

the two conditions separately rather then to consider one illness as the consequence of the other.

The role of dysphoria in contributing to relapse has also been examined. Pickens, Hatsukami, Spicer and Svikis in 1985 studied a group of 590 recovered substance abusers through use of a mailed questionnaire and a telephone survey regarding their relapse rate in the first year following treatment. Of those who had relapsed 31% reported a negative mood state such as depression or anxiety prior to their resumed use of alcohol.

Many subtypes of mood changes in alcoholics have been described (Cummings, Prokop, Cosgrove, 1985). Schuckit, 1985, defined four subgroups of substance abusers which he defined as primary alcoholics, primary drug abusers with secondary alcoholism, primary antisocial personality with secondary alcoholism and primary affective disorder with secondary alcoholism. He felt that the distinctions between these groups had important prognostic and treatment implications.

The persistence of depressive symptoms in an alcoholic study group has been examined. Nakamura, Overall, Hollister, Radcliffe, 1983, compared depressive symptoms at the time of entry into an alcohol treatment program to depressive symptoms after four weeks of treatment in a sample group of 88 patients. They found that at time of entry, based on scores obtained from the Hamilton Depression Scale, the Mood Assessment Scale and the Zung Self Rating Depressive scale, 22 patients had moderate to marked depressive symptoms. An additional 40 had mild symptoms while 26 had no significant depressive symptoms. After four weeks of treatment only four patients could be diagnosed as depressed while 12 had mild residual symptoms and 72 had no significant symptoms. Weddige, 1984, evaluated 139 individuals consecutively admitted to a chemical dependency unit with similar results. Initially 35 fulfilled the DSM-III criteria for depressive disorder and 8 had a MMPI profile consistent with depression but at the time of discharge only 12 met the DSM-III criteria for this diagnosis and only one individual had a MMPI profile consistent with depression. Pettinati, Sugerman, and Mauer, 1982, in a similar study did a four year follow-up of MMPI scores in alcoholics treated in a private psychiatric hospital and found that those who had remained abstinent were characterized by an elevated depression score on the initial MMPI but had a normal score four years later. The worst outcome group initially had elevated psychopathic deviance and mania scores which remained unchanged four years later. An intermediate outcome group (some slips but no regular drinking) initially had elevated depression and psychopathic deviance scores which had normalized at four year follow-up.

The coexistence of alcoholism with major affective disorders has been explored. Winokur, Cadoret, Dorzab et al., 1971, suggested the idea of a depressive spectrum disease. In this study it appeared that in at least one possible type of depressive disorder there was a related increased incidence of alcoholism and sociopathy in male relatives thus suggesting a possible genetic association between one subtype of depressive illness and alcoholism. As previously mentioned, Liskow, 1982, described a patient with coexistent bipolar disorder and alcohol abuse.

The importance of diagnosing alcoholism in patients with other psychiatric diagnoses has been emphasized. Ramsay, Vredenburgh, Gallagher, 1983, found that 35% of patients with some type of psychiatric problem seen in a primary care setting were not questioned regarding alcohol use. In a retrospective chart review it was determined that 23% of such patients on the basis of history, physical findings or laboratory evaluation had signs of possible alcoholism and 6% were definitely alcoholic.

Based on the heterogeneity of mood changes in the alcoholic many treatment strategies have evolved. The patient's course in treatment may also be predicted on the pre-existence or coexistence of an affective disorder. Rounsaville, Dolinsky, Babor, Meyer, 1987, studied 266 alcoholics one year after treatment and found that 3 factors had a predictive effect on treatment outcome over time. These factors included psychiatric diagnosis, global rating of psychopathology and degree of alcohol dependence. In this study any additional diagnosis was associated with a poorer outcome in men. In women the coexistence of major depression was associated with a better outcome in terms of alcohol treatment. Similarly Schuckit and Winokur, 1972, reviewed data obtained from a three year outcome study on 45 female patients divided into two groups of primary alcoholics versus affective disorder alcoholics and found that there was a probable association between a better prognosis and affective disordered alcoholism. The relationship between alcoholism and suicide must also be considered in any discussion related to affective disorders and alcoholism (Goodwin, 1973; Miles, 1977). The current knowledge relevant to affective disorders and alcoholism unfortunately leads to several treatment caveats. It is important when treating patients with a possible dual disorder to avoid initiating pharmacotherapy until at least three weeks post detoxification unless there is a history of bipolar disorder with current evidence of mania or depressive symptoms. If after three weeks the depressive symptoms continue or have worsened use of antidepressant medication may be considered, however psychotherapy may also be an appropriate treatment modality. In fact if the patient exhibits improvement with psychotherapy pharmacological intervention may not become necessary (Nace, 1987; Solomon, 1982). This chapter will discuss the above issues as they impact on treatment.

INCIDENCE OF AFFECTIVE DISORDERS IN HOSPITALIZED ALCOHOLICS

The rates of depression in hospitalized alcoholics vary from 3%-98% depending on the diagnostic tools utilized and the timing of the diagnosis (Keeler, Taylor, Miller, 1979). In one study the incidence of depression as measured by the Zung Self-Rating Scale, Hamilton Depression Scale, and the MMPI was found to be 98% among male alcoholics (Shaw et al., 1975). In a series of studies comparing symptom patterns in primary and secondary depressives, 59% of the alcoholics interviewed were depressed (Weissman, Pottenger, 1977). Weissman and Myers (1980), however, caution that by choosing patients who have actively sought treatment we may be seeing an artificially elevated association of the two conditions.

In contrast to the above reported rates of depression in alcoholics, Hamm, Major, Brown (1979), administered the Zung Scale and the Hamilton Scale to a group of young, healthy alcohol abusers and found that none had clear cut depression. Thus there is conflicting evidence on the incidence of depressive disorders or the subjective experience of depression in alcohol abusers with some studies suggesting a very high association while others report no association.

LIFETIME PREVALENCE OF DEPRESSION IN ALCOHOLICS

Hesselbrock, Meyer, Keener (1985), reported that in hospitalized alcoholics 32% of the males and 52% of the females had a lifetime diagnosis of major depression. The major depression preceded the alcoholism in 50% of the males with a history of major depression and in 66% of the women with a history of major depression. In clinical interviews of the 48 alcoholic patients consecutively admitted to an alcoholism treatment program it was found that 46% had suffered major depressive episodes (Bowen, Cipywnyk, D'Arcy, Keegan, 1974). Alcoholism tended to precede the onset of depression and the depressed alcoholic patients suffered more psychiatric, marital, and legal difficulties than the non-depressed alcoholic patients.

In 20,000 interviews in the general population examining the co-occurrence of alcoholism with other psychiatric disorders, 45% of the males and 65% of females who met criteria for alcoholism also met criteria for affective disorder (Helzer, Pryzbeck, 1988).

In another sample of 1,095 individuals selected randomly from the general population in a community survey the lifetime prevalence rates for alcoholism was 10.1% for men, and 4.1% for women. Among those diagnosed as alcoholic, about 70% had been diagnosed as having had either major or minor depressive episodes during their lifetime (Weissman, Myers, Harding, 1980).

In another study of patients being treated for alcoholism, there was also an elevated lifetime prevalence of depression (Bedi, Halikas, 1985). Forty-three percent of the females and 29% of the males had experienced a major depression.

In a study of 48 alcoholic inpatients, 22 or 46% had a history of major depression. In most, the alcoholism preceded the affective disorder (Bowen et al., 1984). The depressed alcoholics were again described as more likely to be divorced, have had trouble with the law, to have had increased suicidal gestures, to have begun drinking at an earlier age, and to be more irritable and angry than non-depressed alcoholics. In several studies, 14% of alcoholics abstinent for at least one year were found to be depressed (Behar, Winokur, Berg, 1984). In summary, many studies have shown that relatively high percentages of individuals with alcoholism have at some time in their life, also been diagnosed as having a depressive disorder. The studies described above would additionally suggest that in many cases the affective disorder preceded the substance abuse and that the presence of an affective disorder may be associated with a greater morbidity in terms of social functioning, i.e., increased psychiatric, marital, and legal difficulties. Finally, as described above, other studies have shown that many abstinent alcoholics continue to have depressive symptoms.

INCIDENCE OF ALCOHOLISM IN DEPRESSIVES

Merikangas, Leckman, Prusoar, Pauls, and Weissman (1985), in a sample of 133 primary depressives found only 14% to be alcoholic. In an affective disorder program only 6.4% of patients were determined to be alcoholic (Spring, Rothgery, 1984). In a study of primary depressives, (Woodruff, Guze, Clayton, Carr, 1973), of 39 depressed alcoholics, only three were determined to have had a primary depression. The authors emphasized the separateness of primary depression and alcoholism. Alcoholics with depression were more similar to non-depressed alcoholics than to depressed patients without alcoholism when considering such behavioral variables as delinquency and antisocial behavior. Others have failed to document a substantially increased risk of alcoholism in the patient with primary depression (Lewis, Heltzer, Cloninger, Croughan, Whitman, 1982).

DEPRESSION AND RELAPSE

Depression and anxiety are cited as the most common reasons for relapse in alcoholic patients (Pickens et al., 1985; Pottenger et al., 1978). The detection of the emergence of affective symptoms in the abstinent patient thus becomes a key element in aftercare programs. Cooperation and communication between individual counselors and support groups becomes vital in reestablishing an euthymic state in the abstinent individual. As noted previously, depressive-like symptoms may persist for as long as a year following abstinence and may make the individual more vulnerable to relapse.

SUBTYPES OF AFFECTIVE SYMPTOMS IN ALCOHOLISM

An interesting heterogeneity exists among alcoholics including both etiological factors as well as the myriad manifestations of the illness of alcoholism. There is a wide array of affective presentations and subtypes of "mood-like" changes in the alcoholic. Schuckit (1979) has made a plea to clarify terms such as mood, affect, primary and secondary affective disorder, and primary and secondary alcoholism. A primary disorder, for example, is defined as preceding a secondary disorder. For instance, an individual with a several month history of major depression who then begins abusing alcohol is thought by many to have a primary depressive disorder and secondary alcoholism (Weissman, Pottenger, Kleber, 1977). However, experience has shown us that this secondary alcoholism may also be indistinguishable from primary alcoholism, run its own course, and require separate, specific treatment. The current terminology of primary and secondary disorder may therefore be misleading and inadequate since in fact it suggests nothing regarding treatment or long-term outcome (Schuckit, 1985).

PRIMARY DEPRESSION IN ALCOHOLISM

There are many reasons why the alcoholic may be depressed. The alcoholic may also suffer from a primary depressive disorder such as a dysthymic disorder or a major depression. This individual has a dual disorder or co-morbidity. The specific depressive disorder requires specific therapy such as short-term psychodynamic psychotherapy, cognitive therapy, pharmacotherapy, or even electroconvulsive therapy. The timing of the diagnosis is discussed in a subsequent section. The diagnosis of primary depression is best made or confirmed at least three to four weeks post detoxification, is made using standard DSM-III-R criteria, and often entails obtaining collaborative history from friends and relatives as treatment proceeds.

Pitts and Winokur (1966) suggested that perhaps alcoholism and affective illness were different expressions of the same illness. In family studies of individuals with alcoholism and those with affective disorder, interesting trends were observed. The male relatives of alcoholics showed an increased incidence of alcoholism whereas the female relatives of alcoholics showed an increased incidence of depression (Winokur, Reich, Rimmer, 1970).

The role of genetic and environmental factors in the etiology of alcoholism and the subsequent development of alcoholism however remains somewhat unclear. In a study of psychopathology in adopted and non-adopted daughters of alcoholics it was shown that in those adopted away from their biological parents the incidence of depression was equal to the general population whereas in those daughters remaining home there was a higher incidence of depression (Goodwin et al., 1977). Both the nature and nurture factors must be considered when considering the etiology of both affective disorders as well as alcoholism.

Schuckit and Winokur (1972), have reported that women more often have depression preceding the onset of heavy drinking.

Another fascinating type of primary affective disturbance which might precede substance abuse is the individual who suffers from the manifestations of cyclothymic disorder (Akiskal, 1977). Diagnostic criteria include an alternating pattern of drug abuse in addition to irritable periods, explosive outbursts, repeated shifts in line of work, episodic promiscuous behavior, and hypersomnia alternating with decreased need for sleep. These individuals often respond to maintenance lithium carbonate therapy. Flemenbaum (1974) also suggested that chemical dependency might be a parapsychiatric manifestation of affective disorder.

Another type of primary depressive disorder associated with alcoholism is bipolar disorder or manic-depressive illness. In one study, three percent of hospitalized alcoholics were found to have had a manic episode during their lifetime in contrast to one percent of the general population (Hesselbrock et al., 1985; Robins et al., 1984). In a genetic study of bipolar affective disorder, first degree relatives of bipolar patients had the same alcoholism rate as the general population (James, Chapman, 1975). Bipolar illness and alcoholism did not seem to have a strong family link.

Several authors have observed that drinking may increase during the manic phase (Liskow et al., 1982; Winokur, Clayton, Reich, 1969). The association between increased drinking during the manic phase of bipolar illness and the potential periodic drug abuse in the individual with cyclothymia has treatment implications. It may be that a small subgroup of individuals who are dysphoric secondary to increased energy levels are at risk for developing alcohol abuse. Perhaps it is this subgroup of individuals who are more prone to self-medicate. Texas Tech Health Science Center Department of Psychiatry at Lubbock, Texas has treated several such individuals who suffered from a pre-existing affective disorder. The alcoholism and the affective disorder each required separate intervention and treatment.

SECONDARY DEPRESSION IN ALCOHOLISM

Secondary depression in alcoholism is defined as depression occurring after the onset of alcoholism. The signs and symptoms may be similar to a primary depressive disorder. Secondary depression has been attributed to many causes including neurotransmitter changes, personality factors, physical illness, psychosocial stress, familial hereditary factors, and prolonged alcohol consumption (Petty, 1981; Solomon, 1982).

Many agree that the depression or "depressive-like" symptoms occurring in alcoholism are more a consequence than a cause of the alcoholic's substance abuse. The results of chronic experimental intoxication studies have demonstrated that alcoholics become increasingly anxious and depressed as they drink (Mayfield, 1979). Alcohol appears to have a direct depressant effect after prolonged drinking (Tamerin, Mandelson, 1969). A dysphoric state, similar to depression, has been observed during addiction (Cummings et al., 1985). These observations suggest that alcohol exerts a direct chemical depressant effect even if the individual has not otherwise been predisposed to depression. Treatment implications include allowing sufficient time post-detoxification, usually three to four weeks, prior to making a separate diagnosis of depression. These depressive-like symptoms usually clear and do not require additional psychotherapy or pharmacotherapy.

There are many depressive consequences of alcohol use including the potential for many "losses" (Vaillant, 1984). These losses have to be dealt with in treatment to help remove depressive symptoms.

Another state which might appear indistinguishable from clinical depression is "learned helplessness" as described by Seligmann (1975). With prolonged drinking many individuals feel they have no control over their lives and regress to a "depressed-like" state. After regaining control and a sense of mastery associated with treatment and abstinence the associated dysphoric state disappears. The elevation in mood may well be due to the acquisition of coping skills and the instillation of hope.

PERSISTENCE OF AFFECTIVE DISORDER IN ALCOHOLISM

Many clinicians have examined the question of whether or not the associated affective disorder persists. Is it a transient phenomenon secondary to the use of alcohol or is it a primary illness that persists well into treatment and abstinence?

Forty-five percent of 73 alcoholics were noted by the Zung Self-Rating Depression Scale to be depressed at admission to a private university hospital substance abuse treatment program whereas only 10% were shown to be depressed four weeks later (Overall, Reilly, Kelly, Hollister, 1985). In a study examining 50 admissions to a chemical dependency treatment program 78% were depressed at pre-treatment as measured by the Beck Scale as compared to eight percent at post-treatment four to five weeks later (McGovern, 1983). A specific aspect of the treatment consisted of dealing with the resolution of grief and mourning as related to the "losses" associated with alcoholism. In another study by this writer 13 of 132 consecutive admissions to a chemical dependency unit had valid MMPI profiles for depression and appeared clinically depressed. At discharge, about four weeks later, none were clinically depressed (Weddige, 1984).

Schuckit (1979) reports that the "sad affect" produced by the life problems associated with alcoholism often clears within two weeks after the patient enters treatment. In another series consisting of 49 alcoholics who met Research Diagnostic Criteria for depression, only 10 appeared depressed after two weeks of sobriety (Dackis,

Gold, Pottash, Sweeney, 1986). In a VA study only 12 of 84 alcoholics remained depressed after brief treatment (Nakamura et al., 1983). In a four year MMPI follow-up study alcoholics who initially had an elevated D Scale on the MMPI, showed a completely normal MMPI four years later (Pettinati et al., 1982). These individuals had remained abstinent during the four year period. Incidentally, in the same study those patients with the worst outcome had elevated Pd and Ma scores initially and had similar scale elevations four years later. Continued elevation of these subscales may indicate a more significant and persistent type of psychopathology which continued to predispose these individuals to substance abuse.

It does appear that the reported high initial rates of depression in individuals who enter treatment for alcoholism do not persist. It is likely that their mood changes are secondary to the disease of alcoholism and do not represent a primary process. Specific alcoholism treatment appears to be effective in causing a remission of these mood changes, however in primary affective disorders additional treatment modalities such as use of antidepressant medications may be necessary.

DIAGNOSIS OF AFFECTIVE DISORDERS IN ALCOHOLISM

As previously mentioned, the timing of the diagnostic process is crucial in establishing a dual diagnosis of alcoholism and affective disorder. The importance of recognizing alcoholism among patients with other psychiatric problems as well as recognizing alcoholism among primary care patients has been stressed (Coulehan, Zettler-Segal, Block, McClelland, Schulberg, 1987; Ramsay et al., 1983).

The wide range of prevalence of depression associated with alcoholism may reflect differences in the diagnostic criteria or in the instruments used. In one series the incidence of depression varied according to the test instrument utilized. Keeler, Taylor and Miller, 1979, administered different psychological tests of depression to 39 consecutively admitted male alcoholics at a Veterans Administration hospital. All patients were tested between the fifth and seventh days after admission (Keeler et al., 1979). The incidences of depression were eight percent (clinical interview), 28% (Hamilton

Depression Rating Scale), 43% (MMPI), and 66% (Zung Self-Rating Depression Scale).

Sedlacck and Miller (1982) emphasize the importance of distinguishing between alcoholics who are actively drinking, newly sober, or in recovery when diagnosing depression and alcoholism. This allows a more accurate assessment of such variables as the direct depressant effect of the alcohol as well as the various losses associated with the disease. Kammeier, Hoffman, Loper (1973) compared the MMPIs of 38 men in college with their later MMPIs when they had become alcoholic. Only the later MMPIs showed elevated Depression scales. The composite MMPIs (once alcoholic) showed a pathological profile of a self-centered, immature, dependent, resentful, irresponsible person who was unable to face reality.

Predicting the subsequent development and diagnosis of alcoholism and associated symptoms based on childhood premorbid characteristics has also not been successful (McCord & McCord, 1960). In a follow-up study children with strong inferiority feelings, boys with strong encouragement of dependency from their mothers and manifest oral tendencies (thumb sucking, playing with their mouths, early heavy drinking, and compulsive eating), were no more or less likely to develop alcoholism than individuals who did not possess these characteristics. Pre-alcoholics were usually more self-confident, aggressive, and active.

Accurate diagnosis of co-morbidity might be enhanced by the use of routine test instruments specific for alcoholism such as the CAGE [Cutting down, Annoyance by criticism, Guilty feeling and Eye-openers] Questionnaire (Ewing, 1984), and the Michigan Alcoholism Screening Test (Selzer, 1971), as well as utilizing specific psychiatric diagnostic criteria (DSM-III-R), Research Diagnostic Criteria, or the Interview Schedule for Affective Disorders. Some investigators have warned against utilizing screening rating scales such as the Zung, Beck, Hamilton, or MMPI Depression Scales which might lead to highly variable results (Weissman and Myers, 1980).

Differentiating between primary and secondary depression among alcoholics is also important as it relates to evaluating the depth of depression (Bennett, 1985). Even with collaborative history it is often difficult to ascertain primary and secondary diagnostic groups. In general, the authors have found it best to allow an adequate period of detoxification and then make a presumptive diagnosis of primary affective disorder. Usually a 3-4 week detoxification period is adequate. An underlying affective disorder, if left untreated, could jeopardize an individual's potential for maintaining sobriety.

Another diagnostic issue relates to the depression seen in alcoholic patients associated with other coexistent Axis I and Axis II disorders such as schizophrenia, organic mental disorders or severe personality disorders such as borderline and schizotypal personality disorder. Careful diagnosis post-detoxification can lead to individualized treatment for other disorders in the alcoholic patient which might otherwise be seen as uncomplicated primary depression associated with alcoholism.

Diagnosis of affective subtypes in alcoholism often predicts the course in treatment. This precision in diagnosis also allows for more specific individualized treatment approaches.

TREATMENT STRATEGIES FOR AFFECTIVE DISORDER IN ALCOHOLISM

If careful diagnostic procedures and criteria are utilized and sufficient time has been allowed post-detoxification a few alcoholic patients will be found who also meet criteria for a major affective disorder. Simultaneous treatment for major depression or bipolar disorder will then be indicated. Depending on the cognitive and psychomotor activity level, an individual might have to be temporarily transferred to a mental health unit. This decision must be individualized and is also based on the level of expertise of the staff, as well as the ability of the treatment group to incorporate and handle a very depressed or energized patient. Many chemical dependency units can also manage these individuals, however, it should not be at the expense of other patients in the therapeutic community. If the affective symptoms preclude group participation or if the patient takes up all the staff's time then a transfer is appropriate.

Suicidal risk in these individuals must also dictate transfer to a more structured mental health unit. At the Texas Tech Health Science Center in Lubbock, Texas, very depressed patients have occasionally attended group activities on a chemical dependency unit and then returned to an adjacent mental health unit. It is important to continue treating two separate disorders in these individuals and not assume that treatment of the primary depression will automatically take care of the drinking problem. Each disorder will likely continue to run its own course if untreated.

Most AA groups now do not frown on participants who are taking a non-addictive drug such as an antidepressant or lithium carbonate. However, there will be occasional resistance to this practice which must be tempered with education concerning co-morbidity. We occasionally explain the need for this type of medication using the analogy of the medical patient who requires specific medication for thyroid dysfunction or diabetes. These patients will also require specific follow-up, usually from a psychiatrist, for their affective illness as well as an aftercare program for the alcoholism. One treatment should not preclude the other.

Treating alcoholic patients who also have concurrent minor depression or dysthymic disorder allows more flexibility in terms of timing and approach. Many individuals may appear to fulfill criteria for dysthymic disorder during most of an acute inpatient stay. Adopting a "wait and see attitude" often works well for this individual as long as there is little suicidal risk and they can participate in the psychotherapeutic and educational group activities on both an affective and cognitive level. This requires daily monitoring to insure that treatment is being integrated. The temptation in treating these individuals is the premature application of pharmacotherapy or psychotherapy. This is not to imply that individual psychodynamically oriented psychotherapy is unwarranted in these patients. However, it may be more prudent to wait on insight oriented therapy and guide them through a group oriented program and not foster an intense transference relationship with an individual therapist. Brief, supportive visits which foster an identity to the team and program may provide an adequate holding environment to ameliorate their depressive dysphoria. If after several weeks of treatment and aftercare the diagnosis of dysthymic disorder persists then reconsideration can be given to a more specific individual psychotherapeutic approach. Many of these individuals will experience a lifting of their depression without utilizing an additional approach.

Others whose drinking may be predicated on psychodynamic conflict may well later require insight oriented psychotherapy. Various psychodynamic formulations have been developed. These include the dependency conflict model (McCord & McCord, 1960), power conflict (McClelland, Davis, Kalin, Wanner, 1972), and a third model based on self-psychology concepts (Kohut, 1971). The dependency conflict model presupposes an erratic satisfaction of dependency needs as a child resulting in an intensification of these needs and a subsequent conflict over how these need may be appropriately satisfied at older ages. Subsequently the individual finds he must suppress these needs in order to maintain a culturally appropriate "independent facade" resulting in the use of alcohol to satisfy these needs and maintain the individuals self image. In the "Power conflict model" hypothesis the individual uses alcohol to increase feelings of personal power. Theoretically the person prone to alcohol abuse feels that his role in society is undercut by social or other processes. A third model is derived from self psychology. In Kohut's theory assumptions are made regarding the parental relationship. If adequate relationships are not established the child is unable to pass beyond a stage of a grandiose self. The individual is unable to value themselves because of a failure to be valued by the parenting figure. Expectations will be unrealizeable and unreal leading to disappointment and a sense of failure. Alcohol or other drugs may be used to reduce the pain of the depression and guilt and also to restabilize the defensive grandiosity.

An additional secondary type of depression previously mentioned is associated with other psychiatric disorders such as schizophrenia or severe personality disorders. Many alcoholic patients with antisocial personality disorder also meet criteria for major depression (Hesselbrock, in press). The pain of the depressive symptoms may help this group of patients become engaged in treatment. The depressive component in other serious personality disorders, such as the borderline syndrome, may also provide a focus for beginning treatment. The presence of secondary depression again emphasizes the importance of accurate diagnosis.

The group and individual therapy approach may have to be initially modified to effectively treat the above patients with secondary depression. Many, such as the borderline, will be unable to tolerate as much confrontation. They will need to retain some of their defenses to preclude psychotic regression. Individualized strategies which encompass their unique dual diagnoses will have to be developed by the treatment team. However, most of these individuals probably can be effectively managed within a traditional chemical dependency treatment setting if allowances and adjustments are made for their individual diagnoses.

Another secondary type of "depressive-like" symptomatology emerges in the alcoholic patient because of issues related to loss, grief, and hopelessness. It has been shown that during treatment alcoholics develop an increased awareness of losses and show a decrease of both depression and grief (McGovern, 1983). Others have conceptualized depressive symptoms as being related to a grief reaction (Friedman, 1984). A portion of the treatment approach may have to address the phases or stages of grief (Kubler-Ross, 1969), related to the loss of an object. For some patients there are many associated losses accompanying the successful treatment of the disease. This type of "depressive-syndrome" often resolves within weeks of beginning treatment (McGovern, 1983).

Although not designed specifically for treatment of depression, most of the group activities in a treatment program also provide treatment for depressive symptoms. A supportive, empathic holding matrix provides comfort for individuals struggling with losses and decreased self-esteem associated with alcoholism. Aftercare activities including the important role of Alcoholics Anonymous are also helpful in relieving depressive symptoms. The individual is provided with models for identification, is given a mechanism to express resentments, and is supported with increasing control and mastery over his/her life.

Pharmacotherapy is another aspect of treating depression related to alcoholism. When treating depression in recovery it is tempting to respond to complaints of pain, suffering, and apathy with sympathetic prescription writing (Chafetz, 1983). Antidepressants as well as lithium carbonate have been employed in treating alcoholism. Viamontes (1972) reported that none of seven controlled studies showed antidepressants to be more effective than placebo in treating alcoholism. However, seven of nine uncontrolled studies reported positive results in treating alcoholics with antidepressants (Schuckit, 1979). There has also been some suggestion that lithium might be helpful in decreasing alcohol intake (Himmelhock, Hill, Steinberg,

May, 1983). In this study, the effect of lithium was not associated with either the mood level or the psychiatric diagnosis.

Several years ago others also suggested that lithium might decrease alcohol intake in alcoholics. Kline, Wren and Cooper in 1979 performed a double blind study comparing the use of lithium to placebo. They found that over a 48 week follow-up period the number of disabling drinking episodes were significantly less in the lithium treated group. They had excluded patients with bipolar or recurrent unipolar depression from the study. Merry, Reynolds, and Baily in 1976 in a similar study again found that depressed alcoholics treated with lithium had a significant reduction in the number of days that they were incapacitated by drinking compared with a placebo treated group. Non-depressed alcoholics showed no improvement when treated with lithium as compared to a placebo treated group (Kline, Wren, Cooper, 1974; Merry, Reynolds, Baily, 1976). Some studies have not differentiated between depressed and non-depressed alcoholics. Recently two studies reported on the suggested beneficial effects of lithium in alcoholism. Fawcett et al., 1987, in a double-blind, placebo-controlled study examined the effect of treatment with lithium on 104 patients meeting DSM-III criteria for alcohol dependence. It was found that the treatment with lithium was associated with an improved outcome. In this study depressed alcoholics did not show a better response to lithium than nondepressed alcoholics (Fawcett et al., 1984; Fawcett et al., 1987). Despite the positive results of the studies cited above conclusive evidence of the effect of lithium on the treatment of substance abuse is lacking. At this point antidepressants and lithium should be reserved for patients who meet diagnostic criteria, according to the DSM III-R, for specific affective disorders. This diagnosis must persist three to four weeks post-detoxification.

COURSE AND PROGNOSIS IN TREATMENT

It is significant to note the course and prognosis of depressed alcoholics in treatment. In a three year follow-up of alcoholic women, those with primary affective disorder had a comparatively better prognosis than primary alcoholics did (Schuckit & Winokur, 1972). This may be because depression is more common in women and easier to treat than alcoholism. Another study examined the frequency and persistence of depression in the alcohol abuser (Pottenger et al., 1978). In alcoholics treated as outpatients at one year follow-up, 72% of those still drinking were depressed and 75% of those not depressed were abstinent. It has also been shown that in alcoholic men the additional diagnosis of major depression, antisocial personality, or drug abuse is associated with a poorer outcome (Rounsaville et al., 1987). Again in this study major depression with alcoholism in women was associated with a better outcome. For women, the affective disorder was likely to be a primary diagnosis with alcoholism occurring only subsequent to the onset of the depression. The alcoholism may have been an attempt at self-treatment. Others have also reported that the nature and extent of pretreatment psychiatric problems was the single best predictor of treatment response for alcoholics (McLellan, Luborsky, O'Brien, Burr, Evans, 1986). In contrast, O'Sullivan et al. (1983), in comparing alcoholics with and without coexisting affective disorder found a lack of difference in drinking behavior in the two groups. Such contradictory results may be in part due to differences in definition of terms and the methods by which diagnoses are derived.

ALCOHOLISM AND SUICIDE

In the context of affective disorders and alcoholism, suicide must also be considered (Miles, 1977). Actuarial data has suggested that there are 10%-47% alcoholics among suicides and 6% to 21% suicide among alcoholics (Goodwin, 1973). Alcoholics who commit suicide are characterized as being intoxicated, overwhelmed with hopelessness, have a diminished future time perspective, have "chronic" alcoholism, have a past history of delirium tremens, and may have mixed sedative-hypnotic medications (Beck, Weissman, Kovacs, 1976; Lester, Beck, 1975).

It then becomes incumbent upon the treatment team to be alert to this additional risk when evaluating and treating the depressed alcoholic. Some of these individuals who are at high risk for self-destructive behavior may have to be temporarily cared for in a psychiatric unit. For others, the structure and support in a multidisciplinary chemical dependency unit with access to psychological and psychiatric consultation will provide adequate treatment.

CONCLUSIONS

The relationship between alcoholism and affective disorders remains complex. There exists a heterogeneity in both alcoholics as well as in depressive symptoms in alcoholics. Most alcoholics probably do not drink because they are depressed. Depressive-like mood symptoms occur almost universally in the course of alcoholism. Primary and secondary depression as well as depressive-like mood changes often have varying durations. Primary depression and alcoholism often have separate clinical courses. The secondary depressions in alcoholism are often associated with such factors as the direct effect of alcohol or with life's losses. These syndromes often do not require specific treatment for depression and may disappear in three to four weeks. The accuracy of a diagnosis of depression in alcoholics is enhanced by the use of standardized criteria as well as by waiting three to four weeks post-detoxification. Alcoholics will present with a variety of dysphoric mood changes depending on when they are seen in the course of treatment. Depression may persist after treatment for alcoholism and be associated with relapse. Patients with many pre-existing psychiatric problems including depression often do not do as well in treatment. The exception is in women with pre-existing major depression who may actually have a better prognosis than women who present with just alcoholism.

Treatment for primary depression associated with alcoholism is treated as a separate diagnosis. The secondary depressions or depressive-like symptoms which often disappear with time may, however, be associated with grief, loss, and mourning issues or be associated with other non-affective psychiatric diagnosis, and may require specific treatment approaches. Pharmacotherapy (antidepressants and lithium carbonate), is reserved for treating separate, specific affective syndromes and is not prescribed for the drinking behavior.

Alcoholism is also associated with an increased risk of suicide. It becomes increasingly important to assess depressed alcoholics for suicidal risk factors.

The relationship between alcoholism and affective symptoms continues to be fascinating and challenging in terms of etiological and treatment issues. The future is promising with reference to further delineating the heterogeneity of both alcoholism and related affective disorders. Current knowledge does allow us to recognize and treat many of the depressive syndromes associated with alcoholism.

REFERENCES

1. Akiskal, H. (1977). Cyclothymic disorder: Validating criteria for inclusion in the bipolar affective group. *American Journal of Psychiatry. 134*, 1227-1233.

2. Beck, A.T., Weissman, A., & Kovacs, M. (1976). Alcoholism, hopelessness, and suicidal behavior. *Journal of Studies on Alcohol. 37*, 66-67.

3. Bedi, A.R., & Halikas, J.A. (1985). Alcoholism and affective disorder. *Alcoholism: Clinical and Experimental Research. 9*(2), 133-134.

4. Behar, D., Winokur, G., & Berg, C.J. (1984). Depression in abstinent alcoholic. *American Journal of Psychiatry. 141*(9), 1105-1107.

5. Bennett, L.A. (1985, March). *Symptoms of depression among hospitalized and post-hospitalized alcoholics in Yugoslavia.* Prepublication draft.

6. Bowen, R.C., Cipywnyk, D., D'Arcy, C., & Keegan, D.L. (1984). Types of depression in alcoholic patients. *Canadian Medical Association Journal. 130*, 869-874.

7. Chafetz, M.E. (1983). The alcoholic patient: Diagnosis and management, depression in recovery. In *Medical economic books* (p. 154). Oradell, NJ.

8. Coulehan, J.L., Zettler-Segal, M., Block, M., McClelland, M., & Schulberg, H.C. (1987). Recognition of alcoholism and substance abuse in primary care patients. *Archives of Internal Medicine. 147*, 349-352.

9. Cummings, C.P., Prokop, C.K., & Cosgrove, R. (1985). Dysphoria: The cause on the result of addiction. *The Psychiatric Hospital. 3*, 131-134.

10. Dackis, C.A., Gold, M.S., Pottash, A.L.C., & Sweeney, D.R. (1986). Evaluating depression in alcoholics. *Psychiatric Research. 17*(2), 105-109.

11. Ewing, J.A. (1984). Detecting alcoholism: The CAGE questionnaire. *Journal of the American Medical Association. 252*, 1905-1907.

12. Fawcett, J., Clark, D.C., Gibbons, R.D., Aagesen, C.A., Pisaui, V.D., Tilkin, J.M., Sellers, D., & Strutzman, D. (1984). Evaluation of lithium therapy for alcoholism. *Journal of Clinical Psychiatry. 45*, 494-499.

13. Fawcett, J., Clark, D.C., Aagesen, C.A., Pisani, V.D., Tilkin, J.M., Sellers, D., McGuire, M., & Gibbons, R.D. (1987). A double-blind placebo-controlled trial of lithium carbonate for alcoholism. *Archives of General Psychiatry. 44*, 248-256.

14. Flemenbaum, A. (1974). Affective disorders and "chemical dependence": Lithium for alcohol and drug addiction? *Diseases of the Nervous System. 35*, 281-285.

15. Friedman, M.A. (1984). Grief reactions: Implications for treatment of alcohol clients. *Alcoholism Treatment Quarterly. 1*(1), 55-69.

16. Goodwin, D.W. (1973). Alcohol in suicide and homicide. *Journal of Studies on Alcohol. 34*, 144-156.

17. Goodwin, D., Schulsinger, F., Knop, J., Mednick, S., & Guze, S.B. (1977). Psychopathology in adopted and non-adopted daughters of alcoholics. *Archives of General Psychiatry. 34*, 1005-1009.

18. Hamm, J.E., Major, L.F., & Brown, G.L. (1979). The quantitative measurement of depression and anxiety in male alcoholics. *American Journal of Psychiatry. 136*, 580-582.

19. Helzer, J.E., & Przybeck, T.R. (1988, May). The co-occurrence of alcoholism with other psychiatric disorders in the general population and its impact on treatment. *Journal of Studies on Alcohol. 49*(3), 219-224.

20. Hesselbrock, M.N., Meyer, R.E., and Keener, J.J. (1985). Psychopathology in hospitalized alcoholics. *Archives of General Psychiatry. 42*, 1050-1055.

21. Hesselbrock, M.N. (in press). A review of empirical evaluations of common classification schemes. In M. Galanter (Ed.), *Recent developments in alcoholism*. New York: Plenum Publishing Corporation.

22. Himmelhoch, J.M., Hill, S., Steinberg, B., & May, S. (1983). Lithium, alcoholism, and psychiatric diagnosis. *Journal of Psychiatric Treatment and Evaluation. 5*, pp. 83-88.

23. James, J., & Chapman, C. (1975). A genetic study of bipolar affective disorder. *British Journal of Psychiatry. 126*, 449-456.

24. Kammeier, M.L., Hoffman, H., & Loper, R.G. (1973). Personality characteristics of alcoholics as college freshmen and at time of treatment. *Quarterly Journal of Studies on Alcohol. 34*, 390-399.

25. Keeler, M.H., Taylor, C.I., & Miller, W.C. (1979). Are all recently detoxified alcoholics depressed? *American Journal of Psychiatry. 136*, 586-588.

26. Kline, N.S., Wren, J.C., Varga, E., & Canal, O. (1974). Evaluation of lithium therapy in chronic and periodic alcoholism. *American Journal of Medical Sciences, 268*, 15-22.

27. Kohut, H. (1971). *The analysis of self*. New York: International Universities Press.

28. Kubler-Ross, E. (1969). *On death and dying*. New York: MacMillan.

29. Lester, D., & Beck, A.T. (1975). Attempted suicide in alcoholics and drug addicts. *Quarterly Journal of Studies on Alcohol. 36*, 162-164.

30. Lewis, C.E., Heltzer, J., Cloninger, C.R., Crougha, J., & Whitman, B.Y. (1982). Psychiatric diagnostic predispositions to alcoholism. *Comprehensive Psychiatry. 23*, 451-461.

31. Liskow, B., Mayfield, D., & Thiele, J. (1982, April). Alcohol and affective disorder: Assessment and treatment. *Journal of Clinical Psychiatry. 434*, 144-147.

32. Mayfield, D.G., & Coleman, L.L. (1968). Alcohol use and affective disorder. *Diseases of the Nervous System. 29*, 467-474.

33. Mayfield, D.G. (1979). Alcohol and affect: Experimental studies. In D. Goodwin, & C. Erickson (Eds.), *Alcoholism and Affective Disorder*. New York: Spectrum Press.

34. McClelland, D.C., Davis, W.N., Kalin, R., & Wanner, E. (1972). *The Drinking Man*. New York: The Free Press.

35. McCord, W., & McCord, J. (1960). *Origins of Alcoholism*. Stanford: Stanford University Press.

36. McGovern, T.F. (1983). *The effects of an inpatient alcoholism treatment program with two variations on measurements of depression, hopelessness, loss, and grief*. Unpublished doctoral dissertation, Texas Tech University, Lubbock.

37. McLellan, A.T., Luborsky, L., O'Brien, C.P., Barr, H.L., & Evans, F. (1986). Alcohol and drug abuse treatment in three different populations: Is there improvement and is it predictable? *American Journal of Drug and Alcohol Abuse*. *12*, 101-102.

38. Merikangas, K.R., Leckman, J.F., Prusoff, B.A., Pauls, D.L., & Weissman, M.M. (1985). Family transmission of depression and alcoholism. *Archives of General Psychiatry*. *42*, 367-372.

39. Merry, J., Reynolds, C., Baily, J., & Coppen, A. (1976). Prophylactic treatment of alcoholism by lithium carbonate. *Lancet*. *2*, 481-482.

40. Miles, C.P. (1977). Conditions predisposing to suicide, a review. *Journal of Nervous and Mental Disorders*. *164*, 231-246.

41. Nace, E.P. (1987). *The treatment of alcoholism* (p. 2181). New York: Brunner/Mazel.

42. Nakamura, M.D., Overall, J.E., Hollister, L.E., & Radcliffe, E. (1983). Factors affecting outcome of depressive symptoms in alcoholics. *Alcoholism: Clinical and Experimental Research*. *7*(2), 188-193.

43. O'Sullivan, K., Whillans, P., Daly, M., Carroll, B., Claire, A., & Cooney, J. (1983). A comparison of alcoholics with and without coexisting affective disorder. *British Journal of Psychiatry*. *143*, 133-138.

44. Overall, J.E., Reilly, E.L., Kelly, J.T., & Hollister, L.E. (1985). Persistence of depression in detoxified alcoholics. *Alcoholism: Clinical and Experimental Research*. *9*(4), 331-333.

45. Pettinati, H.M., Sugerman, A.A., & Mauer, H.S. (1982). Four year MMPI changes in abstinent and drinking alcoholics. *Alcoholism: Clinical and Experimental Research*, *6*(4), 487-494.

46. Petty, F. (1981, November-December). Secondary depression in alcoholism: Implications for future research. *Comprehensive Psychiatry*. *22*(6), 587-595.

47. Pickens, R.W., Hatsukami, D.K., Spicer, J.W., & Svikis, D.S. (1985). Relapse by alcohol abusers. *Alcoholism: Clinical and Experimental Research*. *9*(3), 244-247.

48. Pitts, F., & Winokur, G. (1966). Affective disorder VII: Alcoholism and affective disorder. *Journal of Psychiatric Research*, *4*, 37-50.

49. Pottenger, M., McKernon, J., Patrice, L.E., Weissman, M.M., Ruben, H.L., & Newberry, P. (1978). Frequency and persistence of depression in the alcohol abuser. *Journal of Nervous and Mental Disorders*. *166*(8), 562-570.

50. Ramsay, A., Vredenburgh, J., & Gallagher, R.M. (1983). Recognition of alcoholism among patients with psychiatric problems in a family practice clinic. *Journal of Family Practice*, *17*, 829-832.

51. Robins, L.N., Helzer, J.E., Weissman, M.M., Orvaschel, H., Gruenberg, E., Burke, J.D., Jr., & Regier, D.A. (1984). Lifetime prevalence of specific psychiatric disorders in three sites. *Archives of General Psychiatry. 41,* 949-958.

52. Rounsaville, B.J., Dolinsky, Z.S., Babor, T.F., & Meyer, R.E. (1987). Psychopathology as a predictor of treatment outcome in alcoholics. *Archives of General Psychiatry. 44,* 505-513.

53. Schuckit, M.A., & Winokur, G. (1972). A short-term follow-up of women alcoholics. *Diseases of the Nervous System. 33,* 672-678.

54. Schuckit, M.A. (1979). Alcoholism and affective disorder: Diagnostic confusion. In D.W. Goodwin & C.K. Erickson (Eds.), *Alcoholism and affective disorders*. New York: Spectrum Publications.

55. Schuckit, M.A. (1985). The Clinical implications of primary diagnostic groups among alcoholics. *Archives of General Psychiatry. 42,* 1043-1049.

56. Sedlacck, D.A., & Miller, S.I. (1982). A framework for relating alcoholism and depression. *The Journal of Family Practice. 14*(1), 41-44.

57. Seligmann, M.E.P. (1975). *Helplessness: On depression, development and death*. San Francisco: W.H. Freeman.

58. Selzer, M.L. (1971). The Michigan Alcoholism Screening Test: The quest for a new diagnostic instrument. *American Journal of Psychiatry. 127,* 89-94.

59. Shaw, J.A., Donley, P., Morgan, D.W., & Robinson, J.A. (1975). Treatment of depression in alcoholics. *American Journal of Psychiatry. 132,* 641-642.

60. Solomon, J. (1982). Alcoholism and affective disorders: Methodological considerations. In J. Solomon (Ed.), *Alcoholism and clinical psychiatry*. New York: Plenum Medical Book Company.

61. Spring, G.K., & Rothgery, J.M. (1984). The link between alcoholism and affective disorders. *Hospital and Community Psychiatry. 35*(8), 820-823.

62. Tamerin, J.S., & Mandelson, J.H. (1969). The psychodynamics of chronic inebriation: Observations of alcoholics during the process of drinking in an experimental groups setting. *American Journal of Psychiatry. 125,* 886-899.

63. Vaillant, G.E. (1984). The course of alcoholism and lessons for treatment. In: L. Grinspoon (Ed.). *Psychiatry Update. 3,* 311-319.

64. Viamontes, J.A. (1972). Review of drug effectiveness in the treatment of alcoholism. *American Journal of Psychiatry. 128,* 100-121.

65. Weddige, R.L. (1984). *The prevalence and persistence of depression in alcoholism*. Unpublished series.

66. Weissman, M.M., Pottenger, M., Kleber, H., Ruben, H.L., Williams, D., & Thompson, W.D. (1977). Symptom patterns in primary and secondary depression. *Archives of General Psychiatry. 34,* 854-862.

67. Weissman, M.M., & Myers, J.K. (1980). Clinical depression in alcoholism. *American Journal of Psychiatry. 137,* 372-373.

68. Weissman, M., Myers, J., & Harding, P. (1980). Prevalence of psychiatric heterogeneity of alcoholism in a United States urban community. *Quarterly Journal of Studies on Alcohol. 41*(7), 672-681.

69. Winokur, G., Clayton, P.J., & Reich, T. (1969). *Manic-depressive illness*. St. Louis: Mosby.

70. Winokur, G., Reich, T., Rimmer, J., & Fitts, F.N., Jr. (1970). Alcoholism III Diagnosis and familial psychiatric illness in 259 alcoholic probands. *Archives of General Psychiatry. 23*, 104-111.

71. Winokur, G., Cadoret, R., Dorzel, J., & Baker, M. (1971). Depressive disease: A genetic study. *Archives of General Psychiatry. 24*, 135-144.

72. Woodruff, R.A., Guze, S.B., Clayton, P.J., & Carr, D. (1973). Alcoholism and depression. *Archives of General Psychiatry. 28*, 97-100.

Schizophrenia and Substance Abuse

George S. Layne, MD

I. INTRODUCTION

The patient with co-existent Schizophrenia and Substance Abuse Disorder represents the epitome of the Dual Diagnosis problem. Not only do the two forms of disability interact in specific ways that exacerbate each other, they are traditionally treated by schools of professionals with such widely divergent philosophies that patients with one problem are typically excluded from treatment by programs that specialize in the other. Thus the patients who need the best of both worlds get the least of each.

The tragedy that this represents to the individual patient is compounded by the effect on the community. While schizophrenia is relatively rare, affecting about 1% of the population, substance abuse among schizophrenic patients runs 50% or more in many studies. Also, since schizophrenia is essentially an incurable brain disease, patients in given areas tend to accumulate if not treated effectively. In years past, this accumulation occurred in state hospitals. This resulted in the paradox that a disease affecting 1% of the population typically filled more hospital beds than any other medical diagnosis, especially when younger age groups are considered. The advent of de-institutionalization led to the closing of many chronic beds and this population has become more and more visible. Community treatment programs have not been able to replace the caretaker function of the state hospital and substance abuse has increased as many schizophrenic patients have had to cope with their illness on their own.

George S. Layne is Assistant Clinical Professor of Psychiatry, Jefferson Medical College, Philadelphia, PA.

The picture is not hopeless, however. Recent studies by Kofoed, McBride, Hellerstein and others have shown that the schizophrenic substance abuser can be effectively treated and returned to a reasonable life. These studies are addressed later in this paper. The answer is the same wherever success has occurred. If the best principles of psychiatric care for schizophrenia can be combined with the classically effective programs for substance abuse, recovery from substance abuse and relief of psychotic symptoms can be accomplished. The goal of most recent writings in this field, and of this paper, is to encourage the development and enhancement of such interdisciplinary programs. This is not different from the situation with other psychiatric diagnoses combined with substance abuse. However, due to the higher degree of disability in schizophrenia, such combined programs are more critical to the care of the schizophrenic patient.

II. PREVALENCE OF COMBINED
SCHIZOPHRENIA AND SUBSTANCE ABUSE

Substance abuse is seen far more often by individuals treating schizophrenics than schizophrenia is seen by those in the substance abuse field. The reason for this has to do with the development of the community mental health systems which have traditionally treated all the mentally ill, regardless of complications. Substance abuse programs have tended to be based on treatment philosophies that excluded the most severely mentally ill patients. So, although the dual diagnosed schizophrenic patients may not have gotten definitive care for their substance abuse, they have generally crossed paths with the mental health system on a regular basis.

McClellan and Druley, (1977), studied Coatesville, PA. Veteran's Administration Hospital patients and found that of a randomly selected group of psychiatric inpatients, none of whom were in primary substance abuse treatment, 50% of 279 patients had a substance abuse problem. About 60% of the sample were schizophrenic.

Richardson, Craig and Haugland, (1985), studied 56 schizophrenic inpatients at the Rockland, New York Psychiatric Center, evaluating their treatment experiences over an average of a 5 year period from time of first treatment. This was a group of post-deinstitutionalization period chronic patients aged 19-44 (average 27). About 55% were substance abusers. Richardson argues that her methods underestimated the degree of substance abuse and quotes other studies of similar groups with rates as high as 74%.

It is difficult to document how frequently the substance abuse problems of the schizophrenic who is in treatment are not addressed adequately, but a good example was given by Alterman, (1980), who reported on schizophrenic patients hospitalized at the Coatesville VA Hospital in 1980. The charts of 1063 patients on *non-substance abuse* wards were reviewed. One hundred and one (9.5%) could be identified and categorized as schizophrenics with a secondary diagnosis of alcoholism. Of these 101 patients, 45% were identified as having become intoxicated while in the hospital. Two-thirds of the drinking patients were intoxicated 3 times weekly yet only 20% of the drinking group were receiving specialized treatment for their alcohol abuse problem.

The above studies are typical. The average schizophrenic patient seen in mental health clinics today probably drinks, smokes marijuana and is not having his/her substance abuse issues dealt with adequately.

III. SCHIZOPHRENIA

What is schizophrenia and what makes the patient with this illness different from any other substance abuser and significantly different, even, from other dual diagnosis patients? Schizophrenia is a brain disease. It is a hereditary illness caused by genetic events set in motion before birth. The schizophrenic patient suffers from an imbalance of the chemicals which cause electrical impulses to pass from nerve to nerve in critical parts of the brain.

The above definition is controversial. There are still psychiatrists who believe that schizophrenia is a psychological illness caused by environmental factors in childhood. There is even a very well known psychiatrist who has stated publicly in the New York Times that schizophrenia is not an illness at all, but akin to a problem of not learning to live well enough. According to this psychiatrist, just as one must learn to play tennis, one must learn to live, and this particular psychiatric professor believes that a "schizophrenic" street person who froze to death on the streets of New York simply hadn't learned well enough.

Such attitudes fly in the face of scientific evidence and I mention them here only because resistance to the psychiatric approach is one of the major impediments to good treatment for schizophrenic substance abusers. Certainly, life skills must be taught to such patients, as they must to any severely disabled person. But, schizophrenic patients can be differentiated from well people by chemicals in their spinal fluid, by the degree of premature atrophy of the brain shown by many on CAT scans and by the neurological "soft signs" found in a large percentage of cases. Fortunately, medications can help alleviate the symptoms of schizophrenia, but to use them properly, one must understand the underlying medical reality of the illness. Psychotherapy can help a schizophrenic person cope with his illness better, or help him abstain from substance use, but it cannot make the hallucinations stop. Treatment of the substance abusing schizophrenic requires an enlightened and liberal attitude toward psychiatric medication or the patient simply will not be there to treat.

Schizophrenia is characterized by symptoms which interfere with verbal forms of treatment to such a degree that they must be controlled before such treatment can begin. This differs from the depressed patient or the patient with a personality disorder who can participate in treatment without much change in his underlying mental state being required first. More than any other condition, schizophrenia attacks the ego, and it is the ego which is the part of the mind responsible for reasonable interpersonal transactions. The acute schizophrenic is in a state of ego dissolution. The result of this process is a series of changes in the patient's behavior and stated feelings which form the basis for diagnostic evaluation.

An oversimplified, but adequate description of schizophrenia may be based on Linn's 7 categories of psychiatric illness, (Linn, 1975). The schizophrenic may show significant symptoms in the area of affect, motor behavior, thinking, and perception. Consciousness is usually not affected. Memory and intelligence are at least impeded by other symptoms. The following is a list of Linn's categories as they apply to schizophrenia.

Affect (emotional feeling tone). The schizophrenic patient may show inappropriate affect where the expressed feeling is out of proportion or contrary to the actual events precipitating the affect. Affect is often described as flat in this illness, but in fact the schizophrenic can at different times show great degrees of affect, mood swings, depression, elation or panic.

Motor Behavior. Schizophrenic patients may show unusual movement responses to requests or suggestions. Catatonia, the classic sign of schizophrenia, is rarely seen except in severe, untreated cases.

What are seen, all too frequently, are the so called negative symptoms, which include lassitude, lack of motivation, inertia and difficulty following through on plans. While not strictly a motor problem, these are particularly troublesome problems since they do not respond as well to medications.

Thinking. Schizophrenia is said to be a thought disorder, since, with affect limited or inappropriate, and behavior not obviously related to reality, it is apparent that the schizophrenic is not thinking the same way as others. This occurs even when affect tone is not great, as opposed to the affectively disordered patient who may act strangely, but usually when obviously greatly disturbed or depressed.

The expressions of thought in schizophrenia are unusual and may indicate delusional ideas which may be quite bizarre. The thought process as indicated by speech may appear to be random with associations that do not make sense. The problem may appear to the outsider to be one of intact thought processes with a delusional idea at the core, or a more disturbed condition in which the processes themselves do not connect in any rational way.

Perception. Schizophrenia is characterized most specifically by disturbances in perception, usually hallucinations, defined as false sensory perceptions not associated with real external stimuli. These may be of any of the senses, but schizophrenics commonly have auditory hallucinations, often hearing voices when no one is speaking. Visual hallucinations are often seen in drug induced psychosis and olfactory hallucinations sometimes indicate brain tumors, but schizophrenics can have any type of hallucination.

The effect these symptoms have on the person suffering from them can be understood from the concept of ego functions. Freud spoke of reality testing, judgment, thinking, impulse control, and psychological defense as the work of the ego. The schizophrenic has profound difficulty in precisely these functions as can be imagined from the type of basic malfunctions of thinking and feeling noted above. Bellak, Hurvich and Gediman, (1973), in their classic work on Ego Functions in Schizophrenics, Neurotics and Normals, quantified these issues with the help of specific psychological tests. They found Schizophrenics to be significantly impaired in all of the 12 areas he tested including reality testing, judgment, impulse control and thinking. More importantly, they found neurotic subjects to be closer to normals than to schizophrenics. To some extent it is appropriate to characterize the neurotic subjects as more like the typical substance abuse patient. The difference between the typical SA patient and the schizophrenic then becomes very clear from Bellak's data.

Those who will quibble about the difference between the neurotic patients in Bellak et al.'s study and the typical personality disordered substance abuse patient may prefer to look at the problem from the point of view of psychological defenses. The schizophrenic, at least when untreated, suffers from ego regression which may be very severe and is characterized by the most primitive forms of defenses, including denial and projection which reach unbelievable degrees of concrete literalness. Denial of reality makes hallucinations possible while projection is the psycho-dynamic basis for paranoia. The regressed schizophrenic has great difficulty making abstract interpretations in conversations. When asked "what brought you to the hospital" the patient responds "a taxi." Pitifully this is neither a joke nor a hostile sarcastic response, but rather the natural response of a severely ego-impaired psychotic patient.

Johnson, (1984), has described the defenses seen under the regressive tendency of alcoholics in an inpatient rehabilitation setting. While he describes a severely impaired population, the denial he speaks of does not reach the level characterized by bizarre delusions and hallucinations which characterize schizophrenia. Furthermore, many of the defenses noted by Johnson, such as isolation, intellectualization, and rationalization through which the typical alcoholic manifests his regression are actually too mature to be available to the schizophrenic in the midst of an acute episode.

While I must mention that schizophrenia is a spectrum disorder and point out that there are milder cases than I describe to illustrate the illness, for the sake of the dual diagnosis issue, the more typical classic presentation should be kept in mind. In the individual case, a patient's strengths help him rise above the expectations presented by his illness, but programs must be based on the more usual cases. It should be clear that the schizophrenic patient represents a different sort of substance abuser, requiring a special approach.

The key to that approach is the use of medication. While an adequate anti-psychotic medication regimen will be listed later as part of every successful program, I raise the issue here since the need for medication is pivotal to understanding the schizophrenic patient. Since the medications needed are more mind-altering than those used in the other major psychiatric illnesses (depression and mania), resistance to their use may be more of a problem in the schizophrenic population treated in a substance abuse program.

Running counter to the classic AA philosophy requiring abstinence from all mind altering substances, the use of medication is a lifesaving measure for many schizophrenics. Since the discovery of the anti-psychotic effect of chlorpromazine in the 1950s the treatment of schizophrenia has moved from the arena of protective custody to one of community treatment and return to productive life.

While the effect of anti-psychotic medication is unfortunately not the same for all, most patients get tremendous relief of the more onerous disturbing symptoms. Delusional thinking and hallucinations, the so called "positive" symptoms, simply stop for many patients, and decrease significantly for many more. The "negative" symptoms, having to do with poor motivation and lack of energy, may not respond as well, and many schizophrenic patients have found relief from their voices, but seem to be still unable to find motivation to get on with their life. This is probably a specific ego deficit which takes the form of the patient remaining regressed and emotionally dependent on others to an inappropriate degree.

This may be as disabling as the "positive" signs, hallucinations and delusions. At any rate, the first step in treatment for the schizophrenic patient, substance abuser or not, is a good trial of antipsychotic medication.

IV. THE EFFECT OF SCHIZOPHRENIA IN THE SUBSTANCE ABUSE PROGRAM

Not all treatment programs are alike, but most successful programs share certain characteristics. These include an abstinence orientation which excludes medications, strict rules, strong focus on responsibility for one's own actions, and a social milieu approach (AA/NA/COA etc.). This is all mixed in a context of confrontation. One is confronted with one's addictive lifestyle and asked, with some degree of pressure, to change. Those who can, do. Those who can't, generally, are invited to try again some other time. Legal pressure may be used to help a person make an initial decision, but the kind of work needed in a typical substance abuse rehabilitation program does not come easily when one is in "to beat a rap."

The schizophrenic patient in need of substance abuse treatment challenges all the above ideas. A typical patient must be on medications, cannot tolerate abstinence in the face of truly terrifying delusions of persecution which may be dampened by alcohol, cannot organize his/her thinking well enough to comprehend the rules, may not be willing to come to treatment voluntarily because of fear and is phobic of large groups of people, making attendance at self help meetings impossible.

All too often, the result of this conflict is the invitation mentioned above, to continue one's treatment at a later time and a different place. But it need not be that way. Programs can be designed to be more flexible, and to understand that treatment of regression by support and gradual institution of responsibility does not have to represent enabling of addictive dependency. Such programs can help the schizophrenic substance abuser reach a stage of development where the traditional treatments will work. In other words, the initial reaching out and orientation to the program, may need to be drawn out and expectations relaxed. The patient will become trusting as he feels safe and substance abuse treatment can begin.

V. THE EFFECT OF SUBSTANCE ABUSE
ON SCHIZOPHRENIA

The question of what effect substance abuse has on the schizophrenic patient's illness is important for two reasons. The first is the problem of management of psychosis in a psychotic person taking a psychotogenic drug. When used to excess, all drugs of abuse have the potential of causing a psychotic reaction at some stage of use, either acute or chronic, or as a withdrawal effect. Obviously, then, these drugs, especially the psychotomimetic or hallucinogenic drugs will cause psychotic symptoms to worsen in schizophrenic patients. They also create diagnostic confusion, to be discussed later.

The second reason is the issue of drug of choice. Is there such a thing? Or is drug abuse such an individualized thing that there is nothing to be learned from drug of choice studies? There are, in fact, patterns, and it is valuable to look at this question, but the ultimate answer in each case must come from the individual patient.

A person uses drugs either because of a sought after direct effect (such as euphoria or excitement) or because of the drugs moderating effect on a pre-existing feeling. Abusers who use drugs to alleviate depression or to bring sleep after stimulant use are said to be "self-medicating." This is a hypothesis which neatly changes the focus on the user from one of "thrill seeker" who might be viewed with disdain, to that of "unfortunate victim," who simply didn't find help for the underlying problem. However, our wish to embrace the self-medication model is thwarted when we review drug of choice studies.

Is the patient choosing a drug for a recreational purpose? If so, abstinence is an issue of saying no to oneself, of avoiding a sought after but damaging experience. But if the patient is self-medicating dysphoria, abstinence may turn out to be a negative feeling state to be avoided. Another issue is peer pressure. If it is true, as suggested by Minkoff, (1988), that some young adult chronic patients use drugs because their peers do, to become one of the group or to gain an identity, then that use cannot be challenged without addressing the identity issue. Self help groups can be useful in this regard, but the issue is to determine just what the drug means to the patient.

Issues of self-medication and identity may be interesting side lights for an adult personality disordered alcoholic, but they are life itself to a 22-year-old schizophrenic.

Most drug of choice studies have focused on general issues in drug use patterns, or psychoanalytic considerations. However, I feel that since we are dealing with powerful drugs, with strong effects, the pharmacologic effects should be looked at first. These are the effects that will lead to psychological conditioning and true dependence.

Richardson et al. (1985), found that the Rockland substance abusing schizophrenics referred to earlier used a variety of drugs. Seventy-nine percent used marijuana, 36% "LSD," 29% stimulants, 14% used Cocaine. Heroin, "PCP" and barbiturates were each used by 11%. Fifty percent used alcohol and 38% used three or more substances. This is clearly a pattern of poly-substance abuse; a typical pattern in young schizophrenics who are engaged in drug choice for all the reasons mentioned above. Marijuana and alcohol are almost universally reported to be the primary drugs of abuse for schizophrenics, but this may simply be secondary to ease of obtaining the drug.

Schneir and Siris, (1987), looked at specific choices, reviewing 18 studies which reported drug of abuse choice in schizophrenia. The following discussion summarizes these studies and their clinical significance.

Stimulants. Schizophrenics are reported to use more amphetamines and cocaine than controls. (Controls may be other diagnoses or normals.) Why would a schizophrenic person use speed? To get high, of course, in the same way as any other young sensation seeking drug abuser. We know that prolonged amphetamine use can result in a toxic psychosis and we, therefore, must ask the following questions. Why would a psychotic person seek to be made more psychotic? Is the patient on medication? Is he taking a stimulant to counteract the sedation of chlorpromazine? Or is he depressed, with the depression being worse, for him, than the voices, which he may have gotten used to? If so, the euphoria of amphetamine may be worth worsening auditory hallucinations to the schizophrenic person on the street.

Marijuana. Schizophrenics are reported to use Cannabis more frequently than other diagnostic groups. Marijuana may have many different effects, from sedation to paranoia production. First ask "What does it do to you," then ask, "why do you want that to happen." The answers should be useful in treatment.

Hallucinogens. Here too, more use by schizophrenics was reported. Why does a schizophrenic want to cause more reality diffusion? Perhaps to gain control over the process, although the idea of a schizophrenic taking a street hallucinogen must also be seen as a self-destructive issue. Loss of control is often reported by non-psychotic people as what they fear most from "going crazy." The psychotic patient, horrified by the idea of psychotic symptoms he/she cannot control, may feel some relief from being able to worsen those symptoms by taking a drug. For other patients, the obvious risk of adding hallucinogenics to an underlying psychosis may in fact represent a self-destructive act, similar to cutting one's skin, or it may be a frankly suicidal act.

PCP. Phencyclidine causes psychotic states, and as with LSD, the diagnosis of schizophrenia made in the face of hallucinogen intoxication begs for more history. Young schizophrenics do take this drug, evidence that the schizophrenic symptoms may not be the primary issue when the choice to take the drug is made.

Alcohol. Surprisingly, in the studies reviewed by Schneir and Siris, (1987), schizophrenics were less likely to use alcohol than other psychiatric diagnostic groups. Of course, all diagnostic groups combined abuse alcohol at a higher rate than the general population and this is true for schizophrenics as well. Alcohol may function as an antidepressant (while the blood level is rising) or, more likely, as an anti-anxiety agent.

Opiates. The self-medication hypothesis would indicate heavy use here, since opiates are anti-psychotic and can mask schizophrenia. Yet schizophrenics are relatively lower in use of these drugs. There may be an underestimation of the prevalence of opiate use since opiate users might be underdiagnosed for schizophrenia.

The results of these studies are counterintuitive, if we look only at the self-medication model. A more open mind is necessary in assessing why each patient uses which drug. Schizophrenics whose positive symptoms are controllable with medication may choose stimulants to counteract the negative ones, or to counteract side effects of medication.

Millman, (1988), suggested that what alcohol, marijuana and stimulants have in common, is a psychological distancing effect. As problems are separated from here and now affect, existential dysphoria is dampened. What is clearly needed is a study of schizophrenic patients' reports of why they use the drugs they do, in the context of their subjective reports of their illness. Meanwhile, we must counsel our schizophrenic patients that all drugs and alcohol are known to exacerbate their symptoms.

VI. DIAGNOSTIC ISSUES

The key to treatment of schizophrenia with or without substance abuse complications is diagnosis. This is not a clear cut issue. In the young adult age group, for example, there are three conditions which commonly cause the psychotic ego disruption under discussion here. Schizophrenia is one, of course. Bipolar affective disorder, or manic-depressive illness is another. Third is substance abuse. If substance abuse is so prevalent in this age group, and if Bipolar disorder is as prevalent as schizophrenia, how can we make the diagnosis? The answer is, slowly and carefully.

Bipolar illness is characterized, classically, by alternating cycles of euphoria and depression. Either can be psychotic in degree. Euphoria or mania, in particular, can look exactly like agitated schizophrenia. The diagnosis can be made by taking a look at the long term history, or by following the patient for several months to see how he/she functions. A return to complete normality suggests Bipolar illness. Schizophrenia tends to have a steady, if slow, down hill course throughout life, at least through ages 20-40. But in the absence of history, looking at a single slice of time, with the patient agitated, illogical, hallucinating and with paranoid delusions,, how can one differentiate schizophrenia from Bipolar illness? It is nearly impossible. Many clinicians think they can and many patients get the wrong diagnosis.

The answer is to be sure that the patient and his family know that the diagnosis isn't clear, so that proper follow-up can be done. This is an important point since the treatment for both illnesses is the same for the acute episode (major tranquilizer type anti-psychotic medication). For long-term treatment, however, lithium is the drug of choice for Bipolar illness and the proper diagnosis can save a young person from a lifetime of trouble with the side effects of major tranquilizers.

If psychotogenic drugs are known to be in the patient's blood or urine, or suspected in the recent past, and there is no prior history of psychosis when drug free, a diagnosis of schizophrenia or one of bipolar illness should not be made. Alcohol can cause hallucinations in extreme intoxication and withdrawal. Schuckit, (1983), warns that one should wait before making a diagnosis of primary psychotic illness in the face of intoxication.

Alcoholic hallucinosis was often confused with schizophrenia in the past with rates reported as high as 30% for schizophrenia in alcoholic populations. This in turn led to the suggestion that schizophrenia and alcoholism were genetically related. Numerous studies have since proven this wrong, including a study of fraternal and identical twins with schizophrenia by Kendler, (1985).

Stimulants can cause psychosis and amphetamine psychosis is perhaps the closest simulator of schizophrenia we know. LSD and PCP cause a psychotic state as their acute effect. Marijuana can cause paranoia and acute psychosis in vulnerable people. It isn't known whether those who become psychotic with cannabis are schizophrenic to begin with, or suffering from a peculiar ego weakness which makes them vulnerable. Andreason, (1987), studied military conscripts in Sweden and suggests a causative effect of marijuana for schizophrenia, but this is controversial.

Schizophrenia, in its classic form, at present, cannot be cured. It may wax and wane, but it generally follows a downhill course. The intoxicated psychotic person should be treated symptomatically, and monitored closely. If after two weeks of abstinence, psychotic symptoms are still severe, schizophrenia is likely. After 4 weeks, the diagnosis is virtually certain. If anti-psychotic medication was used, it should be gradually decreased and stopped after a month.

A return of psychosis suggests schizophrenia. Long term use of street drugs may lead to an organic brain syndrome from a number of possible causes, and, of course, alcohol can cause psychosis from chronic abuse, but permanent psychosis caused solely by substance abuse is rare. Schizophrenia exacerbated by drug use is relatively common. Persistent psychotic symptoms several weeks after drug use calls for in depth re-examination of history and the diagnosis should then be made as if substance abuse was not an issue.

VII. TREATMENT

The treatment of the substance abusing schizophrenic patient is nothing strange or new. It is rather a return to an old idea, the idea that if a patient has two illnesses, treat him or her for both and they'll both get better. For a number of reasons, mostly political, the treatment of psychiatric illness and substance abuse became separated, performed by different people in different institutions. The problems of the schizophrenic substance abuser are so severe that intensive treatment on both fronts is needed from the beginning. Separate programs cannot provide the intensity of psychiatric and substance abuse work needed. Therefore, we need to make the political compromises necessary to bring the two treatment sides together.

Schizophrenia is not an impossible problem for the psychiatrist to treat. Neither is substance abuse for the traditional programs. A combination of the successful elements of both programs can result in an appropriate treatment program for the substance abusing schizophrenic. In the final section I will close with three examples of programs which claim some success in the field. These programs were developed separately in different institutions, but share a number of programmatic similarities, most notably the interdisciplinary approach.

Kofoed, (1986) summarized the controversies which contribute to treatment problems for schizophrenic substance abusers. The list came out of work setting up a dual diagnosis outpatient program in Oregon.

1. Causal relationships between drugs and severe mental illness are not clear. We don't know, often, whether mental illness is the cause or the result of substance abuse.
2. Diagnosis is complicated and difficult.
3. Appropriateness of sequential approach to treatment is not

clear and the choice of sequence is often arbitrary. The patient in need of psychiatric and substance abuse treatment can get lost as the treating professionals argue about which treatment should be done first.

4. There is little data about concurrent treatment programs.
5. Use of medication is controversial outside of psychiatry.
6. Use of disulfiram is controversial even within psychiatry.
7. Timing and degree of abstinence enforcement is not clear once absolute standard is departed from. It is easy to say "all drugs are bad and should be avoided." If we break this rule to allow some drugs; i.e., the "good" ones the psychiatrist prescribes, there is no clear consensus about where to draw the new line.
8. Some programs exclude the "other side" by definition.

Dr. McBride, (1988), whose experience is with the MICA (Mentally Ill Substance Abuser) program in Jersey, has worked with Alcoholics Anonymous to increase tolerance of the special needs of the mentally ill substance abusers. This work begins with MICA AA meetings on the hospital grounds. Additionally there are meetings around the state facilitated by recovering mental health workers. These psychiatrically oriented AA meetings are known as "Double Trouble" meetings.

AA tradition leads to problems for schizophrenic substance abusers for at least two reasons. First, the abstinence approach is often taken so literally that the use of medically necessary anti-psychotic medications is not supported. Thus, if the patient is to make a successful entry into the AA system, it may have to be at the expense of medication. This leads, predictably to relapse in both psychosis and substance abuse. Secondly, many AA members fear the stigmatization of mental illness in society and tend to shun psychiatric patients and programs to avoid being characterized as mentally ill.

These problems can be overcome by using educational methods of overcoming psychiatric stigma. The approach is aimed at the local AA organization leading to a self-help support system that welcomes the newly abstinent schizophrenic.

VIII. SAMPLE PROGRAMS FOR THE TREATMENT OF SCHIZOPHRENIC SUBSTANCE ABUSERS

1. The Beth Israel, New York City Program

Hellerstein and Meehan, (1987), presented the Beth Israel program in New York City in 1987. They showed that an outpatient group therapy program designed for schizophrenic substance abusers could decrease days of hospitalization. Beginning in 1984, they made their first goal keeping the patient in treatment. Traditional expectations of psychiatric and SA programs were relaxed. Compliance with medication regimens and abstinence from illicit drugs and alcohol were goals to work on, not conditions for participation. Initial steps were:

1. Engagement of the patient in the group process by identification and sharing of mutual problems, especially those involving psychosis and substance abuse.
2. Interpersonal skill development, to help the patients be better able to utilize the group process for their own benefit.
3. Problem solving. At this point patients were helped to work on family, housing and work issues.
4. Education about medication and addictions issues.
5. AA/NA encouraged.

For those patients able to make a minimal commitment to abstinence, the program worked. Those who had organic impairment and those who came to group intoxicated did poorly. For the 10 patients who started the program, hospital days decreased from 25/year to 8/year. This included the dropouts.

2. The New Jersey "Mentally Ill Chemical Abuser" Program

Dr. Herbert McBride, (1988) has presented the MICA program, describing an approach to treating the schizophrenic substance abuser adopted by the state of New Jersey. MICA (Mentally Ill Chemical Abuser) was organized to help cut red tape in the treatment of the 50% of admissions to state hospitals which were substance abuse related. MICA provides for the mixing of traditionally separate treatment programs. The program works at the state level by mandating closer ties between drug treatment and mental health treatment bureaucracies. Patients who are identified as meeting the need for intensive services from both sectors are treated in special MICA units in the state hospitals. These become, essentially, substance abuse units for schizophrenics. The essentials of Dr. McBride's MICA unit at Marlboro State Hospital are as follows:

1. Intensive 12 step program
2. Peer oriented milieu
3. Medication for psychosis
4. Mental health oriented group therapy
5. Peer oriented behavior modification program
6. Vocational rehabilitation program
7. Support groups for families
8. MICA oriented half-way houses.

3. The Oregon "Psychiatrically Impaired Substance Abuser" Program

MICA's counterpart on the West Coast is PISA (Psychiatrically Impaired Substance Abuser), the program reported by Kofoed, Kania, Walsh and Atkinson, (1986) in Oregon.

The PISA program follows:

A. Initial focus on symptom control, abstinence and psychiatric medication. This includes psychiatric or detox inpatient stay if needed.
B. Outpatient program begins with assessment group which provides orientation and education into dual diagnosis issues. This can begin in the inpatient setting. This initial group experience helped define the patients roles and was felt to aid retention in the program.
C. Once psychiatrically stable, AA and un-monitored disulfiram use are begun.
D. Goals developed for ongoing treatment. If patient makes commitment to program, enters ongoing treatment group.
F. Treatment group meets weekly.

G. Medications are continued. Compliance is monitored with blood and urine tests and breathalyzer for disulfiram.
H. Abstinence monitored by urine drug screens and breathalyzer.
I. AA continues.
J. As needed, individual psychotherapy, family therapy, day treatment, etc.

The PISA program started out with 32 patients, 16 of whom were schizophrenic. Of these 32, 8 lasted 11 or more months in the program. Five of these 8 were schizophrenic. The non-schizophrenic patients suffered from other psychiatric illnesses in addition to various forms of substance abuse. Thus the schizophrenic patients were retained longer in this program compared to their non-schizophrenic peers.

Kofoed pointed out that previous outpatient treatment was associated with retention in this program, even without prior abstinence. Also, no psychosis due to disulfiram therapy was noted, probably due to use of anti-psychotic medications.

IX. SUMMARY

A composite program, based on the literature and personal experience could embody these features:

1. *Early Engagement.* The schizophrenic substance abuser should be identified and involved in an active treatment program as early as possible. Psychiatric inpatients and detoxification patients should be approached by the outpatient program during the inpatient stay.
2. *Peer Oriented Therapy Program.* Group therapy, behavior modification programs and milieu therapy should use peer pressure and identification with recovering peers.
3. *Life Skill Rehabilitation.* It is hard to learn how to get along in society while suffering from delusions. The time in the program while medicated may represent a rare symptom free period for some patients, and the opportunity should be taken to do some effective life skill training. The education process should include medical and addiction issues as well.
4. *Self Help Groups.* Alcoholics Anonymous and Narcotics

Anonymous networks serve many purposes. The schizophrenic patient needs substance free role models. Furthermore, some substance abuse may represent socialization — self-help groups provide a healthy alternative. The 12-step programs lend needed structure to the patient's life.

5. *Abstinence Orientation*. Substance abuse patients who must take psychoactive medication should be encouraged to see the difference between taking appropriately prescribed anti-psychotic medication and street drug use. Medications do not represent a relaxation of the goal of abstinence. The medicated patient who remains free of illicit drugs and alcohol should be appreciated as abstinent.

6. *Family Involvement*. Family therapy is powerful treatment for many things. Family issues are always present, even if the family isn't. Family work can range from having the patient ventilate hostile feelings about a parent to having networks of dozens of people to help motivate a dispirited patient.

7. *Psychiatric Involvement*. The psychiatrist should be an active, ongoing member of the treatment team. Appropriate psychotropic medication is discussed at all levels and used matter of factly.

8. *1:1 Psychotherapy*. Whether supportive, psychodynamic or behavioral, the 1:1 relationship is important throughout the treatment process. Some of this role is assumed by the AA/NA sponsor.

X. CONCLUSION

Schizophrenic substance abusers are among the most difficult patients to treat for either of their two diagnoses. The nature of schizophrenia makes relaxation of usual substance abuse rules necessary to keep patients in treatment. Application of the usual program techniques for substance abuse treatment can work for schizophrenics. For this to occur, the work must be combined with knowledge of the ego limitations of the patients. Close interdisciplinary cooperation with appropriate psychiatric support with anti-psychotic medications provides a treatment program which has been proven to work.

REFERENCES

1. Alterman, A.I., Erdlen, F.R., McLellan, A.T. & Mann, S.C. (1980) Problem Drinking in Hospitalized Schizophrenic Patients, *Addictive Behaviors*, 5, 273-276.

2. Andreasson, S., Allebeck, P., Engstrom, A. & Rydberg, U. (1987) Cannabis and Schizophrenia. A Longitudinal Study of Swedish Conscripts, *The Lancet*, Dec. 26, 1987, 1483-1486.

3. Belak, L., Hurvich, M. & Gediman, H.K. (1973) *Ego Functions in Schizophrenics, Neurotics and Normals*. New York: John Wiley and Sons, 328-329.

4. Hellerstein, D.J. & Meehan, B. (1987) Outpatient Group Therapy for Schizophrenic Substance Abusers, *American Journal of Psychiatry*, 144, 1337-1339.

5. Johnson, R. (1984) Ego Deficits in the Personality of the Alcoholic, *The Psychiatric Hospital*, 15, 37-40.

6. Kendler, K.S. (1985) A Twin Study of Individuals with Both Schizophrenia and Alcoholism, *British Journal of Psychiatry*, 147, 48-53.

7. Kofoed, L., Kania, J., Walsh, T. & Atkinson, R.M. (1986) Outpatient Treatment of Patients with Substance Abuse and Coexisting Psychiatric Disorders, *American Journal of Psychiatry*, 143, 867-872.

8. Linn, L. (1975) *Comprehensive Textbook of Psychiatry*. Freedman, A.M., Kaplan, H.I. & Sadock, B.J., eds., Baltimore: Williams & Wilkins, 822-824.

9. McBride, H. (1988) Psychiatric Disorders in Substance Abuse. Pragmatic Treatment. *American Academy of Psychiatrists in Alcoholism and Addictions, Annual Meeting*.

10. McLellan, A.T. & Druley, K.A. (1977) Non-random Relation Between Drugs of Abuse and Psychiatric Diagnosis, *Journal of Psychiatric Research*, 13, 179-184.

11. Millman, R.B. (1988) The Abuse of Marijuana and Psychedelics by Psychiatric Patients. *American Academy of Psychiatrists in Alcoholism and Addictions, Annual Meeting*.

12. Minkoff, K.M. (1988) Dual Diagnosis of Psychosis and Addiction. *American Psychiatric Association, Annual Meeting, Course 46*.

13. Richardson, M.A., Craig, T.J. & Haugland, G. (1985) Treatment Patterns of Young Chronic Schizophrenic Patients in the Era of Deinstitutionalization, *Psychiatric Quarterly*, 57, 2, 104-110.

14. Schneir, F.R. & Siris, S.G. (1987) A Review of Psychoactive Substance Use and Abuse in Schizophrenia, *Journal of Nervous and Mental Disease*, 175, 641-652.

15. Schuckit, M.A. (1983) Alcoholism and Other Psychiatric Disorders, *Hospital and Community Psychiatry*, 34, 1022-1027.

Substance Abuse
and Personality Disorder

Edgar P. Nace, MD

Suffering produces endurance, and endurance produces character, and character produces hope, and hope does not disappoint us.

Romans 5:3-5 (RSV)

Each of us is known not only by his or her physical features, occupation, and family background, but especially by what is called personality. Personality is "the ingrained pattern of behavior that each person evolves, both consciously and unconsciously, as the style of life or way of being in adapting to the environment" (APA, 1984).

Personality is a display, however expansive or muted, of our characteristic ways of thinking, feeling and behaving. In common parlance one is known as quiet, shy, bold, reliable, honest, dramatic, serious, good-natured, and so on. Embedded in such descriptions are the patterns, the attitudes, and behaviors that characterize one as an individual across the widest variety of social and interpersonal settings. Such enduring patterns are personality traits. These traits are the apparent and outward manifestation of how we characteristically perceive, think about, and relate to others and to ourselves, and hence, make up our "personality." Personality traits influence, much as do our physical features, how others respond to us, the quality of our relationships, and, ultimately, how we feel about ourselves.

Edgar P. Nace is Chief of Service, Substance Abuse Programs and Director, Health Professionals Program, Timberlawn Psychiatric Hospital, Dallas, TX.

183

If personality traits become inflexible, maladaptive and cause subjective distress or functional impairment, a disorder of personality is considered to exist (APA 1987). Personality disorders are evident by adolescence or early adult life. The disorder continues over the adult life span, but may modify in mid to late adulthood. A salient characteristic of personality disorders is that the traits are "ego-syntonic"; that is, not considered undesirable by the individual. The response of others to such traits is, however, distressing to the individual with a personality disorder. In some cases the traits are experienced as "ego-dystonic" (i.e., not desirable) for the affected person, but changing the troublesome behaviors is difficult.

The American Psychiatric Association (APA 1987) recognizes eleven distinct personality disorders. These can be grouped into three clusters based on predominant features.

Cluster A: This group is characterized by odd and eccentric traits and includes paranoid, schizoid, and schizotypal personality disorders. These disorders may predispose the individual to psychiatric conditions such as delusional disorder or schizophrenia.

Cluster B: This group of disorders is characterized by behavior which is erratic, emotional, or dramatic. Antisocial, borderline, narcissistic, and histrionic personality disorders fall within this category. This cluster of personality disorders has the strongest association with substance use disorders.

Cluster C: This group of disorders is characterized by traits of fear and anxiety and includes avoidant, obsessive-compulsive, dependent, and passive-aggressive personality disorders. Substance use disorders commonly occur in this group but not as frequently as with Cluster B.

An individual may have more than one personality disorder. There is a diagnosis of "personality disorder not otherwise specified" for cases that have features of several personality disorders but do not meet criteria for any one disorder.

A description of each personality disorder is beyond the scope of this chapter and can be found in the *Diagnostic and Statistical Manual of Mental Disorders Third Edition-Revised* (DSM-III-R) published by the American Psychiatric Association.

SUBSTANCE USE DISORDERS AND PERSONALITY DISORDERS: COMORBIDITY

A strong association between personality disorders and substance use disorders has been well-documented in recent studies. The strongest relationship between substance use disorders is with anti-social personality disorder (ASPD). The Epidemiologic Catchment Area (ECA) study is providing data collected in over 20,000 interviews at five different sites in the United States on the comorbidity of alcohol abuse/dependence and drug abuse/dependence with other psychiatric disorders (Reiger, Myers, Kramer et al., 1984). Data on the co-occurrence of ASPD with alcoholism from the ECA study has been reported by Helzer and Pryzbeck (1988). ASPD was found in 15% of alcoholic men. In contrast, non-alcoholic men had a lifetime prevalence of ASPD of 4%. For women the comparable prevalence rates of ASPD were 10% (alcoholic women) and 0.81% (non-alcoholic women). Thus, the alcoholic male is nearly four times more likely to have ASPD than the nonalcoholic male and ASPD in alcoholic women is 12 times more common than in nonalcoholic women.

Further documentation of the increased prevalence of personality disorder in substance abusers is provided by Drake and Vaillant (1985). In a longitudinally followed sample of men, 23% met criteria for an Axis II Diagnosis of personality disorder by age 47. Of the alcoholic men in this sample, 37% appeared to have a personality disorder. This nonclinical sample also provides some information as to which personality disorders may be more common in the substance-abusing population. For example, all the men with ASPD were also alcoholic, whereas alcoholism was rare in the schizotypal personality disorder.

The association between personality disorder and substance use disorder is even stronger when clinical samples are studied.

A Canadian study of 96 abstinent alcoholics found a high incidence of avoidant personality disorder. Using DSM-III criteria, 35% of the sample met criteria for avoidant personality disorder. Alcohol abuse was considered a consequence of this disorder in a majority of cases (Stravynski, Lamontagne, and Yvon, 1986). Koenigsberg, Kaplan, Gilmore, and Cooper's (1985), review of over 2,400 patients found 36% had personality disorders. Patients with a substance use disorder were more likely than other psychiatric patients to have a personality disorder; e.g., 46% of alcoholics and 61% of nonalcoholic/drug abusers had a personality disorder. In this study, the most frequent personality disorders among the substance use disorders were borderline (43%), antisocial (21%), and mixed (17%).

In a study of nearly 100 alcoholic patients admitted to an inpatient substance abuse unit, 13% were found to have a diagnosis of borderline personality disorder when evaluated by a standardized rating instrument using conservative criteria (Nace, Saxon, and Shore, 1983).

When patients are admitted to psychiatric services there is a consistent relationship found between psychiatric diagnosis and degree of substance abuse. The highest levels of substance abuse are associated with patients having severe character pathology (i.e., personality disorder) in contrast to patients who present with schizophrenia or other psychoses where the degree of substance abuse is less (Crowley, Chesluk, Dilts et al., 1974; Ritzler, Strauss, Vanord et al., 1977; Croughan, Miller, Matar et al., 1982; Ghen and Klein, 1970).

The personality disorder most commonly reported in substance abusing patients is ASPD. Hesselbrock, Meyer, and Keener (1985), found ASPD to be the most common additional diagnosis in a hospitalized sample of over 200 male alcoholics. Forty-nine percent of these men met DSM-III criteria for ASPD. Of the 90 alcoholic women in the study, 20% met criteria for ASPD.

Rounsaville, Eyre, Weissman, and Kleber (1983), diagnosed primary ASPD in 27% of opiate addicts and secondary ASPD in another 27% of patients.

In a study of 133 narcotic addicts, 65% met Axis II criteria for a personality disorder (Khantzian and Treece 1985). Again, ASPD was the most commonly diagnosed personality disorder and accounted for nearly one-half of the personality disorder diagnoses.

Antisocial personality disorder should not be thought to be the only personality disorder associated with substance use disorders. In fact the relative proportion of ASPD in the substance-abusing population awaits further results from studies such as the ECA study. In a recent study (Helzer and Pryzbeck, 1988), 15 percent of alcoholic men and 10 percent of alcoholic women had ASPD. We do not know as yet from such general population studies how many would have borderline personality disorder, avoidant personality disorder, etc.

Borderline is most likely the second most common personality disorder found in substance-abusing samples. It has been reported in 43%, (Koenigsberg et al., 1985) 28% (Johnson and Connelly, 1981), 13% (Nace, Saxon, and Shore, 1983), and 6% (Khantzian and Treece, 1985), of samples. The procedures for diagnosing personality disorders in clinical studies vary considerably, but it would seem safe to assume from the clinical studies now available that within the substance-abusing population the prevalence of personality disorder is at least 50%. As standardized interviews are used (e.g., the ECA study Reiger, Myers and Kramer et al., 1984), the accuracy of prevalence studies will improve. In the meantime, we can summarize our current understanding by recognizing a strong association between substance use disorders and personality disorders. This association is strongest for Cluster B of DSM-III-R, in particular ASPD and borderline personality disorders.

PERSONALITY DISORDER SECONDARY TO SUBSTANCE ABUSE

Our discussion up to this point has implied that in those cases where personality disorder and substance abuse coexist the personality disorder would have preceded the substance abuse disorder. This is a logical conclusion since features of personality disorder are usually evident by mid to late adolescence and may therefore precede a syndrome of psychoactive substance dependence. Behavioral disturbances of childhood such as attention-deficit hyperactivity syndrome and conduct disorder are precursors to both the development of substance abuse and personality disorder. Conduct disorder often precedes ASPD (McCord and McCord 1982), and attention-deficit hyperactivity disorder increases the probability of a future substance use disorder (Tarter, Alterman, and Edwards 1985).

At this juncture the reverse situation should be considered—that substance abuse may produce a syndrome diagnostically compatible with the personality disorders. No specific personality disorder as described in DSM-III-R is necessarily found, but rather a constellation of traits which are largely generic to most personality disorders. Diagnostically, the terms "personality disorder not otherwise specified" or "organic personality disorder" may apply.

Etiologically, intoxicating substances produce a combination of toxic-organic effects on brain function and reinforcement of regressive behavior. This combination may result in a "generic" personality disorder which is secondary, not primary, to alcoholism and drug dependence. This point has recently been documented in a community sample of men longitudinally followed ". . . in terms of the childhood variables of boyhood competence, adolescent IQ, environmental weaknesses, and emotional problems, alcoholic men with personality disorders appeared quite similar to men without personality disorders" (Drake and Vaillant 1985). That is, nonalcoholic men with personality disorders in contrast to the alcoholics with personality disorders were more impaired on the childhood variables mentioned above. Thus, the chronic effects of alcohol must be considered as relevant to what eventually appears as a personality disorder. Bean-Bayog (1986) has emphasized the importance of alcoholism as a trauma; a trauma capable of impacting character structure similar to the effects observed following natural disasters or catastrophic human experiences. The components of the "alcoholism trauma" include loss of control over drinking, blackouts, damage to health, stigma, losses, impaired problem solving skills, and assaults on self-esteem and personal integrity. Like victims of other types of trauma, the alcoholic may respond with pathological defenses including projection and denial. The regression to such defenses will enable continued use of alcohol.

We can appreciate that the pharmacologic effects of alcohol and drugs induce personality regression with a weakening of ego functions. The highly reinforcing properties of alcohol or drugs yield immediate gratification which, in turn, fosters regressive behaviors. This relationship is illustrated in Figure 1. (Nace, 1987) The consequence of this sequence is a composite picture of the "addicted personality," i.e., the effect of chronic use of drugs or alcohol on

PHARMACOLOGIC EFFECT OF INTOXICATING SUBSTANCES

- Rapid

- Predictable

- Pleasurable

Immediate gratification with little behavior output

Regressed Ego State

- Impulsivity

- Decreased frustration tolerance

- Self-centeredness

- Grandiosity

- Passivity

- Affect intolerance

FIGURE 1

personality functioning. The resultant traits are commonly described clinically as follows:

—*Impulsivity*—cannot delay gratification; stimulus bound
—*Decreased frustration tolerance*—impatient; overreacts to situations; inconsistent.
—*Self-centeredness*—stubborn and defiant; lacking empathy
—*Grandiosity*—either overvalues or undervalues self; sees things in either/or rather than shades of gray; can't compromise; perfectionism; sees self as unique.
—*Passivity-withdrawn*; isolated; feeling of helplessness; "mentally lazy:" avoids self revelation.
—*Affect Intolerance*—difficulty in recognizing feelings; fear of feelings; decreased ability to endure or regulate painful emotional states.

By the same token, such traits may predate substance abuse and serve as the components of a "generic" personality disorder or "personality disorder not otherwise specified" (Lion, 1974). We have then the possibility of an interaction between a pre-existing personality disorder (of either the generic type or, more specifically, from the Axis II classification) and the regressive effects of chronic substance abuse. This interaction is diagrammed in Figure 2. To summarize, Figure 2 illustrates that a personality disorder increases the individual's vulnerability to substance abuse which is represented in the right half of the circle: Personality disorder → Abuse of Alcohol/Drugs. Secondly, substance abuse leads to a regressive syndrome clinically similar to personality disorder. The latter sequence is illustrated by the left half of the circle: Abuse of Alcohol/Drugs → Personality disorder, Nace, (1987).

WHY PERSONALITY DISORDER PREDISPOSES TO SUBSTANCE ABUSE

When we consider personality disorders in a generic sense two broad areas of dysfunction stand out: Regulation of behavior and tolerance of affect (Khantzian 1981). Defects in behavior regulation include poor impulse control, recklessness, and a failure to anticipate consequences. When these features are dominant, drug experimentation can be expected. Realistic concern about consequences will not be apparent; the inability to delay gratification will compromise efforts to resist; and self-centeredness and lack of empathy will serve as blinders to effects of substance abuse on others.

The second major area of dysfunction concerns affect. The abil-

INTERACTION OF PERSONALITY DISORDER AND SUBSTANCE ABUSE

(Need for rapid predictable gratification)

Regression

Reinforcement of

immature traits

provided by

Alcohol or Drug Abuse

FIGURE 2

ity to recognize, regulate, and tolerate emotions is often limited. Rather than experience discrete focused feelings, which serve as indicators of well-being and sources of initiative, a vague state of dysphoria is often present (Wurmser 1974). The euphoric or stimulating properties of drugs will alter this vague state of discomfort and provide an affective focus. For many patients with a moderate to severe personality disorder, a well-defined affect, pharmacologically induced, is preferable to their more usual state of discomfort. A young woman with borderline personality disorder had experienced mild to moderate anxiety when intoxicated with marijuana. When asked why she continued to use marijuana she explained that the induced anxiety made her more cautious and less likely to act out in an impulsive manner. Her experience illustrates a deficit in the recognition of signal anxiety which was compensated by cannabis intoxication. The case also illustrates that substance abuse in the personality disordered patient is not exclusively hedonistic.

The defects in regulation and tolerance of affect may be briefly "corrected" by drugs through the ability of the drug to provide a defense against emotions or repair deficiencies in ego functions.

The function of defense is provided by the ability of a drug to counter threatening feelings or feelings which are intolerable. According to Wurmser (1974) "the importance of the drug effect in the inner life of patients can perhaps be best explained as an artificial or surrogate defense against overwhelming affects" (p.127). Examples of the defensive function of drugs are provided by Khantzian (1985). The cocaine-dependent individual may be self-medicating against chronic depression or residual attention deficit disorder. The opiate-dependent patient finds relief in the antiaggression and antirage actions of opiates.

The function of repair refers to the enhancement of well being and functioning which the drug effect provides. A reduction in distress occurs which the individual has not been able to find through his or her own mental or behavioral efforts. Wieder and Kaplan (1969), consider drug use to serve a "corrective" or "prosthetic" function. Along the same lines, Khantzian describes the role of cocaine as replacing boredom and emptiness with feelings of self-sufficiency (Khantzian, 1985).

It is apparent that the subjective effect of drugs, particularly the change in affect, ranges from the relatively simple brief period of euphoria; through escape from or "self-medication" for painful feelings; to intrapsychic functions analogous to mental defenses and ego enhancement (repair). These effects occur across the broad spectrum of intoxicating substances and any one person may utilize a variety of drugs for essentially the same result. On the other hand, many drug users will have found one drug or have narrowed their choices to specific drugs for specific effects.

To conclude, the individual with a personality disorder is at increased risk for a substance use disorder. The characteristic impulsivity and poor ability to anticipate consequences promotes drug-taking as well as other high risk behaviors. Secondly, the patient with a personality disorder often finds within the pharmacologically induced effects of intoxicating substances "benefits" beyond those experienced by the better integrated personality. The drug effect is more reinforcing because it serves more functions; the drug accomplishes more, meets diverse needs; and, therefore, increases the potential for compulsive use.

PERSONALITY DISORDER COMPLICATES THE COURSE OF A SUBSTANCE USE DISORDER

The course of a substance use disorder will be impacted by the presence of a personality disorder. The onset of substance abuse is likely to occur at an earlier age in the patient with a personality disorder. Earlier age of onset when a substance use disorder and a personality disorder are combined has been documented across a wide variety of samples. It is especially likely in patients with ASPD or borderline personality disorder (Nace, Saxon, and Shore 1983; Hesselbrock, Meyer and Keener 1985; Schuckit 1985; Stabenau 1984; Cadoret, Troughton and Widmer 1984).

A second complication is the increased likelihood of polydrug use. Although we are discussing substance abusing patients, those with a personality disorder will show greater severity of substance abuse and a more varied pattern (polydrug abuse). Borderline alcoholics show a more extensive history of drug abuse prior to treatment than nonborderline alcoholics and a greater tendency to relapse to drug abuse following treatment (Nace, Saxon, and Shore, 1986). Within a large sample of narcotic addicts polydrug use was significantly greater in patients with a personality disorder and the addicts with a personality disorder were also using greater amounts of narcotics (Khantzian and Treece, 1985).

A third complicating factor is the increased possibility of additional psychiatric symptoms in the personality disordered substance abusing patient. In a study of narcotic addicts depression and personality disorder were found in the same subjects with a high degree of frequency (Khantzian and Treece, 1985). In a follow-up study of opiate addicts a decrease in psychiatric symptoms was noted for nearly one-half the subjects (Rounsaville, Kosten and Kleber, 1986). However, those addicts with a concurrent personality disorder were most likely to have a recurrence or development of symptoms over the two and one-half years follow-up. Other studies have documented that alcoholics with a personality disorder are more likely to have symptoms of anxiety, depression, mania, and schizophrenia or show features of somatization disorder and chronic depression (Cadoret, Troughton, and Widmer 1984).

Although less well-documented, indications are that substance abusing patients with concurrent personality disorders make more suicide attempts (Nace, Saxon, and Shore 1983), have a poorer prognosis, and are more frequently lost to follow-up (Woody, McLellan, Luborsky et al., 1985).

TREATMENT OF SUBSTANCE ABUSE: IMPACT ON PERSONALITY DISORDERS

There are various approaches to the treatment of personality disorders with most falling either into the category that emphasizes an improvement in adaptation or into the category that attempts structural intrapsychic change using modified psychoanalytic psychotherapy (Gordon and Beresin, 1983). In either case change is usually slow to occur, and persistence and patience are required of the therapist and treatment team.

Fortunately, patients with a combined substance use disorder and personality disorder whose treatment is focused on substance abuse will simultaneously undergo a modification of character pathology. That is, as we utilize the therapeutic approach available for the treatment of alcoholism and other substance use disorders (Nace 1987) and combine these with participation in 12-step programs we are, in part and perhaps inadvertently, treating the personality disorder as well. This will be apparent as we briefly examine both rehabilitation and 12-step programs.

Consider the process of recovery as it is initiated in a rehabilitation program: The environment of a rehabilitation program is usually highly structured. Time is ordered, activities tightly scheduled and behavior regulated by rules and regulations. Setting limits is a constant feature of such programs: Limits in terms of use of alcohol or drugs (none); limited visiting; relatively little use of medications; and prohibitions against acting out. A reality orientation is emphasized that stresses coping and deemphasizes and discourages regressive behaviors. These functions — structure, limit setting, and emphasis on adaptation (rather than regression) — serve to shore up and strengthen ego functions. Self-care skills such as the ability to anticipate consequences of behavior and to curb impulses will be reinforced in such an environment.

Emphasis on recognition of feelings and tolerance of feelings — rather than avoidance of painful affect through use of alcohol, drugs, or acting-out — serves an integrating process essential to self-control. The emphasis on abstinence provides a paradigm for therapeutic issues beyond avoidance of alcohol and other drugs. Abstinence will depend on the development of frustration tolerance, patience, impulse control, and an ability to regulate affect. All of the above are major issues in the treatment of character pathology. The latter will be positively influenced *pari passu* with a drug free life-style.

In a similar vein, the program of Alcoholics Anonymous (AA) focuses not only on alcohol but extends its program of recovery to the alcoholic's relationships (Kurtz and Kurtz 1986). Initially, the focus is on the alcoholic's relationship to alcohol. This is expressed in the first step of AA — "We admitted we were powerless over alcohol — that our lives had become unmanageable." As the alcoholic progresses through the twelve step program he or she is called upon not only to accept the limitation of his or her relationship to alcohol, but also to examine his or her relationship to others and to a "higher power." Step 2 states: "Came to believe that a Power greater than ourselves could restore us to sanity." The need to address spiritual relationships is further emphasized in Step 3 — "Made a decision to turn our will and our lives over to the care of

God as we understood him"; Step 5 – "Admitted to God, to ourselves, and to another human being the exact nature of our wrongs"; Step 6 – "Were entirely ready to have God remove all these defects of character"; Step 7 – "Humbly asked Him to remove our shortcomings"; and Step 11 – "Sought through prayer and meditation to improve our conscious contact with God *as we understood Him*, praying only for knowledge of His will for us and the power to carry that out."

Relationships to others are addressed in Step 5 (see above); Step 8 – "Make a list of all persons we had harmed, and become willing to make amends to all"; Step 9 – "Make direct amends to such people whenever possible, except when to do so would injure them or others"; and Step 12 – "Having had a spiritual awakening as the result of these steps, we tried to carry this message to alcoholics, and to practice these principles in all our affairs."

The relationship to oneself in the form of self examination is reflected in Step 4 – "Made a searching and fearless moral inventory of ourselves"; and Step 10 – "Continue to take personal inventory and when we were wrong promptly admitted it."

The therapeutic impact of Alcoholics Anonymous has been described by Chappel (1988). The first three steps are described by Chappel as "surrender steps" – the individual begins to overcome the feeling of helplessness and to gain an internal locus of control. Steps 4 and 5 are inventory steps paralleling a process of psychotherapy by encouraging self examination. Steps 6 and 7 are considered by Chappel to be "personality disorder treatment steps" as they address defects of character. Steps 8 and 9 promote honest relationships and Step 12 is a "sharing step."

The power of "surrender" (facing limitations), self-examination, confession and restitution is rediscovered from time to time in various forms of psychotherapy, (Glasser 1985; Drakeford 1987). The dynamics captured by the 12-steps of AA are reflected not only in variegated forms of psychotherapy, but in the conceptualization of alcoholism by AA. The focus of AA is not so much on the disease of alcoholism but on the alcoholic himself. The focus of the scientist is the disease of alcoholism, but it is the alcoholic (not alcoholism) that is the primary concern of AA. "To be an alcoholic then, is *not* to have alcoholism: it is to *be* an alcoholic" (Kurta and Kurtz, 1986, p.124). Kurtz's skillful analysis of the impact of AA on the alcoholic enables us to appreciate that recovery from alcoholism is more, much more, than not drinking alcoholic beverages. Rather, an impact on character structure occurs, an impact that enables the alcoholic individual to cope with the absence of that substance upon which he or she had been dependent; and which allows the formation of an identity formed on sobriety. From this, integrity and a consistent character can emerge.

This does not imply that treatment of personality disorders is complete or even fully addressed in the rehabilitation process, but that a start is being made through the initiation of treatment for substance use disorders. With the attainment of sobriety, the capacity to observe and modify long-standing trends is greatly improved. A quote from Bill Wilson, cofounder of AA, illustrates this point: "I am beginning to see that all my troubles have their root in a habitual and absolute dependence upon my personal prestige, security, and romantic attachment. When these things go wrong, there is depression. Now this absolute dependence upon people and situations can only lead to conflict. Both on the surface and at depth. We are making demands on circumstance and people that are bound to fail us" (Kurtz 1979).

It can be appreciated, then, that whether we view recovery from alcoholism (and other forms of substance abuse) through the dynamics operating within our rehabilitation programs, psychotherapies, or the 12 steps of AA, a process is occurring that affects and influences personality structure. For this reason, we can be confident that the treatment of the chemically dependent patient with a personality disorder is well conceived by a focus on the substance abuse and the appropriate blend of rehabilitation, psychotherapy, and 12-step programs.

REFERENCES

American Psychiatric Association, *Psychiatric Glossary*, Washington, D.C., American Psychiatric Press 1984.

American Psychiatric Association, *Diagnostic and Statistical Manual* (3rd Edition Revised), Washington, D.C., American Psychiatric Press, 1980.

Bean-Bayog, M. Psychopathology produced by alcoholism. In Myer, R.E. (ed.) *Psychopathology and Addictive Disorders*. Guilford Press, New York, pp. 334-345, 1986.

Cadoret, R.J., Troughton, E., Widmer, R.B. Clinical differences between antisocial and primary alcoholics. *Comp. Psychiatry*, Jan-Feb, Vol. 25 (1). 1984, pp. 1-8.

Chappel, J.N., Gottheill, E., and Nace, E.P. *Alcoholism Update for psychiatrists* Usdin, G. (ed.) The American College of Psychiatrists, 1988.

Croughan, J.L., Miller, P.J., Matar, A. and Whitman, B.Y. Psychiatric diagnoses and prediction of drug and alcoholic dependence. *J. Clinical Psychiatry*, 1982, Sept. Vol. 43 (9) pp. 353-356.

Crowley, J.T., Chesluk, D., Dilts, S. et al. Drug and alcohol abuse among psychiatric admissions. *Arch. Gen. Psychiatry*, 30: 13-20, 1974.

Drake, R.E. and Vaillant, G.E. A validity study of Axis II of DSM-III. *Am. J. Psychiatry*, 142:5, May 1985, pp. 553-558.

Drakeford, J. W. *Integrity Therapy*, Broadman Press, Nashville, TN. 1987.

Ghen, M. and Klein, D.F. Drug use in a young psychiatric population. *Am. J. Orthopsychiatry* 40:448-455, 1970.

Glasser, W. *Reality Therapy*, New York: Harper and Row, 1985.

Gordon, C. and Beresin, E. Conflicting treatment models for the inpatient management of borderline patients. *American J. Psychiatry* 140:8, August, 1983, pp. 979-983.

Helzer, J.E and Pryzbeck T.R. (1988) The co-occurrence of alcoholism with other psychiatric disorders in the general population and its impact on treatment. *J. Studies on Alcohol*, Vol. 49, No. E, pp. 219-224, 1988.

Hesselbrock, M.N., Meyer, R.E., and Kenner, J.J. Psychopathology in hospitalized alcoholics. *Arch. Gen Psychiatry*, Vol. 42: 1050-1055, 1985.

Johnson, R.P., and Connelly, J.C. Addicted physicians take a closer look. *JAMA* 1981; 245: 253-257.

Koenigsberg, H.W., Kaplan, R.D., Gilmore, M.M. and Cooper, A.M. The relationship between syndrome and personality disorder in DSM-III: Experience with 2,462 patients. *Am J. Psychiatry*, 142:2, pp. 207-212, Feb. 1985.

Khantzian, E.J. Some treatment implications of the ego and self-disturbance in alcoholism. In Bean, M.H. and Zinberg, N.E. (eds). *Dynamic Approaches to the Understanding and Treatment of Alcoholism*. New York, The Free Press, pp. 163-188, 1981.

Khantzian, E.J. The self-medication hypotheses of addictive disorders: Focus on heroine and cocaine dependence. *Am. J. Psychiatry* 142:11, Nov. 1985, p. 1259.

Khantzian, E.J. and Treece, C. DSM-III psychiatric diagnosis of narcotic addicts. *Arch. Gen. Psychiatry*, 42: 1067-1071, 1985.

Khantzian, E.J. The self-medication hypotheses of addictive disorders: Focus on heroin and cocaine dependence. *Am. J. Psychiatry* 142:11, Nov. 1985, pp. 1259.

Kurtz, E. *Not God: A History of Alcoholics Anonymous*, Center City, Michigan, Hazelden, 1979, p. 214.

Kurtz, E. and Kurtz, L.F. The social thought of alcoholics. In Watts, T.D. (ed.) *Social Thought on Alcoholism: A Comprehensive Review*. Robert E. Krieger Publishing Co., Macon, FL. 1986, pp. 117-136.

Lion, J.R. *Personality Disorders: Diagnosis and Management*, Baltimore, Williams and Wilkins, 1974.

McCord, W. and McCord. J. A longitudinal study of the personality of alcoholics. In Pittman, D.J. and Snyder, C.R. (eds); *Society Culuture and Drinking Patterns*. New York, John Wiley, 1982, pp. 413-430.

Nace, E.P., Saxon, J.J. and Shore, N. A comparison of borderline and non-borderline alcoholic patients. *Arch. Gen. Psychiatry*, 40:54-56, 1983.

Nace, E.P., Saxton, J.J., Jr., Shore, N. Borderline personality disorder and alcoholism treatment: A one-year follow-up study. *Journal of Studies on Alcohol*. Vol. 47, No. 3, 1986, pp. 196-200.

Nace, E.P. *The Treatment of Alcoholism*, Brunner/Mazel, New York 1987.

Reiger, D.A., Myers, J.K., Kramer, M. Robins, L.N., Blazer, D.G., Hough, R.L., Eaton, W.W., and Locke, B.Z. The NIMH Epidemiologic Catchment Area Program: historical context, major objectives, and study population characteristics, *Arch. Gen. Psychiat* 41: 934-941, 1984.

Ritzler, B.A., Strauss, J.S., Vanord, A. et al. Prognostic implications of various drinking patterns in psychiatric patients. *Am. J. Psychiatry*, 134,(5): 546-549, 1977.

Rounsaville, B.J., Eyre, S. L., Weissman, M.M. and Kleber, H.D. The antisocial opiate addict. *Advances in Alcohol and Substance Abuse*, 1983, Vol. 2(4) 29-42.

Rounsaville, B.J., Kosten, T.R. and Kleber, H.D. Long-term changes in current psychiatric diagnoses of treated opiate addicts. *Comprehensive Psychiatry*, 1986, Sept-Oct., Vol. 27 (5) pp.480-498.

Schuckit, M.A. The clinical implications of primary diagnostic groups among alcoholics. *Arch. Gen. Psychiatry*, Vol. 42 (11). 1985, pp. 1043-1049.

Stabenau, J.R. Implications of family history of alcoholism antisocial personality, and sex differences in alcohol dependence. *Amer. J. Psychiatry*, Vol. 141 (10), 1984, pp.1178-1182.

Stravynski, A., Lamontagne, Y., and Yvon, Jacques L. Clinical phobias and avoidant personality disorder among alcoholics admitted to an alcoholism rehabilitation setting. *Canadian J. Psychiatry* Nov. Vol. 31 (8), pp. 714-719, 1986.

Tarter, R.E., Alterman, A.I and Edwards, K.L. Vulnerability to alcoholism in men: A behavior-genetic perspective. *J. Stud. Alcohol* 46 (4): 329-356, 1985.

Wieder, H., Kaplan, E.H. Drug use in adolescents: Psychodynamic meaning and pharmacologic effect. *In Psychoanalytic Study of the Child*. Eissler, R.S., Freud, A., Hartman, H., Lustman, S. and Kris, M. (eds.) Vol. 24, pp. 399-431. International Universities Press, New York, 1969.

Woody, G.E., McLellan, T.A., Luborsky, L. and O'Brien, C.P. Sociopathy and psychotherapy outcome. *Arch. Gen Psychiatry*, 1985, Nov. Vol. 42 (11) pp. 1081-1086.

Wurmser, L. Personality disorders and drug dependency. In Lion, J.R. (ed.), *Personality Disorders: Diagnosis and Management*. Baltimore, Williams and Wilkins, pp. 113-142, 1974.

Treating Dual Disorders:
A Model for Professional Education
and Training

Thomas E. Klee, PhD

In order to address the educational and training needs of those who provide treatment to dually disordered patients, it is necessary to acknowledge the hierarchy of these service providers. It is a hierarchy easily recognized within the treatment field, as well as by the lay public. It is political, economic, and educational. Psychiatrists are at the top, psychologists are next, followed by master's level clinical social workers, and addictions counselors are at the bottom. In the past each group, except psychiatrists, has struggled for parity with the top of the hierarchy on political and economic fronts. The idea of educating these professionals to treat dually diagnosed patients, when one of the diagnoses involves addiction or substance dependence, challenges the hierarchy on a functional level. While it is true that addictions counselors tend to be the least educated and have the most to learn about the dually diagnosed, it is also true that a significant information gap exists among psychiatrists, psychologists, and social workers about substance dependence, which is the bailiwick of addictions counselors. Consequently, education and training programs need to consider the information and skill deficits of all professions attempting to treat the dually disordered.

This professional hierarchy is reflected in the basic educational systems for each profession, as well as in ongoing professional training. Each group tends to provide training for itself at the implied exclusion of the other groups. This inbreeding of ideas and

Thomas E. Klee is Coordinator, Graduate Program in Counseling Psychology, Chestnut Hill College.

199

therapeutic orientations is stifling as it restricts the exchange of ideas and information. A model for education and training that breaks these barriers by structuring an expanded perspective in the training curriculum is needed.

The primary focus of this article is such a model. It provides a framework for the education and training of addictions counselors, within the larger context of human behavioral science. Given this broader base, the model presented also addresses the educational needs of other professionals who deal with the dually diagnosed. Currently, it is being used effectively by various professionals interested in addictions counseling in general and dually disordered patients in particular.

THE MODEL

Frequently, addictions counselors acquire their credentials via the experiences of their own addiction and recovery. This approach is informally supported by the self-help movements, most notably, Alcoholics Anonymous and Narcotics Anonymous, whose members often distrust mental health professionals, particularly if they have not gone through their own addiction and recovery processes. In the past, this attitude prevented addictions counselors the benefit of a vast base of information for professional decision making, which in turn, gave them a less than professional status in the eyes of the better educated professionals. Over time, some of these boundaries began to loosen, but mostly through regulations of non-treatment entities such as third party payers who required licensed professionals for reimbursement, and the federal government's research efforts which required behavioral scientists as principal investigators. The boundaries did not begin to break down among the practicing professionals until the need for improved treatment for the dually diagnosed became a priority within the therapeutic community.

In 1986 Chestnut Hill College, located in Philadelphia, received approval from the Commonwealth of Pennsylvania to initiate a Master's degree program in counseling psychology with a specialization in addictions counseling. This program was structured with two primary goals in mind. The first was to improve the educational foundation of addictions counselors by providing them with a Master's level program based in a behavioral science, in this case counseling psychology. This goal targeted the needs of those who wanted to become addictions counselors and the needs of existing addictions counselors who wanted to expand their clinical base in behavioral science, as well as their professional status. The second goal was to provide other credentialed professionals, such as psychologists and psychiatrists, with a Certificate of Advanced Graduate Study in Addictions to supplement their existing educational and experiential base. Essentially, the program was designed to combine addictions counseling with the broader based field of counseling psychology. The need for this type of educational and training program was so great that in a two year period of time it has grown to over 180 qualified graduate students, of which over 150 are working toward the Masters degree.

This program at Chestnut Hill College is organizationally within the Department of Psychology and the Graduate School. It is directly administered by a Coordinator who is a faculty member in the psychology department with a background in counseling psychology, psychodiagnostics and addictions counseling. This background of the Coordinator in both psychology and addictions counseling (which is true of other full-time faculty as well) influences the curriculum and helps students bridge the gap between these fields. In addition to teaching, the Coordinator monitors the curriculum, participates in student selection, supervises field placements, and responds to specific student needs in their professional development.

Modifications in Existing Educational and Training Formats

The weaknesses of the existing educational and training programs for addictions counselors have to do with their limited informational base in the behavioral sciences. This becomes a significant problem in working with the dually diagnosed patient. An example of this is that many of those who apply to Chestnut Hill's graduate program from the addictions field are unable to distinguish between the terms hallucination and delusion during their initial interview.

Terms such as perseveration and circumstantiality are like a foreign language to many of the applicants. Ironically, many of these applicants are addictions counselors already working with dually disordered patients, and some claim to be doing formal diagnostic work. During the interviews it became clear that these applicants are diagnosing and working with patients whose disorders they know little about, and lack the resources to develop a clinical understanding of the patients. This lack of knowledge reflects limitations in the existing education and training of addictions counselors working with dually diagnosed patients, which need to be addressed. It raises questions about the professionalism and quality of care being provided. Chestnut Hill College addressed these issues by structuring a graduate level education program for addictions counselors that modified the existing training formats to meet the needs of these students and the patients they serve in five ways. An overview of these five modifications is provided below. Each of these modifications is then discussed in detail.

First, it was recognized that the training and education of addictions counselors needs to be regulated and formalized. Previous attempts to achieve this goal can be seen in the movements in many states to certify addictions counselors. Unfortunately, certification processes often reinforce the isolation of addictions counselors by maintaining a narrow perspective on the definition of pathology, recovery and the counseling process. A broader academic background is necessary, particularly for those working with the dually diagnosed. Without this expanded informational base, addictions counselors will continue to find it difficult to understand human behavior in comprehensive terms or to communicate their thoughts with other professionals. The best way to achieve this goal is to move the training and education into a formal academic curriculum. Colleges and universities have the facilities and access to expertise to provide a full range of academic training. These institutions can develop formal relationships with state governments and credentialing boards to assure a meaningful, quality curriculum. They also have the facilities for continuing education, seminars, workshops, and summer institutes.

Central to the curriculum is the idea that the training of addictions counselors needs to occur within the wider context of understanding human behavior. Psychopathology, assessment, family dynamics, human development, and research design need to be part of the basic repertoire of anyone working within the counseling process. At Chestnut Hill College, it was decided that the best medium for this broader context is counseling psychology. This decision did not minimize the need for courses specific to addictions, but rather distinguished between core courses based in counseling psychology, and specialization courses based in addictions. Both need to be part of the curriculum. Finally, it was recognized that diagnostic and therapeutic issues specific to working with the dually disordered patient need to be addressed as part of the curriculum. Consequently, all courses within the curriculum have been designed to address the dually diagnosed. This is especially important for core courses such as psychopathology, assessment, counseling techniques, and all addictions courses.

Second, it was recognized that addictions counselors who work with the dually disordered need a more structured internship as part of their professional development. Internships are the point at which academics and experience meet. One without the other creates distortion in the counseling process. In the past many addictions counselors got their experience on the job with insufficient supervision. Formalized internships are a way of rectifying this problem.

Third, addictions counselors who work with dually diagnosed patients need a greater sense of professionalism within themselves and as they are perceived by others. One of the reasons addictions counselors frequently discount other professionals, such as psychiatrists, is because of their own fear of rejection on professional grounds. By increasing their level of professionalism, addictions counselors will be able to relate to other professionals more effectively.

Fourth, addictions counselors need to be aware of the similarities and differences between what they do and what is done by other treatment professionals. It was recognized that addictions counseling requires a different theoretical orientation that provides a distinct and necessary contribution to an overall treatment team of various professionals. This, in turn, requires communication skill building so that addictions counselors can relate their perspective to other professionals in verbal and written formats. The addictions perspective, as well as learning efficient methods of communicating this perspective, has been structured into all courses in the curriculum.

Fifth, in establishing this program at Chestnut Hill College there was a perceived need to evolve and avoid stagnation within the program and the profession. Addictions counselors need to understand the value of change as new data from research of the counseling process become available and treatment populations become more heterogeneous. As a result, the program and curriculum has been structured to be flexible in meeting the changing needs of students in this rapidly growing field. This feature addresses the future of training and educating addictions counselors.

Curriculum

The curriculum requirements for a graduate training program for working with the dually diagnosed can be divided into three categories: core courses, addictions specialization courses, and the internship. The first two will be discussed in this section and the following section will address the internship.

Core Courses. Core courses are those that provide the student with a broad based understanding of human behavior and the counseling process. At Chestnut Hill College, each graduate student in the addictions program is required to take seven of the ten core courses offered. Four courses are required of everyone: Theories of Counseling, Psychopathology, and Counseling Techniques I and II. The other three core courses can be selected from the following: Marital and Family Counseling, Human Development, Group Counseling, Legal and Ethical Issues of Counseling, Diagnostics/Testing, and Research Design. Most of these core courses are taught by faculty with expertise in addictions, and each course is designed to include a review of the addictions problem within the scope of the course. Courses in psychopathology, assessment and counseling techniques are always taught by faculty with clinical experience in addictions, and include an emphasis on the problems of the dually disordered.

Addictions Specializations Courses. In addition to the seven core courses, each student is required to take four specialization courses in addictions counseling. Regularly scheduled specialization courses include: Foundations of Chemical Dependency, Counseling Approaches to Substance Abuse, Advanced Therapeutic Issues in Addictions Counseling, and Spirituality and Healing. Special seminar courses in addictions counseling are offered each year to augment the addictions curriculum. These seminars focus on special populations such as adult children of alcoholics, women in addiction, addiction and the family, and personality disorders. Finally, a summer institute on topical issues in addictions is offered to both graduate students and the general therapeutic community.

These specialization courses, as well as the workshops and the summer institute are also open to professionals who want to expand their understanding of addictions counseling or earn a Certificate in Addictions Counseling.

Specific Curriculum Issues for Working with the Dually Diagnosed. In addition to highlighting the addictions perspective in the core courses and providing specialization courses in addictions, there is a strong effort at Chestnut Hill College to teach theoretical and applied models that address the problems of the dually diagnosed. The result of this effort is the bridging of a foundation in counseling psychology with the work done in addictions counseling. This is most effective in the teaching of psychopathology and the various courses in counseling techniques. The following two examples are provided to clarify this issue.

The first example is of a theoretical model that bridges understanding between psychopathology and addictions counseling. Object relations theory as refined by Kernberg (1975, 1976) provides insight into early personality development, especially in regard to how one relates to self and others. Dysfunction occurs when the personality is inadequately organized around these relationships with self and others. Typically, this occurs in borderline and narcissistic personality structures (Kernberg, 1975). The usefulness of this orientation has been understood and applied to addictions counseling by Forrest (1983) who suggests that many alcoholics have similar behaviors, interpersonal styles and internal psychodynamics to individuals with borderline and narcissistic personality organizations. Forrest (1983) develops a psychodynamic theory of addictions and substance abuse which identifies narcissistic need and entitlement deprivation in early life as primary factors in the development of addictive patterns. Interestingly, graduate students at Chestnut Hill College who are experienced addictions counselors, find this theoretical orientation helpful in explaining what they see in their patients; the theory fits their experiences. Forrest (1984) also applies this theory to a form of psychodynamically oriented treatment.

The second example is of an applied counseling model that bridges addictions counseling with counseling psychology by building a therapeutic model on general systems theory. The self-management therapy developed by Kanfer and Schefft (1988) attempts to assess and treat multiple dimensions of existence. Kanfer and Scheff (1988, p. 36) identify environmental, psychological, and biological/genetic factors as the three primary dimensions that need to be considered when providing a therapeutic service. By determining in which domain or interaction of domains dysfunction is occurring, one can target therapeutic interventions to the dysfunctional area of existence. Kanfer and Schefft (1988, p. 60) developed a self-management therapy in which clients learn to control their behavior, their physiological reactions (e.g., emotional arousal), and their cognitive controls including self-reactions. Their model is helpful in training addictions counselors for three reasons: (1) it is structured to look at multiple levels of existence; (2) it is complementary to many theoretical orientations; and (3) it addresses therapeutic problems typical of addicted and dually diagnosed patients. One useful construct developed by Kanfer and Schefft (1988, p. 57) is the difference between "decisional self-control" (pouring a bottle of whiskey down the drain) and "protracted self-control" (maintaining sobriety over time by making changes in the way one processes the world). Learning to deal with the conflicts (alternative decisions) posed by either of these forms of self-control is much of the work that occurs in addictions counseling.

Internships

One of the major problems in the past training of addictions counselors who work with the dually disordered is the lack of a formal internship. Typically, addictions counselors are trained on the job, in one facility, and within one therapeutic orientation. Combined with the lack of an academic background, this experiential deficit leaves most addictions counselors with a narrow perspective of human dysfunction and a limited repertoire of therapeutic interventions. One way of solving this problem is to require a standard internship, following academic training, that brings the student into contact with supervisors who can teach proper diagnostic skills, as well as appropriate interventions for the dually diagnosed.

At Chestnut Hill College the internship is structured to provide the student with a wide range of field experiences. Students in addictions counseling are required to do four part-time field placements, each lasting one semester. The students are at the sites two to three days a week for a minimum of 120 hours per semester. At least 45 of these hours must be spent providing diagnostic and therapeutic services directly to patients. The remaining time is spent in supervision, case preparation, staff meetings, record keeping and observation of other clinicians. Not only does this part-time placement offer the student a range of experiences, but it also meets the needs of students who work and cannot commit to a one year full time internship.

Students are encouraged to do each placement at a different level of the treatment continuum, which includes prevention and early intervention, detoxification, residential rehabilitation, outpatient counseling, and aftercare. Students who are interested in more in-depth learning at a particular site may spend two semesters at one site. However, all students are required to have exposure to at least two sites, or levels of the treatment continuum.

Prior to doing a field placement, students are required to take courses in theories of counseling, psychopathology, and counseling techniques. In addition, they have to take at least two specialization courses in addictions. Without this academic preparation, students would be problematic to supervise. Students are required to be supervised by a licensed or certified professional at the worksite who is experienced in the diagnosis and treatment of the dually disordered. Supervisors are typically psychologists or psychiatrists experienced in addictions or certified addictions counselors experienced in treating the dually disordered.

In addition to providing the students with a greater awareness of dually disordered patients and appropriate methods of treatment, this system of field placements also allows the student to explore more options as to how they define themselves as professionals.

This is achieved by having the students keep a journal of their field experience, as well as, attend bi-weekly meetings of all students doing field placements. The meetings are led by the Coordinator of the graduate program, who monitors the placements. The purpose of these meetings is to have students focus on their own issues as developing professionals. Clinical issues discussed include handling violent patients, confidentiality, relating to supervision, and counselor self-esteem.

Professionalism

By extending the role of the addictions counselor to include the treatment of the dually diagnosed patient, his or her professional identification is also changed. These changes are a result of being better informed and trained. The enhanced professionalism is reinforced via their acceptance by other professionals such as psychologists and psychiatrists. Once addictions counselors are able to effectively communicate within a diagnostic nosology, they can be heard by other professionals. Once they can implement effective interventions based on diagnostic information, they can gain the respect of other professionals. Addictions counselors who attempt to treat the dually diagnosed without formal training are at risk ethically and professionally. The pathology is too complex and the dually disordered patients are too much at risk to allow untrained counselors, without supervision, to attempt to effect positive change.

The issue of professionalism is explored in depth in all the graduate courses at Chestnut Hill College. It is further explored on a personal level during the practicum experience. As mentioned earlier, during the four field placements, the students attend a bi-weekly group led by the graduate program Coordinator to develop insight into their professional identification. Students may also elect a weekly group meeting for a more intensive exploration of professional development and personal issues. Essentially, students learn that a sense of professionalism evolves out of four factors: a well developed base of theoretical and empirically valid information, the ability to translate that information into understanding and intervention for the patient, the ability to communicate that information to other professionals in both oral and written formats, and the esteem in oneself as a professional.

Similarities and Differences
with Other Professionals

The enhancement of the academic base, experiential repertoire, and sense of professionalism of addictions counselors challenges the professional hierarchy outlined at the beginning of this paper. Indeed, there may be a tendency to absorb addictions counselors into other professions, particularly as the treatment of the dually diagnosed becomes more refined. This may be said of the addictions counseling program at Chestnut Hill College because it is contained within a counseling psychology degree program. However, the program is structured so that those interested in addictions counseling do not lose their identity, which would be a mistake because professional differences do exist. The program attempts to expand the information and training base of addictions counselors without eroding professional identity. The professional identity of addictions counselors is, in part, distinguishable in terms of orientation and style.

Addictions counselors are specialized to work with patients who abuse or are dependent on substances. It is a specialization that is quick to see the addictive pathology in patients. Breaking through denial to addictive traits is a basic orientation of addictions counselors that is not typical of other treatment professionals. This orientation has also been helpful in identifying the addictive pathology of other dysfunctions such as eating disorders. However, without the proper educational base, this orientation can also be dangerous.

An example of just how dangerous this orientation can be without an adequate educational base became apparent in a case this writer managed. The identified patient was a 17-year-old male accurately diagnosed as borderline personality disorder. He had an active fantasy life of being a mercenary soldier because he enjoyed the idea of killing people. At times these fantasies crossed-over to delusions and hallucinations. In addition, he had a history of extremely impulsive behavior which included multiple suicide attempts. Ironically, he did not abuse drugs or alcohol even though both parents had histories of alcohol dependence. As with most borderline personality disorders, treatment was difficult. In this case it was more difficult because both parents were addictions counselors with a singular perspective on all human dysfunction. Their orientation as addictions counselors convinced them that all their son had to do was abstain from his destructive thinking and follow a twelve step program, which they communicated to him in a very confrontational style. They also received a great deal of support for their position from other addictions counselors and their A.A. support groups. Unfortunately, this orientation made it impossible for them to understand the psychodynamics of their son's disorder. As a result, they rejected all attempts to help them understand their son's condition and work toward effective treatment by throwing him out of the home. He became homeless and sought out mental health professionals only in times of extreme crisis. This case illustrates the point that the therapeutic orientation of addictions counselors needs to be placed within the context of a well rounded educational base that includes how to differentiate between addictions and other forms of pathology.

This orientation in addictions counselors leads directly to a counseling style that can best be described as confrontational. It is the primary style of addictions counselors from detoxifications programs to residential settings to outpatient treatment. Confrontation is a valuable therapeutic tool in helping the patient break through his or her denial. However, as a singular approach it has limitations, especially in working with the dually diagnosed, where a rigid confrontational style may exacerbate the other mental disorder. The addictions counselors who work with the dually disordered need to be better educated and able to use a variety of therapeutic interventions appropriate for specific disorders. They also need to know how to communicate with other professionals and how to function as part of a comprehensive treatment team. A singular orientation will block communication with other professionals and perpetuate the image of addictions counselors as non-professionals.

THE FUTURE

The model reviewed here sets a direction for the future of educating and training addictions counselors, particularly those working with dually diagnosed patients. In addition to the benefits of the graduate level model already discussed, this type of training paradigm promotes the ongoing development of a profession by bringing the students into contact with new developments in the field:

this is central to any academically based training. Previous training models were rarely in touch with new developments in research and applied clinical skills, which prevented professional growth. This issue of ongoing development is critical as treatment populations become (or are recognized) as more heterogeneous, and as new data about the counseling process with these populations become available at ever increasing rates. If addictions counselors continue to function clinically from a narrow definition of human dysfunction without developing a workable understanding of the larger context of behavioral science, they will stagnate and their competence will always be questioned.

Colleges and universities are perfect settings for the future training of addictions counselors at both undergraduate and graduate levels. They provide a context in which the informational base is current, research and development are encouraged, field experiences can be supervised, professionalism can be developed, and credentialing can be standardized. Given the response of addictions counselors to the graduate program at Chestnut Hill College (number of applications and enrollment), there is a clear need for this type of education and training model. Without it, addictions counselors will experience increasing difficulties in their attempts to treat patients as the identification of the dually diagnosed population increases.

REFERENCES

Forrest, G. G. (1983). *Alcoholism, narcissism, and psychopathology*. Springfield, Ill.: Charles C Thomas.

Forrest, G. G. (1984). *Intensive psychotherapy of alcoholism*. Springfield, Ill.: Charles C Thomas.

Kanfer, F. H., Schefft, B. K. (1988). *Guiding the process of therapeutic change*. Champaign, Ill.: Research Press.

Kernberg, O. F. (1975). *Borderline conditions and pathological narcissism*. New York: Jason Aronson.

Kernberg, O. F. (1976). *Object relations theory and clinical psychoanalysis*. New York: Jason Aronson.

Dual Facilities:
Interprofessional Collaboration
in Treating Dual Disorders

Gail Luyster, PhD
Richard Lowe, PhD

The collaboration of clinically trained professionals with addiction-trained counselors in the treatment of dual disordered patients can create a treatment environment charged with the tension of distrust, envy and power struggles. Psychologists and psychiatrists sometimes tend to view addiction as the less interesting symptom of a complex underlying dysfunction. Counselors may tend to view psychiatric disorders as inherently secondary to addiction, so that sobriety will ensure the disappearance of abnormal functioning. Conversely, such collaboration can enhance patient care immeasurably, as well as provide a mutually rewarding professional experience. Both groups have much to offer their patients and each other in a treatment setting where communication, appreciation of each other's perspectives, and the integration of psychiatric and addiction issues are encouraged.

This article focuses on areas of interprofessional collaboration. The traditional roles of doctor and counselor are examined to clarify differences in perspectives and expectations. The format of a dual disorder unit staffed by psychologists/psychiatrists is described in some detail to demonstrate one hospital's effort to maximize the offerings of professional and paraprofessional staff. This is a unit which over time has developed a strong collaborative bond between

Gail Luyster and Richard Lowe are Attending Psychologists, Charter Fairmount Institute.

213

professional staff and addiction counselors. Priorities on a dual disorder unit are addressed. The issue of whether to medicate recovering patients is discussed with regard to the traditional AA stance, legal pressing issues which all mental health workers should be aware of, and clinical concerns specific to the recovering patient. Finally, the importance of intra-staff communication of transference and countertransference issues is discussed and demonstrated by clinical material.

The goals of this article are to highlight the benefits of a multidisciplinary approach and to identify potential obstacles or pitfalls to successful collaboration.

OVERVIEW OF TREATMENT PROGRAM

When a patient enters the Addiction Treatment Service of Charter Fairmount Institute, he/she is immediately introduced to group members and his/her counselor. On the day (or Monday) following his/her admission, the patient meets *The Treatment Team* consisting of psychiatrists, attending psychologists, certified addiction counselors, social workers, and representatives from nursing. The interview content is largely focused on addiction: what was used, for how long, what problems did substance use cause, why is treatment being sought now, what legal and family problems are pressing. Preliminary observations are made of patient's presentation, level of denial/rationalization, secondary diagnosis, ego strengths and weaknesses, character resistances, (possible) specific needs or concerns for suicide precautions, medications, psychological testing/neuropsychological batteries, apparent transference issues with males or females.

From the initial team interview, the patient is sent to join the community at the daily 9:00 a.m. lecture. Lectures are held twice daily; morning lectures cover such topics as emotional development, physiological effects of respective addictions, ego strengths, compulsive disorders, adult children of alcoholic issues, grief and loss, and spirituality. Afternoon lectures are based upon one of the twelve AA/NA steps.

The patient will meet with his/her doctor[1] each day for individual sessions. He/she will also participate in group therapy daily led by his/her counselor.

The individual sessions are a combination of therapy and ongoing clinical assessment. Psychosis must be ruled out and symptoms which may require medication are identified for observation. Deficits in intellectual functioning suggestive of neuropsychological impairment are noted for referral for formal assessment. Physical complaints are screened for therapeutic import and withdrawal symptoms, and referrals are made to an internist who cares for our patients daily.

For patients who are fragile and/or well motivated, the doctor's office will become the place where patient feels safe, feels listened to unconditionally, and finds support. For other patients presenting different styles of character resistance and denial, support per se may be tempered with identification of destructive defenses and resistances. One treatment goal of hospitalization may be the patient questioning such defenses with the ultimate goal of making them ego dystonic.

Meanwhile, the clinician conducts a daily mental status examination via gaining information about the patient's life. The clinician is consistently assessing patient's attention span, ability to process information, to retain information, and to utilize information to develop or deepen self-understanding. Is the patient able to give a reasonably articulate and accurate description of his/her life? The accuracy will be checked through the patient's social worker who takes a psychosocial history within 72 hours and contacts family members and friends for verification and further information. As the patient talks about his/her functioning, is he/she reflecting progress in using input to apply to himself/herself? Is he/she in touch with the reality and impact of his/her addiction and of his/her psychiatric disorder? Is there progress in identifying thoughts and feelings, in expressing these and in utilizing information?

Often the initial presentation will change daily as the patient continues to detox. A very confused, hypomanic, labile individual coming into treatment after five days of detox from methampheta-

---

[1]For purpose of this article, the term "doctor" will include psychologists and psychiatrists who treat the addicted individual.

mines, cocaine, and alcohol, may clear cognitively and stabilize affectively over a week to ten days. Another group of patients may be *empty*, having essentially anesthetized their feelings for years. It may be unclear at first whether the apparent emptiness is that of the narcissistic/borderline personality, the emotional constriction of the avoidant or schizoid personality, or the emotional sangfroid of the antisocial personality—or a product of the active addiction which will dissolve and give way to emergence of a range of affect.

In group, the counselor is essentially making similar assessments with the addition of patient's style of relating to peers. Here focus will be more on addiction. Does the patient identify self as an addict? Does he/she acknowledge and accept his/her inability to control his/her illness (i.e., his/her powerlessness over addictive substances without the resources of the program)? Does the patient understand that his/her illness has affected everyone around him/her, and does he/she appreciate the impact of his/her addictive behaviors on those he/she loves? Is the patient receptive to a program that can provide "tools" for coping with stresses of living and with the seductions of the addiction? How does the patient relate to peers? What transferences are captured within the group setting?

Two forums are built into the week for exchange of patient information. One is the daily nursing report. The morning report is a compilation of three nursing shifts' observations of patients' behaviors. During morning report any problems the patient may experience in functioning within the open therapeutic community will be illuminated. Note is made of patient's timely attendance of activities, verbal content within the community thought to be significant, or unusual occurrences. These include breaking of restrictions or rules, external events such as family crises, conflicts or exclusive pairing with peers. As patients are discussed one by one, any current treatment information may be exchanged to keep therapists and social worker updated on significant elements of history, therapeutic content, and transference as they emerge daily. If a patient is struggling in treatment or seems to need additional support (or confrontation), one consequence may be the *mini-team*: the doctor, counselor, and social worker sit with the patient during his/her scheduled doctor's appointment to discuss problems, provide support, and/or set limits as needed.

A second forum for communication is the weekly *Case Confer-*

ence. On Tuesdays the treatment staff is joined by therapists from occupational and music therapies. Each patient is discussed, team member by team member. The counselor introduces the patient by age, marital status, addiction history, and depicts his/her work in group therapy. The doctor comments on psychiatric diagnosis, relevant dynamics for treatment process, progress in individual sessions, and treatment needs. The social worker gives feedback from family contacts, any legal contacts, and employer (job performance and status). The art therapist displays the patient's art work and compares it to previous work. The occupational therapist points out any problems the patient has completing tasks in shop, and nursing describes any patterns of behaviors which have not been addressed. What emerges is a quite comprehensive view of the patient's functioning in the treatment setting. This allows the team to ascertain areas of progress and to identify treatment needs in any areas in which patient is not progressing. Disparities in functioning from one modality to another are explored further. Discharge needs — individual psychotherapy, group addiction counseling, psychiatrist for medication, and always *90 and 90*, are discussed at this time so that social worker can make any needed arrangements.

It is hopefully clear from this brief overview that the treatment team, particularly the doctor and counselor, must work in synchrony. Differences in assessing patient's presentations are to be expected; the first assumption must be that the patient is presenting differently to two different individuals in two distinct modalities; only in appreciating both views can the patient be understood and treated effectively. The possibility that different presentations represent transference responses must be considered.

Roles of Doctor/Counselor

Before further discussing the respective roles of doctor and counselor on the ATS unit, some historical perspective may be helpful.

Much has been said about the uneasy — often tenuous, at times even stormy — relationship between so-called professionals and paraprofessionals (Nace, 1987; Brown, 1985). Many recovering individuals have had negative personal experiences with physicians and/or psychologists. Perhaps they were prescribed addictive medications by doctors who felt helpless to treat them by any other method. Maybe they received treatment from a psychologist or psychotherapist who either downplayed/ignored the addiction to get to the *root cause* of the *symptom*, thereby tacitly supporting the person's denial system (Bissell, 1982); or, even more destructively, endorsed *controlled drinking* through a behavior modification regimen. Even without such personal exposure, the recovering alcoholic/addict has certainly known or heard of others who have undergone a similar experience. Thus, even assuming most professionals are well-intentioned, it is easy to see how the recovering individual would view doctors with caution, if not outright suspiciousness or hostility.

Conversely, most mental health professionals value the training they received and believe that it has prepared them to treat a variety of psychopathology, including addictive disorders. They may be alarmed that individuals without advanced degrees are treating patients when they lack understanding of the complexity of patient dynamics, ego strengths, or medical issues vital to proper care. The doctor may view the recovering counselor, therefore, as ill-equipped despite being well-motivated to provide adequate treatment.

This training vs experience issue provides a potential source of disharmony. Each side can become defensive about its own inherent shortcomings and engage in much compensatory devaluing of the other's position. Insecurity about not having the advanced training and degree can lead the counselor to dismiss the doctor for *never having been there*. This can be particularly possible when the counselor struggles with a regressed, psychotic or borderline patient with whom he/she is having much difficulty. Similarly, the doctor may be jealous of the counselor's instant bond with the patient and bemoan the lack of boundaries and overidentification without an understanding of the pathology (especially after experiencing the impotence engendered by treatment-resistant, relapsing patients).

Finally, basic differences in philosophy may serve as a barrier to effective mutual understanding and collaboration. The recovering counselor will likely follow the Twelve-Step Program of AA and NA both for personal recovery and as the essential treatment tool. With its emphasis on admitting powerlessness, turning one's will over to a Higher Power, taking a personal inventory, making amends, and passing on one's experience, this powerfully simple program has helped millions of alcoholics and addicts become and remain sober and straight (Alcoholics Anonymous, 1976). Psychiatrists and psychologists, on the other hand, generally believe in free choice and are trained to view coping problems as the result of maladaptive learning or traumatic early experiences/relationships. The idea of *surrender* and *powerlessness* may seem primitive and blindly following direction dangerous. Furthermore, many of them are uncomfortable with concepts such as *spirituality* and *Higher Power*. Constant, unyielding focus on abstinence can be misconstrued as obsessive, overly narrow, and not as *sexy* as other issues or dynamics.

Awareness of such potentially crippling divisions is crucial to successful interdisciplinary collaboration. Although the number of ATS staff meetings (daily morning report, weekly *Case Conference*, bi-weekly doctor/counselor meeting) is time-consuming, these are essential to the smooth running of the program. Different views and ways of handling various patients can be discussed and usually, ironed out. Mutual respect for the contributions each discipline can make is critical. Needless to say, there are differences in how patients' problems are conceptualized, but compromise and working together are accepted as the group norm.

Each side has had to relinquish traditional roles for the unit to function effectively. The attending is not an imperial doctor who controls the treatment team; instead, he/she defers to the counselor to track the patient's progress on a behavioral level. Counselors often give written assignments (e.g., *a life history*; a letter to a deceased loved one) or make suggestions that certain patients receive therapeutic passes. The counselor, on the other hand, will look to the doctor to suggest medication for a psychotic or severely depressed (or manic) patient,[2] help the team understand certain problematic behaviors, symptoms, or dynamics, and refer patients presenting diagnostic or treatment questions for psychological testing.

---

[2]Each psychologist attending has a consulting psychiatrist for medical *back-up*.

While most of this discussion focuses on the doctor/counselor roles, a word should be said about two other critical disciplines. Social work and nursing form the other basic components of the team treatment approach (along with adjunctive or *allied therapies*). Social workers obtain vital historical data—both from the patient and important family members—and feed this information back to the doctor and counselor. They also contact the patient's employer (supervisor/EAP/union representative) to ascertain job functioning and status. The social worker invites family members for the family education program each Sunday as well as discrete sessions with the patient's treatment team. He/she requests employers to come for a back-to-work conference prior to the patient's discharge. Finally, the social worker is the key to coordinating each patient's aftercare.

Nursing staff consists of a head nurse and various R.N.s and psychiatric technicians for each shift. In addition to dispensing medication and recording vital signs, nursing plays a key role in monitoring patients' behavior. Patients who may be *therapy wise* or otherwise on *good behavior* with their counselor and doctor may show another side in the more relaxed setting of the milieu. Lateness, testing limits, and lack of commitment to treatment are confronted and reported to the rest of the treatment team. Nurses and techs also play a supportive role, listening to and encouraging patients; this function is especially vital during second and third shifts, when other staff members are absent.

The program is structured so that each patient meets with his/her doctor daily for brief (20-30 minute), individual psychotherapy sessions and with his/her counselor for daily group therapy and p.r.n. brief, individual counseling sessions. The doctor tends to work from a more empathic position, remaining somewhat detached from specific behaviors which may have to be confronted by the counselor. The counselor, on the other hand, serves as a role model of a recovering individual and there is more of a peer relationship with the patient. The doctor starts with where the patient is emotionally, while the counselor focuses on addiction and prescribes necessary steps toward recovery. Because of such differences, the doctor tends to elicit more positive transference given his/her position of working to understand the patient; the counselor's more direct emphasis on decreasing denial and avoidance may initially result in more negative transference. Both transferences, of course, are potentially therapeutic.[3]

Despite differences in emphasis, each side is working to help the patient begin (or continue) his/her sobriety and enhance the quality of his/her life. And, perhaps, there are more points of similarity than are readily apparent. Several authors have attempted to bridge the gap between AA and psychiatry/psychology (Brown, 1985; Nace, 1987). The issue of powerlessness which forms the cornerstone of recovery has its parallel in the feeling of dissatisfaction or despair that motivates the individual to seek psychotherapy. Step Four's *searching and fearless moral inventory* begins a process of self-exploration which is the essence of psychotherapy. And both sides believe that recovery is a slow, often difficult process which is ultimately well worth the effort.

Through daily collaboration, the doctor and counselor exchange views on how the patient is doing and what needs to be addressed. A *game plan* is established with goals set, monitored, and often modified as more information is gleaned. For example, a young male with a history of *acting out* against authority will be confronted about rule infractions by his counselor and urged to examine how his addiction has adversely affected his relationships. His doctor will help him explore painful experiences, connect these with current attitudes and behavior, and assist him in developing more adaptive ways of coping with anger/frustration.

It is critical that doctors and counselors support each others' positions; otherwise, splitting will inevitably occur. The patient will either be confused about receiving *mixed messages* or exploit the rift in a manipulative manner. This is especially important for patients with primitive ego functioning who cannot easily integrate disparate signals or reactions. The borderline patient who tends to present different fragments of self to different staff members, benefits greatly from staff working closely together to help him/her integrate fragmented and split off parts of self and others. As noted

---

[3]These roles are presented in a more dichotomous fashion than is actually the case for illustrative purposes. There is considerable overlap and flexibility in functions.

above, a particularly valuable tool is the *mini-team*, in which the doctor, counselor, social worker and when possible, a nursing representative meet together with the patient. A patient may be working well in individual therapy but be disruptive in group and non-compliant with program guidelines. With the mini-team, the doctor is in essence saying that he/she may not address such behavior but supports the counselor's position; he/she will not *rescue* the patient nor tacitly approve of the patient's behavior.

Some examples may help illustrate how the team approach can prove invaluable in handling *difficult* patients, and how each discipline can aid the other in promoting successful outcomes.

The patient was a 41-year-old, divorced, white, male alcoholic, whose previous treatment in a didactically-based rehabilitation program had helped him achieve several months of sobriety; however, the patient was not able to maintain long-term abstinence. He was intensely dysphoric and exceedingly anxious, reporting *panic attacks*, disturbed sleep, appetite, and concentration, and a sense of helplessness and hopelessness about the future. After three weeks in treatment he had made only modest progress and his symptoms were still pronounced. One day he announced to the Program Director that he had a secret that was too dreadful to divulge but that he was desperate to share. The Program Director contacted his doctor immediately. Because of the positive, non-threatening nature of the relationship, the patient felt able to describe graphically the compulsion of which he was so ashamed. He sobbed and wailed, feeling mortified but then relieved. Always assuming he would be laughed at or ridiculed, he instead received unconditional acceptance and support. With his doctor's encouragement, he was then able to unburden himself to his group, another profoundly moving experience. Again, he received reassurance and caring and was given a sense of belonging rather than being isolated and different. He felt that these cathartic sessions were the turning points in his treatment. Along with his intellectual grasp of alcoholism, he was now able to *forgive himself* and begin giving himself permission to recover. The special nature of the individual therapeutic relationship allowed the process to start, and then the patient was able to share more openly with his counselor and group, which ultimately provided the support and validation he so desperately needed.

For other patients, such support and empathy, while important, may be insufficient. In particular, patients who are unmotivated, in denial of their addictions, or who are not complying with program structure, may well need firmness and even confrontation. The following example illustrates how the counselor can provide such direction:

The patient was a 21-year-old, male alcoholic who was admitted to a general psychiatric unit of the hospital following an incident in which he was driving while intoxicated and caused an accident, killing two people. After being transferred to the ATS unit, he presented as uninvested in treatment and denying an alcohol problem (claiming this had been an isolated occurrence which ended tragically). His involvement was minimal and he passively tested limits. His doctor urged a cautious approach, emphasizing the young man's underlying depression and terror at the prospect of going to jail; in addition, he pointed to psychological test results indicating an empty young man with dull to borderline intelligence and inadequate coping skills. While this supportive stance helped the patient feel somewhat more at ease, he continued to deny and minimize. His counselor, a middle-aged male with a reputation for *toughness*, then began taking a more confrontational approach, challenging the young man's destructive avoidance while serving as a firm but caring *father figure*. Gradually, the patient responded, as he was forced to face his drinking history and the consequences of his behavior. He was then more able to utilize individual sessions to express his long-standing inadequacy, identify strengths, and prepare emotionally for incarceration. He remained in touch following his discharge, and at last contact, had been transferred to a halfway house from jail and was active in AA.

A third example will illustrate how the team approach can be beneficial even when treatment is not completely successful.

The patient was a 45-year-old, single, female alcoholic and drug addict, a nurse who was four years sober when she entered treatment because of depression and dissatisfaction with the quality of her recovery. It was clear from initial assessments that the patient suffered severe ego deficits, including sexual identity disturbance, a history of stormy interpersonal relationships, and feelings of emptiness and rage. Her counselor, also a middle-aged female, attempted to confront her manipulative, demanding behavior to help her make changes which would enhance her sobriety. Instead, she felt misunderstood and even *destroyed* by her. Rather than continue to battle with the patient in the group setting and risk overwhelming her because of the intensity of her affect, she encouraged the patient to deal with her anger in individual psychotherapy. With a younger male psychologist, she was able to express her underlying self-loathing and sense of despair. This therapist helped her examine the intense negative transference reaction she was having toward her counselor by exploring her relationship with her cold, rejecting mother. It was critical for the therapist to support the patient while at the same time not encourage her devaluing of the counselor. Despite her positive experience in therapy—especially feeling accepted and validated—the patient was unable to move beyond her angry, withdrawn position vis-a-vis her counselor. She was willing to enter outpatient therapy with another middle-aged female counselor, however, and later reported excellent progress in establishing a positive relationship, and, in general, feeling much better about herself and her sobriety. If the counselor had viewed such treatment as overprotective and pushed the patient further, she might have terminated treatment prematurely, or worse, decompensated into a psychotic episode.

Priorities of Treatment

While the different disciplines may vary with regard to their roles and type of input, it is made clear to the patient that the overriding goal is sobriety—abstinence from all drugs and alcohol. Some patients have never attained any significant periods of abstinence, some relapse after doing well for a time, and others remain dysphoric or overwhelmed even years into their recovery. While the specific treatment plan will differ for each of these types of patients, the *bottom line* remains abstinence and improving quality of life.

Treatment priorities will certainly shift as the patient's treatment progresses, but the basic components are assessment, adjustment, acceptance, active involvement, and aftercare.

The issue of *assessment* has already been discussed above, and its importance cannot be overemphasized. The patient is assessed in terms of addiction history, medical condition, psychiatric problems, and psychosocial status. Although there are often many commonalities among patients and abstinence is the primary goal, it is not assumed that *every addict is alike* and will receive the same treatment. A highly anxious, dependent patient will need support and learn to develop improved coping skills; an antisocial individual will require limit setting and group confrontation; a manic-depressive patient will need to work toward accepting his/her need for Lithium as well as meetings and therapy.

The first few days of treatment are critical for the patient to begin to *adjust* successfully to the program. Rules, regulations, and being on time are emphasized to help the alcoholic/addict gain a sense of structure that he/she has lost or never actually developed. For the most fragile or psychiatrically-impaired, the individual psychotherapy sessions can be particularly important; counselors, nurses, and techs will spend individual time with those patients as well.

Acceptance of one's addiction plus any concomitant disorder — perhaps a physical problem such as diabetes or psychiatric one such as bipolar disorder — is heavily stressed throughout the patient's treatment. The counselor will assign a *First Step Work Paper* to help the patient see how powerless and out of control he/she has been. Lectures are given twice daily which cover a myriad of topics, mostly related to addiction and its consequences. Family members attend anywhere from one to three sessions during a patient's treatment stay; a major function of these family sessions is to help promote acceptance by having the patient hear (with sober ears) how his/her addiction has affected loved ones.

After allowing for a period of adjustment, *active involvement* is expected of the patient. In addition to attending all therapies and meetings on time, patients are urged to become truly invested in the program. Quiet or resistant patients may be urged to sit in the front at lectures and AA/NA meetings and share something in each session. Patients with especially debilitating psychiatric disorders will be given extra time and attention in individual sessions. If the patient continues to struggle in treatment, a mini-team will be held to provide support, confrontation, or a combination of the two as needed.

Finally, *aftercare* is obviously viewed as critically important to help ensure a positive transition to the community. From the time of the initial assessments, aftercare planning begins. In addition to *90 meetings in 90 days*, will the patient need group addictions counseling? Individual psychotherapy? Some patients, because of severe ego deficits, impulsivity, or lack of any positive home environment, may require a halfway house setting. Is there one available which will be appropriate given the patient's needs (e.g., accept someone on medications; allow him/her to return to work)? The social worker helps coordinate this aspect of treatment, in collaboration with the counselor and doctor.

Medication

Medication is an increasingly multifaceted issue at this time. Traditionally the bias of AA and therefore of CAC's has been adamantly anti-medication for reasons enumerated in the section on doctor/counselor roles. The clinician should be aware that there are AA meetings where patients who have been carefully tutored regarding their psychotropic medications will be told they are not *sober* or *clean* if they are on any kind of medication. Fortunately, the number of such meetings seems to be few and few counselors would argue with the need to medicate an immobilizing depression or blatant thought disorder. This *radical AA* position seems to be on the wane. Still, because of the recovering person's identification with the patient, there can be denial of the patient's psychiatric illness and intense resistance to medication.

At the other end of the spectrum is the *radical psychiatry* stance, in which addiction is either medicated directly or viewed as secondary to a psychiatric disorder which requires medication. Many psychiatrists and psychologists lack training in addiction and may ignore or minimize the role of the patient's substance abuse. Symptoms which appear to represent a primary affective disorder may in fact be the result of residual withdrawal from the chemical. Unmotivated or otherwise slow to respond patients may make talk therapy frustrating; therefore, medication may appear to be the treatment of choice. Many psychiatric residencies stress the biologial basis of psychiatric impairment, with medication the logical *tool* for treatment.

In addition, the pressure to medicate mounts. When depression is part of a diagnosis, the first question asked by the insurance reviewer is, "Is this patient being medicated?" When the answer is *no*, defense must be made. This is not simply a shift in attitude and theoretical perspective. In 1984 a patient sued a private psychiatric facility for failure to diagnose a biological depression based upon vegetative signs and for failure to treat him with drugs. The malpractice tribunal awarded the patient $250,000.

It must be pointed out, however, that there can be powerful external pressure not to use medication. Alan Stone (1984) cites the Mass. Supreme Judicial Court's 1983 support of patients' rights to refuse medications. This decision was based on recognition that drugs were often prescribed ". . . as a method of chemical restraint . . ."; that some physicians practicing in public psychiatric hospitals lacked adequate training in psychopharmacology; failure at times to recognize the seriousness of side effects, including tardive dyskinesia; and the profession's difficulty distinguishing symptoms of the drug from symptoms of the underlying psychiatric disorder.

Therefore, psychiatrists on a dual disorder unit may find themselves between the proverbial "rock and hard place." In addition to the patient's presenting symptoms, they must assess the appropriateness of the pace of progress based on the individual patient, they must deal with urging from recovering staff not to medicate, and they must take into account pressure from external sources to use medication.

Given these considerations, two questions must be answered: Does the patient need medication? How can this determination be made? Primary indications and contraindications will now be addressed.

If the patient has a history of a thought disorder, preceding heavy use of alcohol or drugs, anti-psychotic medication is essential. This is not as easy to determine as it might seem. The patient may appear to have a schizophrenic history due to previous psychiatric hospitalizations with a diagnosis of schizophrenia and treatment with neuroleptics. Conversely, many schizophrenics cannot accept the devastating nature of their illness and may therefore over-emphasize or exaggerate the role of their substance abuse ("I'm an addict but I'm not crazy.''). The patient's behavior within the therapeutic milieu is closely observed, and the social worker attempts to obtain historical information from reliable family members.

Another indication for medication is the presence of an endogenous, or biological depression. Depressive episodes in the absence of significant external events or extensive substance abuse (e.g., preceding the addiction; persisting during periods of abstinence) may suggest a biological depression requiring medication. The ongoing presence of vegetative signs such as sleep and appetite disturbance, decreased libido, anergy, and anhedonia may provide additional support, although dual disorder patients have been taking in chemicals that have grossly affected CNS functions via intake or withdrawal. Again it is important to obtain information from reliable outside sources. Also DST and TRH tests can potentially provide verification when biological depression is suspected. Certainly there has been much research confirming a link between addiction and affective disorders (see for example, Nace, 1987 and Meyer, 1986).

Finally, whether biological, reactive, or drug-related, some depressions are so debilitating and unresponsive to psychosocial therapies that a brief trial of medication is essential to enable the patient to benefit from such therapies. Despite heroic efforts from staff, some patients are simply too severely depressed to respond without medication. In such cases, the dose would be tapered and eventually discontinued once the patient is able to connect with treatment.

There are some contraindications to using medication as well. Even when psychiatric symptoms are dramatic and pronounced, they can be the direct result of withdrawal. If the patient has not demonstrated psychiatric impairment independent of the addiction, medication for symptoms beyond a safe detoxification would not be the initial treatment of choice. Benzodiazepines are often used for detoxification from alcohol. Some patients are highly anxious, and it may be tempting to use these agents to stabilize them emotionally (Nace, 1987). However, their abuse/addiction potential is very high, and they are therefore contraindicated for recovering patients.

Differentiating between the effects of stimulant toxicity and psychiatric diagnosis can be difficult when the patient is unwilling or unable to report his/her history of drug use. It is not unusual for a patient to give quite varied accounts of substance intake up to ten days after detox, due to lingering drug-related confusion and disorganization. Even a "reliable history" may not indicate quality and mixtures of street substances which can affect toxicity. Presenting symptoms of stimulant amphetamine/cocaine toxicity may resemble paranoid schizophrenia, mania, anxiety neurosis with panic states, a hyperthyroid crisis and pheochromocytoma (Seymour & Smith, 1987). Toxic reactions are related to dose, physical tolerance, length of use, and physical health. They may be exacerbated by CNS depressants used to "come down" from the stimulants. The picture may be further clouded by adverse reactions to Haldol, Librium or any medications used by detox unit when the patient is admitted to a treatment unit.

While depression may signal the need for medication, this is not necessarily the case. Our patients typically suffer varying levels and degrees of depression. Those who are not in a reactive depression are not in touch with the reality of their addiction or its impact on themselves and those around them. Recovering individuals must face the reality of their illness. The drug which has seemed to be a comfort, a reward, an unconditional and reliable friend, a key to social acceptance, an integral part of celebrating and of compensating for injury or loss must be seen for the poison that it is. This literally means grieving this substance.

Further, the recovering individual must confront and assimilate the effect of his illness on his spouse and children. Whether he/she has been violent, verbally abusive, neglectful or physically absent, his/her failure to be the husband and father he/she wants to be and his/her family members' suffering will be overwhelming as his/her reality testing and ability to process information improve. This *hitting bottom* is inevitably humbling and depressing but must truly be experienced for the patient to begin the road to recovery.

The issue of whether to medicate does not end with the patient's treatment in the hospital. The first year of sobriety is well known for its affective vicissitudes. Stephanie Brown (1985, pp. 156-7) notes the vulnerability, dependency and child-like need for direction that characterizes this period of recovery. Patients are not expected to make reasonable decisions on their own (i.e., without discussing them with their sponsors), and are told not to make any major decisions at all the first year. The recommendation of a treatment team to refrain from medication or the failure of the treatment team to validate the use of an antidepressant if the patient is unable to sustain progress will be critical to the patient. Why should a patient flounder when medication might ease emotional lability and discomfort?

Gawin and Ellinwood (1988) in fact report that stimulants such as cocaine, amphetamines, and methyphenidate ". . . induce chronic damping of reward systems in the brain, and their results are consistent with clinical observations of protracted anhedonia" (p. 1778). They report on a number of preliminary studies indicating that long-term treatment of Desipramine and Imipramine resulted in ". . . increased abstinence rates and decreasing cocaine use, craving, and withdrawal symptoms" (p. 1179).

However, when a patient is diagnosed with a disease which by definition involves impulsivity, compulsive use of substances despite adverse consequences, what are the implications of prescribing a mood elevator on an outpatient basis?

These are obviously critical questions to which there are no easy answers. Extreme, rigid positions on either side (never medicate vs. medicate freely) are not in patients' best interests; instead, the pros and cons of each case must be weighed carefully.

The philosophy of our unit with regard to medication is to err on the side of caution. It is often difficult to obtain information verifying an independent psychiatric disorder. Families can rarely give accurate drug information, because the patient has been secretive and deceptive to protect his/her drug use. Thus, the only ways to assure accurate diagnosis is to allow sober/straight time, with ongoing assessment of changes in symptomatology, ego strengths and weaknesses.

Depressed or confused patients will be given a period of time to adjust to the supportive milieu before medication is prescribed. The counselors recognize its efficacy — and even necessity — in certain cases. And the doctors are extremely sensitive to the feelings of recovering staff.

If the patient is unable to respond to verbal therapies, medication is discussed within the treatment team. The doctor may then determine the patient's attitude toward medication, and, if there is hesitation or concern, treatment teams may well meet together with the patient to reinforce the collaborative nature of the decision and the reasoning behind the recommendation.

Doctor, Counselor, Transference and Countertransference

This article has indicated in several ways that a treatment team is working well when a doctor and counselor (and other team members) are sharing observations and information. This is particularly critical when a specific transference or countertransference must be considered in the overall treatment. The role of the doctor is to identify transference and countertransference issues in the process of working to understand the patient. When the patient's transference, or team member's countertransference must be addressed, the counselor can utilize this information to alter or shape his/her work with the patient. Several case reports will follow to illustrate how transference and countertransference issues can be identified and used effectively to enhance treatment.

Patient's transferences are significant sources of therapeutic material. Recently, a 30-year-old, single, white male began to withdraw emotionally from treatment after a positive beginning. He had felt very much neglected by both his parents. Father had left the household when the patient was 14, so had been emotionally and then physically absent throughout patient's youth. Mother had become absorbed in patient's brother who was one year younger than the patient, and had been unable to respond to patient's needs for attention and care until quite recently. Patient was unable to identify thoughts and memories of the past as significant. Material emerged in a haphazard and fragmented way until one day patient noted to his doctor in passing that he felt neglected in group. This led to recognition of his rage with his male counselor for not actively attending to him in group. He was gradually helped to increase his awareness of his longing for his father and of ways that he fought this longing by actively rejecting and discounting his father's tardy overtures. When the doctor communicated the patient's transferential feelings and repetition to the counselor, the counselor was able to demonstrate to the patient the unconscious messages he conveyed that prevented him from having needs recognized and possibly met.

A 29-year-old, divorced, white female was admitted to the unit in a state of agitated anxiety. She became immediately involved with a male peer (who had recently attempted suicide over a broken romance). The patient was empty, desperate for emotional nurturance, and fled her feelings via drugs prior to admission and currently through romance. When the treatment team stepped in to discuss her behavior and therapeutic needs with her, she was furious. She felt unable to tolerate the loss of this peer as a source of narcissistic supplies. If she was not receiving his attention then his interest in her did not exist; she was as unlovable as she felt, and the treatment team was the cause of her suffering. She threatened to leave treatment. She vilified her counselor and then her doctor, complaining to each of the other's coldness, unfairness, and failure to be sensitive to her needs. She was mentioned extensively in nursing report each morning for some form of (mild) acting out which secured for her staff's attention. The team sat with the patient every few days to maintain consistent support of her, to minimize her splitting, and to address her resistance to following the rules. She was helped to verbalize her thoughts and feelings rather than act them out, and to see the difference between focusing on her inner growth and sense of self rather than relying on external sources to camouflage her emptiness and loneliness.

If the team had not worked closely together with this borderline woman, the patient's acting out would have escalated to dangerous proportions, she would have gained little from treatment, and the team would have acted out the patient's internal conflict and fragmentation as they represented their separate perspectives and convictions regarding the patient's treatment needs.

Identifying counter-transference feelings that impede the therapeutic process is critical. With communication between counselor and doctor, the patient can be understood and unhelpful counter-transference feelings dissipated, so that therapeutic work proceeds.

A counselor and doctor recently worked with a patient who was in treatment for the second time after having lost a limb in a drug-related episode of violence. The patient had a history of numerous losses, chaotic relationships, and addiction throughout his family.

The patient was flat, lethargic, hopeless, with much repressed rage surrounding the loss of his limb and his prosthesis. His presence in her office induced in the doctor a sense of physical heaviness and futility. The patient continued to deflect focus on his feelings as he had largely done to his initial treatment team with his denial of feelings and evasive, ponderous presentation. His counselor rejected the induced feelings which were diluted in the group and confronted the patient for his refusal to deal with his anger and pain. The patient reacted strongly, coming to life for the first time. Only when confronted did the patient feel that others cared about him, and when the team worked together to confront the deflection and evasion, the patient gradually allowed himself to acknowledge his fear of his anger and pain. The doctor's counter-transference was the feeling patient had induced in a series of caregivers, and the feeling that pervaded the patient's wife and children. The counselor's reaction to the patient's hopelessness with strong confrontation and challenge, elucidated the doctor's insidious counter-transference, was responsive to the patient's needs, and marked the beginning of progress in the patient's treatment.

Recently an attractive 30-year-old, married woman entered treatment very frightened and overwhelmed. She was quite paranoid, suffered threatening auditory hallucinations, and had been maintained on a low dose of Haldol one year prior to admission. She had grown up in a very chaotic family; she, her husband and child still lived with her parents and her brother. She had suffered periods of neglect and intrusion and had been sexually abused. Thus, ego boundaries were fragile and self-esteem had been devastated. She was preoccupied with whether she was evil or good. She had a history of heavy drug use, but had struggled to remain sober over the course of the past year. When she *picked up*, her outpatient psychiatrist referred her to us for treatment. The patient formed a strong, positive one-to-one relationship with her doctor. She was initially put off by her counselor and group who, she felt, judged her without knowing her. The group's confrontational style was overstimulating; the patient felt incapable of protecting herself. She resisted revealing any personal material within the group. The counselor felt that her refusal to participate in group constituted denial and resistance. Her reticence elicited feelings of inadequacy and failure in her counselor. When the doctor pointed out to the counselor the patient's emotional fragility and legitimate need to maintain her defenses and to be supported in doing so, the counselor was able to see that her reluctance to self-disclose was not a reflection of his competence: his feelings of anger, frustration, and inadequacy dissipated. He was then able to sit with the patient individually, to listen to her, and to give her the support she needed in group. The patient was gradually able to express her fears in group and to establish relationships with the group members. The patient experienced a decrease in confusion, dysphoria, and distrust. She reported that the hallucinations, which had been threatening sexual assault were no longer distinguishable. If the counselor had been unwilling to listen to information available from the doctor, the patient might well have decompensated further either by leaving treatment and deteriorating or by fragmenting under the pressure of confrontation.

SUMMARY AND CONCLUSIONS

The preceding discussion summarizes and illustrates some of the key issues involved in interprofessional collaboration for dual disorder patients. Our perspective was skewed in a positive direction, as we believe strongly in a collaborative, team approach. We have witnessed the benefits time after time, as patients previously considered *too sick* or *chronic* have responded and taken the crucial first step toward recovery.

Of course, the simplicity of having a single or even primary treatment provider can sound appealing. Fewer meetings, less need to *check in*, no competing alternate treatment, no need to compromise. We strongly maintain, however, that the rewards justify the additional effort. Patients benefit from the combined talents, knowledge, and experience of professional and recovering staff. In addition, they can have the powerful experience of others working closely together; many patients come from dysfunctional families, and treatment team cooperation in itself can be part of a "corrective emotional experience." Finally, staff members grow personally and professionally by broadening their knowledge base and expanding their perspectives.

How are tension minimized and positive relations promoted? The very philosophy of the unit — that doctors and counselors are both vital and co-equal members of the treatment team — is the cornerstone of effective collaboration. New staff members are *socialized* regarding the program's orientation and functioning. Most are quite comfortable with the process, either having worked on multidisciplinary teams previously or having the flexibility to recognize the benefits. There are exceptions, however: some doctors cannot relinquish their role as primary caregiver and see all other staff as ancillary; some counselors are accustomed to and relish their identity as chief therapist. These individuals tend to have difficulty and ultimately self-select themselves out to other *situations*.

Finally, it is understood that flexibility is paramount. Counselors may at times be a *second doctor*, exploring dynamics or assisting the patient in achieving an emotional breakthrough. Doctors may have to change focus and emphasize the reality of the patient's addiction or the importance of speaking at AA meetings. Through frequent contact, both formally (scheduled meetings) and just *touching base*, lines of communication remain open, turf battles are minimized, and the basic goal of optimal patient care is reinforced.

REFERENCES

1. Nace, E. (1987) *The Treatment of Alcoholism.* NY: Brunner/Mazel, pp. 197, 198.

2. Brown, S. (1985) *Treating the Alcoholic: A Developmental Model of Recovery.* NY: John Wiley and Sons, pp. 156, 157.

3. Bissell, L. C. (1982) Recovered Alcoholic Counselors. *Encyclopedic Handbook of Alcoholism,* E. M. Pattison and E. Kaufman (Eds.). NY: Gardner Press, pp. 810-821.

4. *Alcoholics Anonymous.* (1976) AA World Services, Inc., NY.

5. Stone, A. (1984) Occasional Notes: The New Paradox of Psychiatric Malpractice, *New England Journal of Medicine,* 311: *21,* 1384-1387.

6. Gawin, F. H. and Ellinwood, E. H. (1988) Cocaine and Other Stimulants. *New England Journal of Medicine,* 318: *18,* 1173-1182.

7. Seymour, R. and Smith, D. E. (1987) *The Physician's Guide to Psychoactive Drugs.* NY: The Haworth Press.

8. Meyer, R. (1986) *Psychopathology and Addictive Disorders.* NY: Guilford Press, pp. 18-24.

Treating Drug Addicts
with Mental Health Problems
in a Therapeutic Community

Jerome F. X. Carroll, PhD

Two coincidental developments have presented contemporary therapeutic communities (TCs) with an unusual opportunity and challenge: the spread of Acquired Immune Deficiency Syndrome (AIDS) among substance abusers and the increasing number of persons with significant mental health problems who also abuse drugs and/or alcohol (Gilbert & Lombardi, 1967; Sutker, 1971; Frederick et al., 1973; DeLeon, 1974; Robins, 1974; Zukerman et al., 1975; Weissman et al., 1976; Harris et al., 1979; DeLeon, 1984; Allison et al., 1985; Carroll & Sobel, 1986; Daley et al., 1987). Both groups are already in our TCs, regardless of whether or not our admissions policies say they should be there. The question therefore, is whether or not they can be successfully treated in our TC.

In New York State, the term Mentally Ill Chemical Abusers (MICA) has been used to describe those with "serious" (typically meaning psychotic) mental illness who also abuse substances (drugs and/or alcohol). Another designation for this group is the "dual diagnosis" patient (Bauer, 1987; Daley et al., 1987; Galanter et al., 1988). That this population contributes a growing and significant challenge to our existing mental health and substance abuse treatment centers has been well documented (McGloughlin & Anglin,

Jerome F. X. Carroll is Director, Substance Abuse Services, Project Return Foundation, Inc., 133 West 21st Street, New York, NY 10011.

The author wishes to acknowledge the help of Marlene Cruz, Kevin Deal, Jesus Delgado, Eunice Edelman, Pamela Everette, Susan Ohanesian, Rudolph Palmieri, Carole James-Richardson, Jeffrey Richardson, and Sandra Thomas.

1981; Safer, 1982; Rounsaville et al., 1982; Schuckit, 1983; McLellan et al., 1983; Woody et al., 1983; Schuckit et al., 1985; Fowler et al., 1986; Rounsaville et al., 1987; Bauer, 1987; Sciacca, 1987; Galanter et al., 1988).

Unfortunately, the MICA concept has two potential disadvantages for those of us who work in TCs. One, by definition, it implies that the mental illness problem is the predominant issue—otherwise, the concept would have been "chemical abusers with mental illness" (CAMI). Two, nearly everyone using the MICA concept tends to confine its use only to the most serious forms of mental illness, that is, those with psychosis.

Regarding the first issue, most MICA people seeking entry into our TC do not present with the classic symptoms/signs of an active psychotic process. Their symptoms are typically in remission and/or under control as a result of the medications they are taking. Thus, at that point, the predominant problem is their addiction, even though their past history of mental illness should not be ignored or overlooked.

Regarding the second point, nearly all residents at Project Return's TC show evidence of some degree of psychopathology, even though it seldom is of a psychotic nature.

Some of the variety of symptoms of emotional dis-ease (Carroll, 1975; Carroll, 1978) to be found among our residents would include the following:

Varieties of Symptoms of Emotional Dis-ease

1. Acute and chronic forms of impaired cognitive functioning (memory impairments of varying degrees; a tendency toward concrete and absolute thinking; inability to take the other's point of view; poor ability to discriminate and generalize; and poor ability to plan ahead).
2. High levels of tension and anxiety (check for badly chewed finger nails and signs of restlessness).
3. Numerous fears (e.g., fear of sex, school, making a mistake, and especially fear of intimacy).
4. High levels of distrust of others.
5. Loneliness, despair, and alienation.

6. Feelings of helplessness, hopelessness, failure, and inadequacy as evidenced by expressions of guilt, shame, self-doubt, and suicidal ideation.
7. Sexual maladjustments.
8. Inability to accept and give love (generally, difficulty in expressing feelings of any kind in socially acceptable and effective ways).
9. Uncontrollable outburst of anger and violence — including disorders of impulse control — pathological gambling and intermittent explosive disorder.
10. Poor communication skills.
11. Occasional episodes of psychosis.

In an informal study done at Eagleville Hospital in 1986 by my colleagues and me,[1] of 45 admissions to a six month TC-oriented residential program, the following diagnoses were made by the program's psychiatrist and psychologists (see Table 1).

The study points to the more common occurrence of personality disorders among the 45 admissions. While personality disorders are viewed as "less severe" in that they typically do not require someone to be hospitalized, personality disorders have been consistently described in the mental health literature as intractable to treatment.

Over a period of nearly 10 years, my colleagues and I studied the nature and extent of psychopathology found among men and women addicted to alcohol and/or drugs who were admitted to Eagleville Hospital (Carroll, 1982). The principal source of data for these studies was the Tennessee Self Concept Scale (TSCS) developed by Fitts (1965).

Our findings clearly documented significant depression in nearly all subjects tested with the TSCS. Their single, best measure of self-esteem (the Total Positive scale of the TSCS), typically was below that of 90% of the general population taking the test. On three other measures of self-acceptance/self-esteem, their TSCS scores were even lower (the Behavior, Moral-Ethical, and Family scales). These findings were consistent across 10 years of testing.

I think few mental health professionals would argue with the contention that low self-esteem/self-acceptance is one of the major causes of most forms of "mental illness." Yet low self-esteem was,

TABLE 1

	Principal Diagnosis		N	Totals	%	Totals
I	Personality Disorders					
	A. Paranoid	301.00	1		2.2	
	B. Schizoid	301.20	2		4.4	
	C. Histrionic	301.50	2		4.4	
	D. Dependent	301.60	3		6.6	
	E. Antisocial	301.70	13		28.8	
	F. Avoidant	301.82	5		11.1	
	G. Borderline	301.83	1		2.2	
	H. Passive-Aggressive	301.84	1		2.2	
	I. Atypical	301.89	8		17.7	
				36		79.6
II	Affective Disorders					
	A. Dysthymic	300.40	3		6.6	
	B. Bipolar	296.6x	1		2.2	
				4		8.8
III	Schizophrenic Disorders					
	A. Residual	295.6x	2		4.4	
				2		4.4
IV	Conduct Disorder					
	A. Social Non-Aggressive	312.21	1		2.2	
				1		2.2
V	Impulse Control					
	A. Intermittent Explosive	312.34	1		2.2	
				1		2.2
VI	Not Diagnosed Left after 1 day		1		2.2	
				1		2.2
				45		99.4

with rare exception, the one problem (in addition to their addiction) which was common to the patients at the hospital. My clinical experience at Eagleville and now at Project Return continues to identify low self-esteem as a major cause of emotional dis-ease among our residents and a significant impediment to their recovery.

Most people with significant emotional dis-ease experience an array of difficult problems, with self, with family and friends, on the job, etc. Addicted men and women are no different, and when their addiction is compounded by low self-esteem and other varieties of emotional dis-ease, these problems tend to mount. These problems can be readily identified by using the Substance Abuse Problem Checklist (Carroll, 1984).

In a study[2] comparing the self-reported problems of alcoholics, drug addicts and multiple substance abusers (those who abused both drugs and alcohol), the groups were more similar than different, when adjustments were made for race and sex. All groups identified many problems (alcoholics averaged 74 problems; drug addicts 75 problems; those abusing drugs and alcohol, 88 problems; and those abusing alcohol and drugs, averaged 92 problems) which needed to be addressed at some point in their treatment if the goal of quality sobriety was to be realized.

REQUIREMENTS FOR TREATING RESIDENTS WITH SIGNIFICANT MENTAL HEALTH PROBLEMS

Probably the most important requirement is to convince the TC staff that residents with significant mental health problems can be successfully treated within the TC. Many TC line staff make a sharp distinction between the "mentally ill" and those addicted to drugs and/or alcohol. They do not feel confident that they can treat those with significant mental health problems. They prefer that these residents be "referred out" to psychiatric treatment centers. Unfortunately, many psychiatric centers are reluctant to treat people who are addicted, and until very recently, the success rate of those psychiatric treatment centers willing to work with this special population was not very high.

The irony in this is that as long as these "dual diagnosis" residents were not identified as "psychiatric," TC staff were able to help many of them to obtain quality sobriety. Most likely these successes stemmed from the staff's deeply held belief that recovery was possible and that people could change their behaviors, if they were motivated to do so. TC staff are particularly adept at motivating people to change their behavior. The fact that staff served as models of recovery also contributed to these successes, as did their insistence that all residents of the TC play an active role in assuming personal responsibility for their own recovery (Carroll, 1978; Carroll & Sobel, 1986).

STAFF DEVELOPMENT AND TRAINING

Once staff see the inevitability of working with residents with significant mental health problems, staff development and training becomes a critical factor. Where TCs have clinical support staff available (e.g., psychologists, social workers, etc.), these staff can be used to teach the TC counselors how to recognize and respond to the many varieties of emotional dis-ease they may encounter. Such instruction can also be supplemented by encouraging and allowing staff to attend outside training available through government and/or university sponsored programs.

The three major points which should be made through such training/education are:

1. residents with significant mental health problems can also achieve quality sobriety;
2. the proper use of prescribed psychotropic medications (antipsychotic or neuroleptics such as Mellaril, Thorazine, Prolixin, Navane, Haldol, and Loxitane; antidepressants such as Tofranil, Elavil, Sinequan, Norpramin, and Parnate; and the bi-polar medication Lithane) is essential for the more seriously mentally ill residents in order that they can control the symptoms of their disorder. These psychotropic medications do *not* produce a "high," as evidenced by the lack of their sales on the streets.
3. more flexible treatment strategies are needed when working with the dual diagnosis resident, especially non-judgmental interventions, providing support, and assisting the individual to

stay grounded in reality. To a large extent, these more flexible treatment strategies are already being integrated into those TCs which have opened their staffing to traditionally trained mental health professionals and whose counselors have begun to obtain additional training and education.

ACCESSIBILITY OF CLINICAL SUPPORT STAFF AND THE NEED FOR TEAMWORK

Another requirement for serving the dual diagnosis resident is that the TC have ready access to clinical support staff (i.e., psychiatrists or psychologists, social workers, physicians, nurses, etc.). These staff may be employed full-time, part-time, or serve as consultants.

However they serve, the clinical support staff must understand and value the TC process. This means they appreciate the importance of role models, peer support and confrontation, the value of work, and the assumption of responsibility for self, others, and the TC.

The need for clinical support staff arises from the fact that the treatment needs of the dual diagnosis resident can not be successfully met *solely* by the traditional TC counselor. The added severe impairments to family, social and family relationships, schooling and the job, as well as the occasional threat of suicide and violence demand that the burden of service be shared and distributed as the situation dictates. In a word, real teamwork, with shifting, functional leadership is the key to success, even though the counselor will continue to serve as the case manager (refer to the case of Mr. R.).

Probably the biggest challenge to creating an integrated team of counselors and clinical support staff is how people respond to the need for change. Where real teamwork is happening, staff resist taking unilateral action. They suspend decisions to demote, to discontinue schooling, to refer out, and to administratively discharge residents, until they have first conferred with the other team members. It also means they seek out the advice and counsel of one another in developing and implementing the treatment plan. In addition, it means that each member of the team reads the documentation of the other team members, at least on a weekly basis.

This is a major challenge for those TCs in which counselors have had to shoulder the entire treatment responsibility for their residents. It is also somewhat threatening to them to have others observing and commenting on their work and decisions. This experience, however, is not unique to the counselors, since the clinical support staff has the same circumstances and feelings to contend with.

Leadership is critical in building effective teamwork between counseling and clinical support staff. Leaders, at all levels, must perceive the necessity of such teamwork and understand that it is in the residents' best interests that such teamwork occur. The leadership must also be wise enough to appreciate the value of the counselor and clinical support staff's work, how the efforts of each complements and fulfills the work of the other. This knowledge is acquired faster by some than others. Unfortunately, some staff never do grasp the significance of this truth.

Before leaving the topic of teamwork, it is important to mention that the concept must be expanded to include external mental health specialists. It is not uncommon for residents with dual diagnoses to be referred out for brief periods of time for more intensive psychiatric/psychological treatment not available in the TC. More often than not, these residents seek to be readmitted to the TC once their psychiatric conditions have improved. In such cases, it is essential that the TC's clinical staff maintain good working relations with the referral source — something which does not always occur, even when the TC staff wish it to happen (refer to case study of Ms. B.).

ADMISSION GUIDELINES

The primary principle which should guide those in the admissions process in deciding which dual diagnosis applicants to admit or not to admit is "functionality." Functionality refers to the *ability* and *willingness* of the applicant to abide by the program's structure and values.

In the case of the dual diagnosis applicant, the following questions need to be addressed at the Admissions Office:

—Is the applicant's sense of reality strong enough, consistent enough to allow him/her to appreciate and participate in the program? Is the applicant willing and able to discuss his/her thoughts and feelings with others?

—Is the applicant taking any psychotropic medications? If yes, which medications? Does s/he have an adequate supply of medication?

—Is s/he taking these medications as prescribed? Is the applicant willing to allow our medical staff to monitor his/her use of these medications?

—Is the applicant free of the symptoms of serious mental illness (i.e., hallucinations, delusions, suicidal and homicidal urges, and sudden, unpredictable mood swings)?

—Is the applicant likely to abide by the TC's cardinal rules against possession and/or use of substances, violence, stealing, and violation of confidentiality?

NEED FOR FLEXIBLE CRITERIA

Most TCs have criteria which must be satisfied in order for a resident to move from one level to another and to graduate from the program. At Project Return, our criteria have been codified in clearly worded behavioral language. In the case of the dual diagnosis resident, exceptions must sometimes be made to our criteria (refer to the case study of Mr. D.).

Having the latitude to suspend and alter criteria is most important to the delivery of quality "individualized treatment," an essential characteristic of any effective treatment program. This is especially true for programs serving residents with significant mental health problems.

GUIDELINES FOR REFERRING OUT

There are various situations which would warrant referring a dual diagnosis resident to an outside psychiatric treatment center. Basically, they would indicate that the resident was no longer capable or willing to function in the program.

Examples of some situations of non-functionality would include:

—instances of bizarre, uncontrollable behavior (e.g., urinating in public places, attempting to jump out a window, hallucinating)
—refusing to do assigned work tasks, blatantly and repeatedly disrespecting peers and/or staff
—breaking a cardinal rule (e.g., using substances, threatening violence, and stealing)

When such instances occur, the dual diagnosis resident should be referred to the staff psychologist for an evaluation in order to determine the next course of action. Typically, this entails a case conference involving the treatment team, followed by a referral to an appropriate psychiatric treatment facility.

AFTERCARE PLANNING

Aftercare planning takes on even greater significance in the case of the dual diagnosis resident. If the resident is taking psychotropic medications, for example, s/he must be able to continue obtaining these medications after leaving the program. Where can these medications be obtained? Can the resident afford them? Who will monitor their effectiveness? A good aftercare plan addresses these questions.

Typically such residents will need to continue with some form of individual and/or group psychotherapy. Again, where will the resident go to get these services? Can s/he afford them?

In addition, some dual diagnosis residents will need special housing and work arrangements. To accomplish these objectives, the expertise of a social worker, housing specialist, and vocational rehabilitation counselor will likely be needed.

And lest we lose sight of a primary concern, such planning should include Narcotics Anonymous (NA) and Alcoholics Anonymous (AA), as well as any early sobriety groups the TC may make available to its graduates. At Project Return, our residents are required to become involved with NA and AA throughout their stay in the program. Before making "Live-Out" (moving into independent living quarters), our residents must have obtained an NA and/or AA sponsor.

However, dual diagnosis residents planning to use NA and AA need to be prepared to deal with those members of NA and AA who argue that no recovering person should ever take any drug, including prescriptive medications. They also need to be warned about those in NA and AA that would deprecate going to a mental health specialist for assistance.

MONITORING THE DUAL DIAGNOSIS CENSUS

Since a dual diagnosis resident will require more careful monitoring and more staff time, TCs need to develop an effective mechanism for determining the total daily census of dual diagnosis residents in the house, for each program (where multiple programs exist in the house), and for each counselor's caseload. Not only is the numerical count important, but so too is the qualitative status of the dual diagnosis resident, that is, whether or not the resident is improving, remaining the same, or regressing.

When individuals with a past history of significant mental illness apply for admission to Project Return, they must be screened by one of our staff psychologists. This screening includes a thorough review of any accompanying documentation relating to previous treatment episodes for mental illness.

Whenever someone accepted for admission to our TC is taking prescribed psychotropics (major tranquilizers only are accepted, as opposed to so called minor tranquilizers such as Librium or Valium, which can produce a "high"; the latter are not acceptable), the nursing staff is alerted. The nurse then is responsible for briefing the counseling staff regarding the nature of the medication, the reason for its use, and any negative side effects that might occur from its use. The nurse should also inform the counseling staff what might happen should the resident on his/her own decide to stop taking the medication.

In cases where signs of serious emotional distress occur after admission, with residents with no known history of mental illness, the resident is immediately referred to one of our psychologists.

The psychologist sees the resident and then decides whether or not to convene a case conference or to arrange for referral out; the latter is done only after first consulting with the other team members working with the resident.

CASELOAD ADJUSTMENTS

Generally speaking, at Project Return, we seek to limit each counselor's caseload to no more than one more seriously impaired dual diagnosis resident. We also do our best to equally distribute the dual diagnosis residential caseload among our clinical support staff.

WHAT CONSTITUTES SUCCESS

Relatively few of the dual diagnosis residents we have admitted to date have graduated from the program. On the other hand, nearly all were able to achieve several level movements before leaving the program. Since each level movement demands specific behavioral changes which favor sobriety and responsible living, we believe some benefits were realized by these residents in our TC.

In addressing this question, how a resident leaves the program must also be considered. For example, did s/he split, get administratively discharged for failure to abide by one of our cardinal rules, or was s/he referred out for specialized treatment? In one instance (refer to the case of Mr. P.), the resident was referred out to a psychiatric half-way house closer to his home. At the time of this referral, Mr. P. had advanced one level. He had, in fact, achieved six months of drug-free living in our community. His psychiatric condition, however, had worsened, and he needed more attention and treatment than our staff could provide.

Was this an instance of treatment failure or treatment success? We believe our treatment constituted a qualified form of success. Mr. P. achieved what he could from our TC, then he was moved along, in a responsible way, to another facility to get treatment we could not provide.

Much in the manner of a relay race, where victory is achieved through the combined efforts of all the runners, Mr. P. continues to move in the direction of quality sobriety, which includes good mental health. That, after all, is the major treatment goal for all of our residents. As with most dual diagnosis residents, the pathway to this goal is somewhat more complicated. To achieve the goal, TCs must learn how to integrate their efforts with those of other service providers.

NOTES

1. Psychiatric diagnosis of 45 patients admitted to Eagleville Hospital's Continuum Program in 1985-86. Unpublished survey, 1986.
2. Carroll, J.F.X. & Chambliss, C.A. A comparison of the self-reported problems of alcoholics, addicts, and multiple substance abusers at admission. Unpublished manuscript, 1984 (Available from [J.F.X. Carroll, PhD, Project Return Foundation, Inc., 133 West 21st Street, NY, 10011, USA]).

REFERENCES

Allison, M., Hubbard, R.L., & Ginzburg, H.M. *Indicators of suicide and depression among drug abusers: 1979-1981 TOPS admissions cohorts.* [DHHS Publication No. (ADM) 85-1411] Rockville, MD, U.S. Department of Health and Human Services, Public Health Service, 1985.

Bauer, A. Dual diagnosis patients: The state of the problem. *The Information Exchange Lines,* 1987, *4*(3), 1-4, & 8.

Carroll, J.F.X. "Mental illness" and "disease": Outmoded concepts in alcohol and drug rehabilitation. *Community Mental Health Journal,* 1975, *11*(4), 418-429.

Carroll, J.F.X. Mental illness and addiction: Perspectives which overemphasize differences and undervalue commonalities. *Contemporary Drug Problems,* 1978, 7, 227-231.

Carroll, J.F.X. Personality and psychopathology: A comparison of alcohol and drug-dependent persons. In J. Solomon and K.A. Keeley (Eds.) *Perspectives in alcohol and drug abuse: Similarities and differences.* Boston: John Wright PSG Inc., 1982, Ch. 4, 59-88.

Carroll, J.F.X. The Substance Abuse Problem Checklist — A new clinical aid for drug and/or alcohol treatment dependency. *Journal of Substance Abuse Treatment,* 1984, *1,* 31-36.

Carroll, J.F.X. & Sobel, B.S. Integrating mental health personnel and practices into a therapeutic community. In G. DeLeon and J.T. Ziegenfuss, Jr. (Eds) *Therapeutic communities for addiction.* Springfield, IL: Charles C Thomas, 1986, Ch. 17, 209-226.

Daley, D.C., Moss, H., & Campbell, F. *Dual disorders: Counseling clients with chemical dependency and mental illness.* Center City, MN: Hazelden, 1987.

DeLeon, G. Phoenix House: Psychopathological signs among male and female drug-free residents. *Addictive Diseases*, 1974, *1*(2), 135-151.

DeLeon, G. *The therapeutic community: Study of effectiveness.* [DHHS Publication No. (ADM) 84-1286] Rockville, MD, U.S. Department of Health and Human Services, Public Health Service, 1984.

Frederick, C.J., Resnick, H.L.P., & Witten, B.J. Self-destructive aspects of hard core addiction. *Archives of General Psychiatry*, 1973, *28*(4), 579-585.

Fowler, R., Rich, C., & Young, D. San Diego suicide study: Substance abuse in young cases. *Archives of General Psychiatry*, 1986, *43*(10), 962-965.

Fitts, W.H. *Tennessee Self Concept Scale Manual.* Nashville, TN: Counselor Recordings and Tests, 1965.

Galanter, M., Castaneda, R., & Ferman, J. Substance abuse among general psychiatric patients: A review of the "dual diagnosis" problem. Manuscript submitted for publication to *The American Journal of Drug and Alcohol Abuse* (in press).

Gilbert, J.G., & Lombardi, D.H. Personality characteristics of young male narcotic addicts. *Journal of Consulting Psychology*, 1967, *31*(5), 536-538.

Harris, R., Linn, M.W., & Hunter, K.I. Suicide attempts among drug abusers. *Suicide and Life-Threatening Behavior*, 1979, *9*(1), 25-32.

McLellan, A. T., Luborsky, L., Woody, G.E., O'Brien, C.P., & Druley, K.A. Predicting response to alcohol and drug abuse treatments. *Archives of General Psychiatry*, 1983, *40*(6), 620-625.

McGloughlin, W., & Anglin, M. Long-term follow-up of clients of high and low-dose methadone programs. *Archives of General Psychiatry*, 1981, *38*(9), 1055-1063.

Robins, P.R. Depression and drug addiction. *Psychoanalytic Quarterly*, 1974, *48*, 375-386.

Rounsaville, B. J., Weissman, M.M., Kleber, H., & Wilber, C. The heterogeneity of psychiatric diagnoses in treated opiate addicts. *Archives of General Psychiatry*, 1982, *39*, 161-166.

Rounsaville, B. J., Dolinsky, Z.S., Babor, T.F., & Meyer, R.E. Psychopathology as a predictor of treatment outcome in alcoholics. *Archives of General Psychiatry*, 1987, *44*(6), 505-513.

Safer, D. Substance abuse by young adult chronic patients. *Hospital and Community Psychiatry*, 1982, *38*(5), 511-514.

Schuckit, M.A. Alcoholism and other psychiatric disorders. *Hospital and Community Psychiatry*, 1983, *34*(11), 1022-1026.

Schuckit, M.A., Zisook, S., & Mortola, J. Clinical implications of DSM III diagnoses of alcohol abuse and alcohol dependence. *American Journal of Psychiatry.* 1985, *142*(12), 1403-1408.

Sciacca, K. New initiatives in the treatment of the chronic patient with alcohol/substance use problems. *The Information Exchange Lines*, 1987, *4*(3), 5&6.

Sutker, P.B. Personality differences and sociopathy in heroin addicts and non-addict prisoners. *Journal of Abnormal Psychology*, 1971, *78*(3), 247-251.

Weissman, M.M., Slobetz, F., Prusoff, B., Mezritz, M., & Howard, P. Clinical depression among narcotic addicts maintained on methadone in the community. *American Journal of Psychiatry*, 1976, *133*(12), 1434-1438.

Woody, G. E., Luborsky, L., McLellan, A.T., O'Brien, C.P., Beck, A.T., Blaine, J., Herman, I., & Hole, A. Psychotherapy for opiate addicts: Does it help? *Archives of General Psychiatry*, 1983, *40*, 639-645.

Zukerman, M., Sola, S., Masterson, J.W., & Angelone, J.V. MMPI patterns in drug abusers before and after treatment in therapeutic communities. *Journal of Consulting and Clinical Psychology*, 1975, *43*, 286-296.

APPENDIX I: CASE SUMMARY — MS. B.

Ms. B. is a 21-year-old Hispanic who entered Project Return's Women's Special Services Program (a program for homeless women who abused substances) on 7/30/87. Upon admission, she reported abusing heroin, cocaine (crack), PCP, and Valium. She stated she had been using heroin and cocaine since age 17. She reported no history of any mental health problems.

On the unit, Ms. B's behavior was very erratic. She was able to participate in group, giving feedback and confronting the negative behaviors of her peers. She was also able to share personal material. However, she would also ramble and suddenly switch from one topic to a totally unrelated topic. She would also interrupt others and suddenly leave the group.

She reported "seeing men in the showers." Once, she urinated in a trash can. She had difficulty sleeping at night. She often wandered into staff offices and off the floor. She also had great difficulty following the program's structure. At house meetings, she was typically observed curled up in the lap of a peer, much in the manner of a child with a parent. Most residents were overly protective of Ms. B.; the minority feared her because of her unusual behavior.

Chronology of Events

8/3/87 Ms. B. was sent to Lincoln Hospital because of her bizarre behavior. She was prescribed Mellaril, 200 mgs. 2x/daily, for seven days and returned to us. This medication was not renewed, and Ms. B. received no medication after 8/17/87.

8/13/87 Ms. B. was sent to Metropolitan Hospital, but they returned her to our facility.

8/17/87 Susan Ohanesian, our Director of Social Services, then took the following actions:

1. A call was made to the HEART Project, the original referral source. They provided a local number.
2. Called the local number and spoke to Mr. M. who advised her to call Mr. H.
3. Called Mr. H who advised her to call the Harlem Rehabilitation Center for Problems in Living.
4. Called both facilities; both refused to accept the client.
5. Called Samaritan, SuCasa, and Odyssey; they were unwilling to accept our client or offer any advice.
6. Called Project ADAM which served dual diagnosis clients. They lost their funding, but they suggested contacting Interfaith Hospital and New Directions.
7. Called Interfaith Hospital and New Directions, but they would not consider accepting client.
8. Called Mr. M. at HEART Project who again referred her to Mr. H.
9. Called Mr. H. who stated that the only alternative was to discharge the client to a shelter for the homeless.
10. Called Mr. M. to advise him of this. He said his supervisor, Mr. R., was on vacation, but that he would speak to another supervisor and get back to us.

8/18/87 Called Mr. M. again. He had no information, but again he promised to speak to someone and get back to us.

8/19/87 Called Mr. M. who suggested contacting the Bronx State Hospital.

Called Bronx State Hospital. They said they only accepted patients through city hospital screening.

9/8/87 Dr. Palmieri, our Director of Psychological Services, wrote a letter to Bronx Lebanon explaining the situation.

9/9/87 Ms. B. was sent to Bronx Lebanon. They stated they could not accept her, because they did not see psychotic symptoms severe enough to justify admitting her.

A case conference was held, and it was decided to keep Ms. B. in our program to see how she progressed.

9/10/87 Ms. B. complained of drowsiness and requested bedrest. The Director of her program was concerned about the possibility of pregnancy. An appointment with a gynecologist was arranged for Ms. B. for Monday, 9/14/87.

9/14/87 Ms. B. went to the gynecologist. On the way back, Ms. B. decided to split.

1/22/88 Ms. B. attempted to re-enter Project Return by giving a false name. She was rejected for admission.

1/29/88 Ms. B. appeared without authorization at our TC; she was disheveled, hungry, and very upset. She was fed, given new clothing, and escorted to a women's shelter for the homeless.

Letter — 9/8/87

Bronx Lebanon Hospital Center
Grand Concourse & East Mount Eden Avenue
Bronx, NY

To whom it may concern:

Ms. B. is a 21-year-old Hispanic female who entered our drug free rehabilitation residence on 7/30/87. After exhibiting bizarre behavior, she was referred to Lincoln Hospital on August 3rd. She was prescribed Mellaril, 200 mgs. 2x/daily, for seven days and returned to our facility. Since then her functioning has continued to deteriorate. She reports having visual, auditory, and tactile hallucinations. There is a loosening of associations, flight of ideas, and paranoid thought processes. Her memory is impaired, and her insight and judgment are poor. Moreover, she exhibits psychomotor agitation.

Specifically, Ms. B. reports being threatened by the Governor, the Mayor, and men with "white hair and green eyes." She sees and feels snakes crawling up her legs. Her walking lacks fluidity, and, while seated, there are obvious and severe repetitious leg movements. She is unable to follow directions or remain in one place for more than a short period of time. She wanders around our facility, and, during one such incident, she urinated in a garbage can.

It is clear that Ms. B. is not suitable for our facility. Her psychotic behavior meets the criteria for a diagnosis of Schizophrenia, Disorganized type (295.10). All our attempts to have her placed in a psychiatric facility have proved fruitless. The last attempt was at Bronx State Hospital. We were told that all patients had to be screened at a city hospital before being admitted to their facility. The city hospital covering our area for screening is Bronx Lebanon. Ms. B. is being referred to Bronx Lebanon so that she can be transferred to a suitable psychiatric facility.

If I could be of any further assistance, please contact me.

Sincerely,

Rudolph Palmieri, Ph.D.
Director, Psychological Services

APPENDIX II: CASE SUMMARY – MR. P.

Mr. P. is a 22-year-old white male who entered Project Return Foundation, Inc., in March, 1987. He had a history of substance abuse since age 7 and was addicted to cocaine, alcohol and marijuana at the time of his admission. At age 18, he had been diagnosed as paranoid schizophrenic. At the time he entered our program, he was being treated at an outpatient mental health program and was stabilized on Stellazine and Cogentin. Since he was not exhibiting any psychotic symptoms at the time of entry, he was accepted into the program with the proviso that he continue his outpatient therapy and medication.

Mr. P. was raised in a middle class family. His mother was chronically depressed and had abandoned the family when Mr. P. was quite young. His father was very active in politics and his efforts to help his son had resulted in Mr. P.'s admission to and discharge from a variety of programs, including military schools, hospitals, and drug treatment centers.

Soon after his admission, Mr. P. began to have difficulty in the program. He could not complete work assignments, had difficulty relating to staff and other residents, and began to exhibit some paranoid delusions. He was demoted in level twice. In July, the staff psychologist ascertained that Mr. P. was not complying with his medication regimen. Contact with his psychiatrist disclosed that Mr. P. had a history of non-compliance. He was placed on a behavioral contract, part of which stipulated that he had to take his medication.

By September, it was clear that Mr. P. would not or could not meet the conditions of his contract. An interdisciplinary case conference was held with the clinical, social service, psychology, vocational/educational, and medical staffs. It was determined that, since Mr. P. had been drug-free for more than six months, his primary problems, at this time, were psychiatric. The decision was made to attempt to find a residential mental health program for Mr. P. where he could receive psychotherapy, medication, and supervised living. Mr. P. also required continuing drug treatment, as well as, supportive counseling due to his HIV positive status.

The Social Service Department contacted many agencies but encountered difficulty due to Mr. P's dual diagnosis. In November, a placement was located for Mr. P. He was transferred to the Hugenout Center, a psychiatric day treatment program, and the Crisis Center, a supervised residence. Close communication between agencies also insured that Mr. P. would be able to attend a weekly substance abuse support group. After one month in his new placement, a follow-up call to the new agency found Mr. P. adjusting well to the program.

Eunice B. Edleman, CSW
Social Worker, Project Return

Susan Ohanesian, CSW, ACSW
Director, Social Services

February, 1988

APPENDIX III: CASE SUMMARY — MR. R.

Mr. R. is a 33-year-old black male who was admitted to our facility on 9/24/87. He was referred by a psychiatrist, Dr. S. from the Charles H. Gay Shelter Care Center for Men on Ward's Island. Because of the psychiatric history, Mr. R. received a psychological evaluation as part of the admission process. During the evaluation, he was oriented X3 and showed no hard signs of psychotic thought processes. Moreover, there was no history or sense of hostile behavior. However, Mr. R. admitted to a history of auditory hallucinations and psychotropic medications, and that he continues to have hallucinations, even while on medication. Soft signs of psychosis were evident in terms of somewhat slurred, slow speech and walking that lacked the expected fluidity.

My assessment was that Mr. R. was no threat to himself or others, and that he would have no particular problem going through orientation. I considered it unlikely that he would graduate from the program. My guess was that he would make Level I, and possibly Level II, but that Level III was beyond him. The factors that influenced my decision to admit him were:

1. Minimal risk (he would require more attention, but there was not likely to be a crisis).
2. Our facility was better for him than the shelter (other alternatives would be adult homes or half-way houses which could be considered later).

3. Our program's willingness to admit dual diagnosis or MICA clients.
4. My general inclination is to give the client the benefit of the doubt.

I contacted the referring psychiatrist, Dr. S., to assure that he would maintain medication responsibility. He was very willing to do this. Moreover, he was eager to maintain contact with our staff concerning Mr. R.'s progress, so that he could determine the best psychiatric treatment. Dr. S. refused to label Mr. R. a schizophrenic. Instead, he used terms suggesting a prevailing depressive condition (possibly bi-polar), questioned whether Mr. R. really experienced hallucinations, and suggested that any apparent psychotic behavior was the result of substance abuse. However, in determining medication, he prescribed both Tofranil (an antidepressant) and Navane (an antipsychotic). Regardless of Dr. S.'s diagnostic opinions (I think that he was influenced by the need to find a suitable placement for Mr. R.), it is my opinion that Mr. R. is schizophrenic, Paranoid Type.

Within the first week that Mr. R. entered Olympus House, a case conference was convened. It seems that he spoke to counselors about his hallucinations, and they became extremely concerned. I assured them that:

1. I was aware of the situation.
2. Mr. R. was on medication, and that this was being followed by his psychiatrist.
3. There was minimal probability of his acting out. In other words I provided support.

Initially, complaints from clinical staff were relatively minor. They did not know how to describe him. I would seek out descriptions and be told that more time was needed to make an evaluation. I even contacted Voc/Ed and was told only that he "showed motivation." About two and one-half months into treatment, Bill S. (his Level I supervisor) described these features about Mr. R.:

1. He seeks too much individual attention.
2. He lacks concentration.
3. He stops speaking in mid-sentence.
4. He exhibits adequate communication when the focus is on others in group.
5. His communication is often irrelevant when the focus is on himself.

Toward the end of January, 1988, I started receiving reports of impulsivity. Specifically, Mr. R. approached his counselor and expressed his desire for a sex-change operation; he yelled at Eunice (his social worker), exclaiming that she was not his counselor, and he asked to be removed from a relatively minor responsibility.

While some of this impulsivity caused concern (his counselor was alarmed at the talk of a sex-change operation), the combination of my support and the growing recognition that the impulsivity was short-lived and quickly forgotten eased much of the staff's anxiety. However, they were left with the issue of: "Where do we go from here?"

A case conference was convened on 1/28/88. In addition to what has already been said, Voc/Ed suggested that while Mr. R. probably has the intellectual ability to obtain a GED, his anxiety level increases during testing and diminishes his performance. It was felt that he would not be able to hold himself together long enough to pass such an examination. It was determined that Mr. R. had progressed as far as he could here (he did achieve Level I status), and it was time to refer him to another facility. His social worker is in the process of finding the most appropriate placement.

> Rudolph Palmieri, Ph.D.
> Director, Psychological Svs.
> Project Return
> February, 1988

APPENDIX IV: CASE SUMMARY – MR. D.

Mr. D. is a 34-year-old black male who entered Project Return's Olympus House on 8/16/85. He has been on psychotropic medication since 1/86 (Tegretol and Mellaril for seizures and impulse control). He has been seeing a psychotherapist at an outside facility on a regular basis since January, 1987.

There have been a number of case conferences on Mr. D. One of these (1/7/87) was convened to determine whether he should be readmitted to Olympus House upon his being discharged from the psychiatric ward of North Central Bronx Hospital. He had been referred to the emergency room there following a determination that he was overtly hostile and perceived as a threat to himself and others. This hostile behavior appeared to be a decompensation associated with non-compliance with his medication schedule. He was readmitted to Olympus House.

Another case conference was convened on 9/17/87 because of concerns about his Voc/Ed progress. It was determined that he would probably not obtain a GED. However, he was allowed to continue with us to see if he could obtain benefits from our program, despite this deficiency.

Currently, Mr. D. has completed porter/maintenance training at the Federation for The Handicapped, and he is attending GED classes two times per week at the Fortune Society. It is expected that the Fortune Society will provide documentation confirming Mr. D.'s GED deficiencies. The Federation of The Handicapped found Mr. D. an evening position that provides no benefits and interferes with his GED classes and individual psychotherapy. Voc/Ed is working with the Federation to make the appropriate changes.

Mr. D. entered our facility with a number of problems in addition to substance abuse. There is evidence suggestive of both neurological impairment (seizures, possible mental retardation/learning disabilities) and a problem of impulse control. Despite these problems, and the acting out associated with them, Mr. D. has never been "shot down" (i.e., down graded from one level to a lower level). He is currently a Level III resident. On several occasions, he was put on a behavioral contract and given special attention, and there have been concerns expressed about whether, in fact, he is capable of completing our program. The result of these concerns, so far, has been to give him more time than usual to adjust to the demands of our program and progress through it. Apparently, clinical staff senses, whether or not they can put it in words, that Mr. D.'s emotional condition is different from that of other clients whose condition necessitates discharge.

Clinical staff can relate to limited cognitive ability, learning disabilities, and unproductive, self-defeating attitudes (character disorders). They can even relate to temporary, acute psychotic states and impulsivity. What they have difficulty relating to is a prolonged narcissistic condition that manifests itself as an inability to relate.

In short, clinical staff cannot relate to "unrelatedness."

Mr. D.'s condition may, in fact, be more intense (quantity) than the condition of others who have already been discharged. However, he has retained an ability to relate that lends itself to the therapeutic community process. Other conditions may lack this relatedness quality. While these other conditions may be less intense in their own right, the qualitative difference may effectively prevent progression through a therapeutic community. It seems that clinical staff is picking up these qualitative differences even though they may not be able to describe them. What may be lacking in formal training is compensated for by life experience. This life experience is beginning to incorporate a "clinical feel" that may allow a greater variety of clients to benefit from our services.

Regardless of whether Mr. D. actually graduates, he has already achieved a level of competence and control that we previously believed was beyond his abilities. This can be attributed to his own personal efforts and a growing sophistication of staff.

Rudolph Palmieri, Ph.D.
Director, Psychological Svs.
Project Return
February, 1988

Concluding Comments

David F. O'Connell, PhD

A number of significant developments over the past decade are, I believe, spawning a cause for optimism in the treatment of dually diagnosed patients. In this final section of this special edition, I have included my thoughts and ideas on these developments.

Firstly, our society's awareness of and attitude towards addictive diseases appear to be rapidly evolving. Chemically dependent people are increasingly being seen as individuals suffering from an incurable but controllable disease and the moral stigma attached to these disorders is rapidly fading. In our culture it has become much easier for individuals to come forth and seek treatment for chemical dependency. A comparable trend has been operative in regard to mental illness also. Schizophrenic and manic depressive individuals now regularly appear on popular talk shows to educate the public about mental illness and the benefits of treatment. Celebrities and sports figures have come forward over the past decade to discuss their mental illness and inspire others suffering from mental illness to not despair and to seek appropriate treatment. In this climate of greater awareness and acceptance of addiction and mental disorders the problem of dual diagnosis has attracted greater attention from both the public and health professionals. The hard realities of our nations addiction problem have awakened mental health professionals to the pervasive drug and alcohol abuse and dependence found in psychiatric patient populations and the limitations of psychotherapeutic approaches to treating addictive diseases. As this has happened, the chemical dependency treatment field has "grown up" and gained greater credibility and respect as a profession. Consequently, addiction professionals have begun to be increasingly sought out by mental health clinicians for their expertise in treating chemically dependent patients in psychiatric settings. Dually diagnosed patients have benefited from this greater level of collaboration.

Thus, as society's awareness of the problems of mental illness and addictions has grown, professionals from both disciplines have had to take a deeper look at the dually diagnosed members of their respective patient populations. With professionals more sensitive to the dually diagnosed patient's needs and our culture's greater acceptance of both types of dysfunctions, afflicted individuals have been identified in increasing numbers and given appropriate clinical care.

Within the field of rehabilitation, in particular the field of psychotherapy, several trends are having a positive impact on the problem of dual diagnosis. The influence of the self psychology movement has had important implications for the treatment of chemically dependent patients, particularly those with personality disorders. The conceptualization of addiction has both a manifestation of a severely damaged sense of self and an effort, albeit futile and destructive, to repair the self has provided addiction clinicians with much needed direction in the long term treatment of addicted individuals, particularly relapse prone patients. It has provided a unified perspective from which to understand patients who suffer from multiple addictive disorders such as eating disorders, sexual addiction and compulsive gambling. At the same time it has provided insight into the association of severe personality disorders such as borderline narcissistic personality disorder, and addictive diseases. Recent literature in this area (for example Levin, 1987) has given legitimacy to the pioneering ideas of the founders of AA and 12 step approaches to addictions treatment. These individuals intuitively understood the characterological dysfunction associated with addictive diseases and developed effective programs to offset and arrest this dysfunction. Research on the effectiveness of AA with dually diagnosed patients (for example, Nace, Saxon and Shore, 1986) validates these ideas and efforts and demonstrates that mentally ill, addicted individuals can benefit immensely from traditional self help programs.

The emphasis on short term intensive psychotherapy, particularly cognitive behavioral methods, is another important trend in the psychotherapy field that is having an impact on the treatment of dual disorders. As chemical dependency counselors grow in clinical competence through more solid professional preparation they have been able to use these proven psychotherapeutic approaches to treat chemically dependent patients. Dually diagnosed patients, especially those with anxiety, depressive and eating disorders, can and have benefited immensely from cognitive psychotherapy methods. Cognitive behavioral methods of treatment have enjoyed a successful track record with a wide variety of emotional and behavioral disorders. The application of these methods to the treatment of addictive disorders is growing steadily and enjoying similar success (e.g., Marlatt and Gordon, 1985). As they become integrated into mainstream drug and alcohol treatment, dually diagnosed patients will receive better quality clinical care.

Improvements in assessment and diagnosis in the fields of psychiatry and clinical psychology are having significant impact on the treatment of dually diagnosed patients. The proliferation of sensitive neuroradial techniques and the development of increasingly sophisticated neuropsychological assessment techniques are leading to more precise identification of mental disorders, especially organic disorders and have contributed to the development of specialized rehabilitation programs for such patients. The increasing use of personality testing in particular is assisting in the early identification and treatment of dual disorders in many chemical dependency treatment settings. Such improvements in the assessment process reinforce the reality that addicts are a heterogeneous group and that traditional treatment approaches often need to be supplemented by specialized medical and psychiatric treatments. Increasingly this is transpiring in many addictions treatment programs.

The greater frequency of bachelor's and master's degree programs in chemical dependency counseling is another encouraging development that will have a positive impact on the quality of care for dually diagnosed patients. Although many in the field would lament it, the paraprofessional model of chemical dependency counseling appears to be rapidly giving way to a more professional model of education and training similar to that in other helping professions. Such professional preparation can make drug and alcohol treatment professionals more sophisticated, sensitive and hopefully more successful clinical care givers. Thus, the more complex, complicated patients such as dually diagnosed individuals can be better understood and treated. The increasing inclusion of courses in addictive diseases in the curricula of physicians, clinical psychologists and psychiatric social workers augurs well for the treatment of the mentally ill chemical abusing (MICA) patient treated in mental health environments. As a consultant and trainer for the MICA Project in Trenton, New Jersey, I have seen first hand the positive impact of training in chemical dependency counseling on the service delivery for MICA patients. The tools and programs of addictions rehabilitation have much to offer psychiatric patients with chemical abuse and dependency histories and my own experience is that mental health professionals are coming to realize the wisdom and benefits of these approaches.

The spiritual dimension of the patient/therapist relationship continues to attract interest from treatment professionals. Perhaps the growing interest in religion, spirituality and "new age" healing and self help techniques in our society is ushering along this trend. In my own education and professional preparation as a psychologist, the spiritual aspect of human functioning in general and patient functioning in particular was barely addressed. The same could be said for many of my colleagues. However this is less often the case in today's treatment environment. The ACOA movement over the last decade appears to have moved spirituality to a more visible position in the understanding and treatment of both addiction and co-dependency. In my own experience this has had a great impact on the treatment of relapse prone and dually diagnosed patients. As a long term practitioner and prescriber of the transcendental meditation program I have witnessed the profound benefits of a daily meditation program for many chemically dependent patients especially dually diagnosed patients with anxiety, depressive and severe personality disorders. Initial research efforts in the use of meditation and other spiritual approaches to rehabilitation for both chemically dependent (e.g., Aron and Aron, 1980) and psychiatric patients (e.g., Carter and Meyers, 1979) is quite promising. I believe the growing emphasis on spirituality will have a major impact on treatment delivery for dually diagnosed patients in the years to come and will help brighten the picture for greater success with this population.

A major challenge facing treatment professionals and researchers over the next decade will be the development and evaluation of specific treatments for dually diagnosed patients in the full spectrum of clinical care from detoxification to continuing care programs. The aforementioned development in psychotherapy may play a role in these programs as may advances in pharmacotherapy and the trend towards specific self help groups for dually diagnosed patients.

Although the formidable problems posed by the dually diagnosed patient appear to be outweighed by our therapeutic solutions, the trends and developments listed here may contribute to the balancing of the scales and tip them in favor of the patient. There appears to be a cause for optimism. If nothing else the realization that a very troubled patient population is finally receiving the much needed professional attention and help they deserve can stand as a source of pride for the dedicated professionals in both mental health and addiction treatment who have worked so hard to make this a reality.

REFERENCES

Aron, A. and Aron, E. (1980) The Transcendental Meditation Program's Effect on Addictive Behaviors *Addictive Behaviors*, 5, 3-12.

Carter, R. and Meyer, J. (1979) The use of the Transcendental meditation technique with severely disturbed psychiatric patients. Institute for Social Rehabilitation Pacific Palisades, Los Angeles, CA.

Levin, J. (1987) *Treatment of Alcoholism and Other Addictions: A Self Psychology Approach* North Vale, New Jersey: Jason Aronson.

Marlatt, G. and Gordon, J. (1985) *Relapse Prevention Maintenance Strategies in the Treatment of Addictive Behaviors*. New York: Guilford Press.

Nace, E., Saxon, J., and Shore, M. (1986) Borderline Personality Disorder and Alcoholism Treatment: A one year follow up, *Journal of Studies on Alcoholism* 47, *3*, 196-200.